Contents

Figures

Tables

Prologue and Acknowledgements

To examine the history of abortion laws in Mexico is to follow a complex, multifaceted, and, especially, ongoing story. It is no doubt an emotionally charged topic which, ever since mid-2015 when I chose it for a doctoral dissertation and discussed it with colleagues or peers, would leave nobody indifferent. Mexico itself is legalistically complex, as a country with a federal system of government and various overlapping 'layers' of laws. As I write this book in mid-to-late 2023, two major milestones have recently been reached: with Mexico's Supreme Court first ruling against the criminalization of abortion in 2021, and then declaring in 2023 that the *Federal* Criminal Code should not penalize abortion anymore and that *federal* healthcare institutions should offer the procedure.

The italics are because, in Mexico, we are fond of saying that 'the devil is in the details' *('el diablo está en los detalles')*. And while the Mexican *federal* laws apply to federal institutions, at the moment of writing these lines, more than half of the subnational states still criminalize abortion in their local laws, which do not immediately lose validity through the Supreme Court's rulings. *Subnational* healthcare institutions (i.e. state-by-state local health departments) will, for now, stay unaffected by the federal reforms. There are still some women in Mexico – though admittedly few – who have been incarcerated because of abortions (or late stillbirths assumed to have been abortions), for whom these recent Court rulings will not prove helpful either. While the topic is already complex in any nation's circumstances, the intricate legal system in Mexico (including concepts like *'amparo'*, which give even wider room for case-by-case interpretation, or for a certain relativity in applying laws and sentences) makes for a considerable number of *devilish details*.

Interest on issues such as abortion tends to come from personal stories – whether our own, or from someone close to us. In my case, what was powerfully attractive about this topic was the intensity of the controversy itself and how quickly it developed into discussions fraught with emotion, especially online behind veils of anonymity. I was mesmerized, as well, by how fundamentally opposed the viewpoints were. The topic also happened to emerge (through no influence of my own) during sessions of a coaching group that I was a part of, in 2015 and 2016, by which time I had already chosen it for doctoral research. When discussing it with friends, relatives, or members of the aforementioned group, more people than I would have expected revealed having had abortions or intimately knowing someone who did – sometimes having changed their minds about the issue in one direction or the other.

Said emotions could range from intense relief, to anger, to mixes of many others, but what became abundantly clear was that many more women than expected had had abortions, legal or otherwise – the issue still being a strong taboo in Mexico as in other traditional cultural contexts. This taboo status of abortion biases the issue and the discussions around it; it merits study and is itself part of any proper academic analysis.

In the Epilogue, I explain the evolution of my doctoral research path, recounting how several conceptual frameworks were examined until I ultimately found a 'fitting' one: *norm contestation* and a *norm-typological analysis* of the clashing ideas surrounding abortion. I use these concepts in the book, for a parallel analysis of opposed ideas. Some fellow academics challenged my decision to give an equal voice to advocates 'for' as well as 'against' legal abortion and my weighing their normative proposals as equivalent. These peers, as well as some of the advocates themselves, questioned whether I engaged in a form of criticisable *'two-sides-ism'*, because I gave an apparently equal voice to two sets of strongly clashing ideas. And while throughout the book I question this perceived binarity in itself, of being *'for'* or *'against'* legal abortion (suggesting that more nuance is desperately needed), I indeed use the term 'both sides' a few times throughout the book: referring either to similarities in concepts or (more often) to ideological clashes and opposed interpretations of human rights and principles of justice. Or to showcase, as well, their respective convictions about moral righteousness: their mirrored certainty of *'definitely standing on the right side of History'*.

This may indeed cause some academics to disagree with my view: seeing that I have not chosen to construct a book that aims to delegitimize one or the other group of advocates, nor to posit why, academically speaking, they have *'been wrong all along'*. Such might have even been my own early aim, my intellectual 'temptation' when beginning my career as a doctoral student and PhD candidate: to finally find *the* argument, to discover *the* ultimate reason why this debate should just end already. Not only did this prove impossible, but also, any such conclusion on my part would still not erase the fact that opposed groups on abortion are unlikely to ever see eye-to-eye.

This ideological clash remains part of the reason why the topic stays *'pendular'* in so many places: with the laws constantly changing, only to meet everlasting contestation, and with even the firmest-seeming, '*set-in-stone-est'* appearing laws (like *Roe vs. Wade* in the United States) changing due to blows of political winds. Or, more often than we would like, due to strong pushes by partisan currents. In Mexico as in other parts of the world, on abortion and other issue areas, I have seen intense pushes in one or another direction of social change be met with furious backlash, and with unintended consequences when not carefully constructed on solid, strategically cooperative ground.

Others, however, would nod in agreement with my supposed *'two-sides-ism'* and jump to the conclusion that as an academic I am supposed to 'stay neutral indeed'. But I disagree with such an interpretation, too. Not only is 'neutrality' or 'objectivity' impossible in social sciences, but one can also defend a particular legal solution while still searching for a 'middle ground' where opposed views (at least those within a range of reasonability and agreement with basic human rights) can be freely expressed. A supposed 'neutrality' is the furthest from my aims – but not so a consideration of ideas perhaps opposed to mine, to a mainstream discourse, to current social policy, or to widely accepted academic concepts.

This view of the issue responds also to analytical reasons, with *norm contestation* being a lens through which I studied abortion during my doctoral research. Related concepts that I used during research, such as the "legitimacy gap", or the various "typologies of norms" (both explained throughout this book) lend themselves to an analytical style consisting of comparisons between opposed sets of meanings and clashing interpretations of concepts, laws, or principles of justice. Such a lens allowed me to examine abortion from different angles and to propose at least a few *'pathways to dialogue'* – not *'pathways to creating immutable solutions to a complex problem'*. To some, I am aware, the alleged *'two-sides-ism'* may come across as lukewarmness. But in these polarized times, I stand by the idea that clashing views on one same topic should at least be listened to in their reasoning and that any potential solution to a debate can only be enriching, satisfactory and, ultimately, *durable*, if most advocates have at least felt heard and considered.

We live in polarized times indeed, throughout the Western world and Latin America – where the capacity for debate, for agreement on certain basic principles, or for even exposing oneself to opposed views seems to be diminishing. In these turbulent days of disagreement on almost everything (often along political-partisan lines, rather than actual collision of ideologies or principles), I see the potential for a similar analytical framework to be applicable to other issue areas. For instance, other issues related to gender (such as policies concerning gender-affirming care in minors), or climate change mitigation in balance with economic development, or gun control in the United States, are all current topics meeting acute controversy and opposed views, all claiming to defend human rights and to protect vulnerable people. An analysis using similar concepts, such as *norm types* and *norm contestation*, can give useful insights as to which principles are clashing in a debate. Such thought exercises can be used to eventually design durable, conciliatory public policy.

This many-year endeavour would have been impossible without the treasured support from many persons and institutions. The research effort was possible through financial support from CONACYT (*Consejo Nacional de Ciencia y Tecnología*), the National Council of Science and Technology in Mexico. I thank my doctoral supervisors, Prof. Dr. Antje Wiener (University of Hamburg) and Prof. Dr. Detlef Nolte (GIGA, German Institute of Global and Area Studies), for their guidance in the realization of this project. My acknowledgement also goes to the GIGA for their support towards my completing the doctoral research programme, especially Dr. Maren Wagner, Dr. Merike Blofield, Dr. Miriam Prys, Dr. Sabine Kurtenbach, and Dr. Bert Hoffmann. My thanks also to Dr. Cristina Herrera from COLMEX (*El Colegio de México*), who gave invaluable support during my fieldwork in 2018.

I dedicate this book to my parents, Carlos Franco and María Yáñez, without whose support I would not be who and where I am today. To my siblings, Aurora and Carlos, for being an immense joy in my life; Hilda Franco, whose affection and support I forever cherish; and Magdalena Franco, for filling so many moments with joy and for having accompanied me to the pro-abortion protest in Saltillo in 2019. Immense thanks to those friends near and far, for believing in me – wholeheartedly to the members of our PhD *'ScrumAdemia'* group, for being 'on the same boat', for their understanding, and for all the shared moments, high and low: Markus Kirchschlager, Anna Fünfgeld, Désirée Reder, Rebecca Lohmann, Swantje Schirmer, Sabine Mokry, and Regina Schnars.

I owe very special mentions to Viviana García for our priceless shared experiences as immigrant academics in Hamburg, and to colleagues Leonardo Bandarra and Lisa Hoffmann, as well as to my colleagues and flatmates Jorge Rincón and Rafael Castro, for having weathered the better part of a global pandemic along with me. Very special thanks to Jan Klenke for not only the enriching friendship but also the moments of reflection and brainstorming that led to the creation of the *"Cartesian chart of norm typologies"* here presented.

And to my dear friend Myriam Gómez, remembering those Saturdays spent in Mexico City, applying to our respective PhD programmes. Even if now in different countries, together we came far.

1 Introduction

Abortion, Advocacy in Latin America and the Mexican Case

In late 2019, I was in Mexico City, nearing the end of my second period of fieldwork for the research that ultimately became this book. While the last decade had seen much advocacy throughout the country, for and against legalizing abortion, the case remained that Mexico City (as the former *Distrito Federal*) was the only subnational state[1] to have decriminalized – and later legalized – abortion. With only a few days remaining before the end of my fieldwork, an advocate working at the Lower Chamber of the National Congress, whom I had interviewed a few days prior, sent me a video via *WhatsApp* along with the message: *'the initiative to decriminalize abortion in the state of Oaxaca has advanced . . . Local Congress will vote it today'*.

The video featured a local congresswoman from Oaxaca, who at that moment was allegedly standing in the lobby of her local Congress, speaking directly to the camera with a message that was both a plea and a denouncement of foreign intervention: *"They want to amend the Oaxacan Constitution to allow abortion . . . illegally, through an extraordinary Congress session, and Argentinian pro-abortion advocates are standing here, telling Mexican women what to say, threatening priests. It is foreign terrorism, no less. No foreigner is allowed to influence Mexican politics. Speak up! Share this video to let them know that we, the 'pro-life' women, we are the real feminists."*

By then, unfortunately, it was too late for me to arrange a last-minute trip to Oaxaca and be present outside the local congress at the moment of voting, or to verify the alleged presence of Argentinian advocates and their supposed threats, or their interference with local politics. A few days later, the state of Oaxaca would make national news as the first subnational state, 12 years after Mexico City, to follow suit and decriminalize abortions carried out before the 12th gestational week. It was not too late, however, to guess that other subnational states might soon follow suit (which they did), or to ponder on the political *'pendularity'* of the issue, or to reflect on this curious case of opposed advocacy groups, each basking in the certainty and inevitable-ness of their victory. And to truly watch, in the words of more than one advocate: *'Mexican federalism come to life'*.

This book is the result of those fieldwork trips, carrying out extended expert interviews in 2018 and 2019. I explore the recent evolution of abortion laws in Mexico, as a story of advocacy that has been constructed using human rights

DOI:10.4324/9781032642338-1

concepts – diving deep into the ongoing *"lawfare"*[2] of two polarized and estranged groups. I have studied the unique landscape of abortion norms and laws in Mexico, and the story of how activists (for and against its legalization) have shaped them, analyzing their proposals for legal and public policy reforms. I map out this sociopolitical and legal landscape throughout the past decade, roughly beginning with the legalization of abortion in Mexico City in 2007, throughout the political backlash that ensued in other subnational states, and culminating with the Mexican Supreme Court's statements in 2021 and 2023, in favour of decriminalizing abortion.

I examine the Mexican case through a 'bifocal' lens of sorts: firstly and predominantly, by 'zooming into' Mexico as a country case where federalism makes for a complex and fascinating legal landscape and secondly, by 'zooming out' to also look at the Latin American and global context of abortion-related norms, as well as to examine networks of transnational advocates and their activities on this topic. *"When federalism came to life"* refers to the idea, shared by advocates on the ground in Mexico (for and against legal abortion), that this issue truly 'awakened' the various subnational states within the country, pushing them into a legislative diversity which did not exist previously.

During my doctoral research, I studied abortion advocacy as a case of *norm contestation* within opposing discourses on human rights. This refers to the controversy surrounding women's right (or the prohibition) to resort to abortion as a reproductive choice or a health-related matter. *"Contestation"* refers to the act (most often carried out by groups of activists or advocates on specific causes) of engaging with those norms which said advocates find inadequate or illegitimate, by protesting against them or by attempting to have them reformed. I apply this lens of *norm contestation* to the analysis of the Mexican case, at the national and subnational level, while touching as well upon the transnational dimension of a parallel debate unfolding at the global level.

The analysis focuses on the Mexican advocates' discourses, where I find varying (and often, competing and clashing) interpretations of human rights in relation to abortion. Also explored are advocates' proposals for *"organizing principles"*[3] of justice. This refers to principles which in theory should help policy makers to decide how best to organize competing ideas, around a basis of protecting human rights. Advocates use discourses to engage in a form of *"lawfare"* as explained by Rachel Sieder and others.[4] In a highly polarized sociopolitical climate, it can become a struggle to find middle ground solutions or second-best policy agreements which fill the "*legitimacy gap*"[5] encountered in such a contentious matter as that of the legality of abortion. In such a climate, the possibilities for meaningful dialogue are often left behind.

The reader will get a detailed understanding of concepts and meanings that these expert activists in Mexico have used in advocacy practices for and against legal abortion, in a journey through the norms and ideas that they propose, protest, and contest proactively or reactively, through discourse and behaviour. This analysis showcases the way in which advocates attempt to fill this "legitimacy gap" with their own proposals of law, norm, and principle, as well as potential solutions within competing norms, differing discursive frameworks, and colliding interpretations of principles of justice.

'Advocacy' is defined as 'the act or process of supporting a cause or proposal'. Throughout this book, the term *'advocate'* is used interchangeably with *'activist'*. They are, however, not exactly the same. The word *'activist'* places higher emphasis on the practice itself of supporting a cause, through actions which have that purpose; it is more strongly related to the realms of politics and social change. Activists often apply the word willingly to themselves, as a label tied to individual identity. *'Advocate'*, on the other hand, more strongly emphasizes the specific cause or policy being embraced; the word is somewhat less tied to realms of policy and social causes – but tied nonetheless, in our modern understanding of the concept.

Being that my empirical work focused on interviewing individuals who are willingly active within a pro- or anti-legal abortion movement; for the purposes of this study, the overlap between both concepts is almost total.[6] *Advocacy* will be understood as the practices carried out by individuals or organizations in their efforts to defend specific courses of action, and '*advocates/activists*' as the individuals, groups, or organizations that publicly support or recommend a particular policy or course of action, with regard to access to legal abortion. Their supported 'course of action' can be to maintain the existing *statu quo*, 'defending it' from the changes proposed by other advocates. The term will not be applied to individuals who merely affirm to be for or against abortion on a purely personal level, or to those who publicly state their opinions on the issue but without defending a policy change or stance.

The Endlessly Contested Issue: A Background to Abortion and Related Laws

Women's rights have gained recognition as a globally relevant matter: one that concerns justice, human rights, and social development. Since the first major steps towards an equal right to participation in the public and political spheres – beginning in the late 19th century, when some of the first jurisdictions worldwide granted women the right to vote – the advancement of women's equal rights has had a diverse and multi-faceted history. It has progressed at different paces depending on nation-state contexts as well as within subnational, racial, ethnic, and other differences. Voices of opposition and contestation (involving sometimes the use of force and violence) have been raised throughout every major step of attaining equal rights, invoking arguments such as tradition, religious belief, moral conviction, or the necessity of *'differentiated rights'* in order to 'protect the family'.

Surprisingly similar arguments have been used in the contestation of (and opposition to)[7] matters as seemingly diverse as women's right to work outside the home and to equal pay, their right to political participation, as well as the issue in focus here: sexual and reproductive rights, especially the issue of abortion. Yet such ways of opposing and contesting rights, norms, and principles are hardly exclusive to *women's* rights and indeed hardly new at all. In some ways, the history of human rights has been a history of expansion, inclusion, and redefinition. Throughout the years we have re-signified *who* should be considered a holder of *which types* of rights; *why* should such rights be granted, and *by whom*; who 'loses' or *forfeits* a certain right and *why*; and, very importantly, *how* should the nation-state act as an upholder and guarantor of rights. Almost every single step forward in this path of expansion and inclusion has been met with questioning and contestation (when not outright resistance or aggressive pushback) to some degree.

Social movements aiming to change the gendered understandings of the world are often met with fierce resistance by conservative social forces; any attempt to change these bedrock principles is often perceived as an unacceptable upheaval of 'the order of things' and usually takes several generations to be fully accepted. For instance, as normal as it seems today in western societies for an unmarried woman to use contraceptives, the introduction of modern contraceptive methods to those same societies around 60 years ago was initially met with resistance, with discourses about the 'immorality' and 'destruction of family values' that *the pill* would represent . . . not to forget regulations in the United States, initially making contraceptives legally available to married women only.[8] To this day, many conservative and religious groups still discourage *any* form of modern contraception, arguing on moral grounds.

As women's rights have gained recognition, the specific dimension of *sexual and reproductive health and rights* (SRHR, the established acronym in international institutions) remains controversial to numerous groups, societies, and traditional-minded communities. It is controversial because issues related to reproduction and 'the family' (often understood as an immutable and universal monolith) lie at the very core of people's ideas about how society ought to be, about how 'proper women' and 'proper men' are supposed to behave within their families and communities, about gender roles at large, and about what constitutes 'an acceptable social order'. This gives way to preconceptions about which practices are acceptable or unacceptable, concerning how people should reproduce and arrange their family life.

Controverted as SRHR already is, few aspects remain as controversial as abortion. It is unique as a social issue, presenting a striking kind of 'rights collision': in *every* instance of abortion, we find two recognizable holders of specific rights (the pregnant woman and the unborn, if at least 'potential' rights in the case of the unborn), in a unique situation of *'rights at odds'* within the body of one of them. To state the obvious, it is a gendered issue by default, as no similar case involves the body of an adult male. It is impossible to draw comparisons within discussions of gender equality, as can be done when debating equal rights to work, education, or political participation. We conclude that rights are violated when one is treated less favourably than someone in a comparable position.[9] In this case, 'comparable positions' are impossible to find. What to make of cases with no obvious comparator?. . . Discrimination laws are of limited use in an issue that affects only women (or those with bodies capable of gestating) and with no comparable instance as of today, where a (potential) individual exists within the body of another.

The practice of voluntarily interrupting a pregnancy has thus been controversial throughout various historical contexts – particularly in modern, Judaeo-Christian ones. Several factors converge to create complicated, often irreconcilable worldviews: social norms regarding gender roles, religious ideas and paradigms on morality, debates on women's agency over their own bodies, rules on what constitutes acceptable sexual behaviour, the legitimacy of an individual choice regarding reproduction (as opposed to a couple's or family's choice), philosophical and legal views concerning the point at which 'life' begins – and chiefly the point at which its judicial protection *should* begin, among other aspects.

The uniqueness of the case comes as a built-in feature, laying the ground for opposing views: the clash does not come about because of religious dogma (although religious dogma often plays a part), but from a quality of legal incomparability. We will be hard pressed to find a more controverted case of rights collision than that of consented abortions[10]: one with less definitive or 'universal' answers, where the normative lines are fuzzier, and where the traditional appeals to human rights lend themselves equally useful to such diametrically opposed worldviews, while providing *less* legal clarity.

The history of abortion's legal status throughout the world is much less straightforward than some advocates would want to simplify it into. In many historical, temporal, and national contexts, it has fallen into normative 'grey areas', legal loopholes, or a state of vagueness and lack of legal precision.[11] In a thoughtful analysis of abortion and human rights (with references also to international human rights documents), Zúñiga ponders both the legal difficulties of attributing personhood (and thus judicially meaningful human rights) to an unborn child while also acknowledging the social interest of protecting its independent life, for example, in cases of medical emergencies not related to abortion (premature birth, in utero surgeries, etc.).[12]

Being a highly complex legal issue, we can never simply say that abortion is 'legal' or 'illegal' in a certain country: most nation-states' laws on the matter are situated along a spectrum ranging from 'complete prohibition in all circumstances with no exceptions', to 'complete permissiveness on request and with no gestational limit'. Very few states are located on either of those extremes.[13] Most countries allow for at least *some* cases where abortion is permitted, the most common such cases being rape, fatal abnormalities in the unborn, or risks to the mother's life if the pregnancy is continued. Near the other end of the spectrum, wherever abortion is allowed more liberally, there is almost always a *gestational limit*: a certain number of weeks along the pregnancy where abortion is considered legitimate. These limits are typically in the near of 12–14 weeks, though other states allow until 24 weeks – by the end of the second trimester.

Different criteria have been used to decide where to place gestational limits. Some 'pro-choice' advocates use *foetal viability* as a threshold to indicate when an abortion should no longer be lawful, but this is bound to stay a 'moving line', prone to future changes. '*Viability*' is the point at which the foetus can survive outside the womb. Before it, the developing embryo needs to be inside another's body to stay alive and eventually be born. Modern developments in medical technology have lowered the viability threshold and are likely to further do so: currently it hovers around the 24th gestational week. Babies born at this point of extreme prematurity can survive but only with state-of-the-art medical technology. They are almost guaranteed to have physical and/or mental disabilities, often needing intensive and lifelong medical care (this has been another subject of advocacy in its own right: cases of extreme prematurity, and the attainable quality of life and medical care).

As some countries have currently established a limit of 24 gestational weeks for legal abortion; today there could already be a potential clash (or at the very least, an uneasy overlap) between the areas of medical law that advocate for better care of the extremely premature infant and the threshold for legal abortion. Such was the case in the United States, where the abortion debate took renewed force in the past decade, and *Roe vs. Wade* was eventually overturned in 2022, paving the way for re-criminalization.[14] The argument for overturning *Roe* was supposedly to 'restore the decision to the subnational states', but one cannot deny that 'pro-life' activism was intensely busy during previous years, with a clear intent to ban abortion – partially on the grounds that the 24-week threshold was too high and too close to viability. Reflecting on these issues serves as a reminder that our understandings of rights are constantly changing, allowing for the shaping and re-shaping of legitimate governing norms, and allowing for the inclusion of new developments in a particular field.

While the concept of *viability* has grounds on embryological and medical science, its limitations must be kept in mind if used in a legal setting related to abortion. Its boundaries are blurry and moving downwards into earlier stages of pregnancy. Because of a similar reasoning, already since the late eighties, the establishment of a viability threshold based on gestational trimesters had been called 'obsolete'[15] – with solid reasonings. As the advancements in embryology change our knowledge about development stages pre-birth, it becomes apparent that any system of 'lines' dividing a pregnancy into trimesters is rather arbitrary, and the same might happen in the future with the concept of 'gestational weeks'.

These advancements are used by some to justify stricter anti-abortion laws. Furthermore, viability is only one of many possible criteria to decide on a threshold at which abortion should be legal or illegal. Post-fall of *Roe vs. Wade,* several states in the United States changed their abortion-related norms using a different threshold: that of the existence of a heartbeat in the foetus. The medical definition of 'a heartbeat' is variable: it can refer to proto-tissue that eventually becomes a heart, sometimes detected as early as six weeks (long before many women realize their pregnancy). This stricter threshold translates into abortion laws that *de facto* ban the practice.

Others focus on the detection of pain signals in the foetus (semblance of a nervous system begins to appear at around ten weeks' gestation), or on the point at which *sentience* or self-awareness begins (a blurrier concept, often confounded by religious belief). For the intents and purposes laid out here, the usefulness of looking at various thresholds is to further emphasize that due to the nature of pregnancy and embryological development, and how unknown the pre-birth stages still are to us, decisions related to abortion laws can be informed by a myriad of criteria, all of them changing, moving, and with some degree of subjectivity. New medical developments also have the potential to introduce new potential stakeholders to the debate: drug companies, medical practitioners, biotech firms, etc. But it also serves us well to remember that legal decisions like these are much more often informed by ideological principle, advocacy messages built on emotion, or partisan loyalties – not necessarily on scientific or medical grounds.

Another sub-discussion concerns the point at which the issue of abortion meets that of the public-private dichotomy. Some theorists ponder: what to make of the right to privacy in this context?[16] Meaning: when should the state intervene, and why?. . . Many who strongly defend the right to privacy, and to non-interference by the state in private or family matters (adopting what is known as a 'libertarian' stance on other issues), make however great exception to this one case, suggesting that the state should actively criminalize and punish women who interrupt a pregnancy, as well as anyone who might assist her (medical personnel or others). That these personal decisions related to reproduction can easily become such 'public affairs' is baffling to others.

The *reasons* to have an abortion are another factor for encountered opinions, beyond whether abortion itself should be allowed or not: rather they become discussions on whether some reasons are legitimate while others aren't. These distinctions can quickly come across as arbitrary, perhaps unfair in some scenarios – when not outright hypocritical if some reasons perceived as 'illegitimate' are allowed while others perceived as 'legitimate' are not. For those opposing legal abortion, the issue is a matter of which few reasons (if any) should be acceptable for actively interrupting a pregnancy. Most commonly accepted are: fatal abnormalities in the unborn (meaning it has no chances of surviving outside the womb), if a woman's life is at risk should the pregnancy continue (to some, this is the only scenario where her rights override those of the foetus), or in cases where pregnancy is the result of rape (where the deciding criterion becomes whether a sexual act was consented to or not, disregarding whether *the pregnancy itself* is wanted or not).

For those in favour of legal abortion, 'number of gestational weeks' is often the only relevant criteria – but this can have problematic implications, as mentioned. Other possible reasons can clash with different human rights concepts, for example, aborting for reasons of (non-fatal) disability, clashing with disability rights. In some countries, it is legal to opt for abortion when a disability is detected in the unborn, often granting even a higher number of gestational weeks for this choice. This can be construed as discrimination, opening also a dangerous window for too broad definitions of what 'disability' means (should blindness, deafness, Down's syndrome, or missing a limb provide enough reasons for terminating a pregnancy?).[17] Gender discrimination is also at play, in societies where especially female foetuses are aborted for reasons of gender preference towards sons – usually happening in contexts where family expectations are stronger than the woman's own 'choice'.[18]

In such a context, simplistic catchphrases trumpeting a woman's '*right to choose*' become an empty slogan at best, and at worst, an oblivious disconnect with many of those women's lived realities. *Who is actually doing the 'choosing'?. . .* Clearly these considerations could (and perhaps ought to, for good measure) cause ethical conflict for any strand of feminism that defends the right to terminate a pregnancy – but not precisely for reasons of gender discrimination, nor to trump over disabled people's equal rights. Should abortion then be legal *except* when it constitutes some clear case of discrimination? And *how* to distinguish between such cases and any other?. . .

Discussions about which of these visions would 'best' fit a particular scenario for the woman, for the unborn, for other family members, for medical professionals, for state institutions, etc., are likely futile and certainly not within the scope of this book. Yet by looking at the various human rights-related dimensions that this issue can touch upon, we can begin to understand the strongly opposed responses, even in persons who would not appear to be so 'ideologically distant' on other sociopolitical topics. Abortion is a sort of 'oddest-case scenario' for contested norms: it is difficult to find a topic where the ideological clashes are more frontal, where worldviews are more opposed, and where solutions suggested by advocates are more at odds with each other. *Mutually exclusive*, if we will.

Advocacy 'on the ground' shows these collisions clearly. The opposing sides of the debate are opposed, in a very general sense, because they each focus on one of the two differing rights holders. The self-labelled *'pro-life'* advocates place their discursive focus on defending the rights (or 'potential' rights, if they can be so described) of the unborn, in full equality to the woman's rights – or at least, as legally meaningful enough to restrict abortion in all but a few cases. Meanwhile, so-called pro-choice advocates view the woman's right to choose over her own body as trumping any potential rights of the unborn – at least during the early stages of pregnancy.

We perceive the many instances of '*except if*', '*or at least*' and '*or maybe only*' in each position: they signal that most abortion-related norms (and thus the lawmakers and advocates who put them into place) are not absolutist or strictly binary in their ideas. They recognize limits, exceptions, caveats, or circumstances where abortion can or should be either permitted or restricted (for 'pro-life' and 'pro-choice' discourses, respectively).[19] These nuances tend to be acknowledged by advocates, however, only through further prodding – after initial expressions of knee-jerk, black-and-white, 'for' or 'against' militancy. Most activists concerned with abortion have opinions falling somewhere on a spectrum ranging from absolute prohibition to absolute permissiveness, with only few vocal minorities actually standing on either of those extremes. But the nuanced positions, again, can take several further nudges within a long, constructive discussion to be finally revealed.

It is often the political 'pulls and pushes' of specific places and periods, more so than the medical sciences, that have defined abortion-related policy and continue to do so: as it is being currently witnessed, with many contextual specificities, in the United States after the repeal of *Roe vs. Wade* in 2022. Advocacy and politics, local and global, play a large role in shaping the proposed abortion policies and the attempts to find *organizing principles*. Currently there is no global or regional consensus on what the precise legal status of abortion ought to be; nor on specific boundaries of a '*right to life*' or a '*right to choose*'. There isn't a firmly set position by international organizations on what should nation-states' role be in relation to abortion: whether to provide, regulate, finance, or to just keep 'hands off' and deregulate it. The issue is still mostly left for countries to decide domestically, save for a few general recommendations such as not criminalizing women for abortions and providing them with post-abortion care regardless of whether a procedure was legal or not.

I look at various international human rights documents, chiefly those created within the United Nations and Inter-American legal systems, and how they can be interpreted within this issue. What these legal documents specify is as relevant as what they (more often) do *not*. Their frequent ambiguities, which exist for the sake of accommodating domestic and contextual interpretation (taking, for example, the very *un*specific articles of the Convention on the Rights of the Child), make them suitable to be construed as supportive to opposed groups within the debate.

A crucial note should be made on the label of '*pro-life*'. Throughout this book, the advocates against abortion will often be referred to as 'pro-life' advocates. Although this labelling, with their appropriation of the idea of 'protecting life', is problematic for a multitude of reasons, they are self-identified as such, in a way which merits study in itself as a reframing of their own narrative (with the obvious implication that advocates opposed to them are '*pro-death*'). In each instance of using this term, it should be understood that it is meant as 'the self-proclaimed, *pro-life* advocates'. It is somewhat simpler to refer to them using their self-chosen 'pro-life' wording, for the sake of avoiding constant repetition to clarify that they are 'anti' or 'against legal abortion'.

In a similar vein, it should be noted that the term '*pro-choice*' comes from the Anglo-Saxon linguistic landscape of pro-legal abortion movements. In the Spanish language, advocates in favour of legalizing abortion tend not to use a direct translation of the term 'pro-choice'. Such a translation, like '*pro-elección*' or similar ones, comes across as rather ambiguous and un-specific of what kind of 'choice' one is defending, or even which issue one is referring to. For all its potentially useful conciseness, '*pro-elección*' is not a commonly used term across the Spanish-speaking world of legal abortion advocates. These advocates are instead more divided between calling themselves 'pro-abortion', 'in favour of abortion', or 'pro-decriminalization' (*pro-despenalización*), with the latter term carrying less stigma. Using 'pro-choice' often throughout this book responds to reasons of it being a familiar term in the Anglophone sphere and importantly to convey many of these advocates' message that, though they may feel *personally* opposed to abortion themselves, they defend any individual's right to legally choose abortion for herself.

The Odd Legal Case: Abortion in Latin America and Related Advocacy

Women in Latin America have, in recent decades, seen significant advancements in terms of equal legal rights, political participation, and their general status in civil and economic life.[20] Yet the matters pertaining to sexual and reproductive rights remain controversial in many countries and within many conservative and tradition-oriented groups across the region, and no issue is as highly contested as the legality of abortion. It is still an acutely debated issue in Latin America, including Mexico, and a frequent topic of public controversy, where any change in related laws or public policies (in any direction) rarely goes without contestation by activists, religious representatives, government officials, and diverse NGOs. It stands out among other legal debates in its '*contestedness*', and in its fickle (what I deem '*pendular*') legal history.

Religious institutions, political parties, important political figures, and international NGOs have played an active role in placing this issue on social and political agendas at the local, national, and transnational scale, advocating for various possibilities on a spectrum ranging from complete liberalization to full bans (including criminalization at times). Every such change tends to be highly contested, and the debates tend to stall when addressed through frameworks of morality, human rights in a general sense, or even gender equality. Debates about abortion in the region are highly politicized: a gamut of institutions and prominent individuals from many walks of life carry out strong advocacy for or against its legalization, often with clear objectives of policy and legislative change – and sometimes as an easy 'political flag' for advancing a candidate in an election. The influential Catholic Church has not shied away from trying to influence debates, votes, and minds,[21] using abortion as a major cornerstone of debates on family life, gender roles, social life, and political activity.

We find different 'legality statuses' across the region,[22] ranging from full bans with no exception in countries like El Salvador and Nicaragua to liberalized access (up until a certain number of gestational weeks) in Uruguay, Cuba, recently Argentina and Colombia,[23] as well as Mexico in five subnational states (as of late 2021).[24] Most countries in the region prohibit abortion except in three common cases, very often known as 'the three causes' (*'las tres causales'*), because these three tend to be the most frequently admitted exceptions to abortion bans: risks to the mother's life if the pregnancy is continued, fatal malformations in the unborn, or if the pregnancy results from sexual assault. Throughout the book I will often refer to these as 'the three causes' or 'the three *causales*', using the word in Spanish. These *'causales'* are, today, the most frequent legal compromise[25]: three instances where even those who oppose abortion (be they advocates or the public at large) tend to agree that an exception is warranted. It tends to be only in those three situations that the usual focus of the debate shifts from '*When does life begin?*' into '*When is it unacceptable to force a woman to carry a pregnancy to term?*'

The three '*causales*' don't necessarily come together: some countries may allow for only one or two, or these three plus others. Other, less common exceptions are when the pregnancy is a result of incest, risks to the mother's 'health' more broadly (which can sometimes include mental health), impairments in the unborn even if they are not fatal (the aforementioned disability reasons), or other 'broad socioeconomic grounds'. We find rules with various nuances, including differentiated sanctions depending on contexts and circumstances (or differentiated for the woman and the personnel carrying out the abortion).

Moreover, one should not forget that in Latin America, there are often considerable disparities or gaps between what is *stated by law*, and what is *actually implemented on the ground*. It is the case on many issues, including access to abortion as a public or private medical service. This is markedly the case in Mexico with the penalties to abortion: while codified in law, illegal abortion is rarely persecuted in reality. During some of the field interviews, this very fact was brought up by some 'pro-life' advocates as a good reason to keep abortion illegal *and* criminalized in the law: the fact that those penalties are rarely enacted but still act as "a good enough deterrent".[26] This is telling about the impunity culture in Mexico at large but also about a potential argumentative flaw of a pro-criminalization argument, if its strong point is *its non-implementation in reality*.

Gaps can also exist between the legal reality of abortion in a particular time and place, and the public's awareness of it (meaning it can be legal or illegal in a certain place, while most of the public believes otherwise), not to forget the convoluted ways in which medical and legal judgment can collide.[27] Written norm does not necessarily align with the realities on the ground, with the public's awareness of those realities, or with the possibilities for successful implementation of an idea.

Advocates for and against abortion in Latin America have resorted to a wide array of arguments, through different conceptual frameworks, in order to influence public and political debates, in their attempts to change or maintain the legal status of abortion in a given place.[28] Abortion has been framed as an issue of religious morality,[29] of women's human rights,[30] of children and the unborn's human rights,[31] as well as public health and maternal mortality, touching upon dimensions of class, sexual and reproductive mores, family planning practices, and, of course, gender roles.

If we analyze recent cases of successful legalization, Mexico City in 2007 and Argentina in 2021, when abortion was legalized until gestational weeks 12 and 14, respectively, or Chile in August 2017,[32] when abortion was legalized only in the cases of the three "causes", we often find that advocates relied on a framework of *public health* to advance their cause: placing abortion on political agendas by advancing the idea that it is an issue of women's health, instead of a criminal or moral issue. In the Mexican case, only when the debate was framed as an issue of health rather than 'morality' or 'personal choice' (prevention of maternal mortality in women who did not have access to expensive, private and safer illegal abortions) was decriminalization and eventual legalization achieved.[33]

Advocates often act as representatives of NGOs or as political representatives, claiming to speak on behalf of larger constituencies, groups, or populations. In the Latin American context of this topic, such advocates are often immersed in an ongoing process of challenge and contestation of the current legal status of abortion in their area (whatever that status may be),[34] often furthering a particular legislative course of action: be it to legalize abortion with no restrictions other than gestational weeks, or to legalize it only in specific legal circumstances (rape, fatal medical abnormalities, etc.), or to illegalize it as well as make it punishable by law. In contexts where abortion is already illegal, often the *'pro-life'* advocates are defending the *statu quo* of illegality against proposed changes, although occasionally some advocates defend the further toughening of already strict anti-abortion laws or penalties. It is rather the 'pro-choice' groups which, in this context, face the uphill battle towards change.

In public protests and media debates, we find strong tendencies towards moral reductionism, where opposed groups of advocates attempt to summarize their ideas in highly simplistic and context-devoid manners, using emotionally charged terms. This simplification was observed in the protests attended in Mexico during 2018 and 2019, as can be also seen in other protests elsewhere, documented online through photographs. Signs and posters often display slogans such as, '*Abortion is Murder*', '*We will never allow this in Chile/Mexico/El Salvador, here we protect children and the family*'. Discourses show an appropriation of 'true morality' on the opposed groups. Those pushing for more liberal abortion laws have not been exempt from moral reductionism and *'sloganism'*, also attempting to capture what is a complex and context-sensitive issue into short catchphrases: '*My body, my rights*', '*If I give birth, I decide*', or '*Stop the rosaries in my ovaries!*'.[35]

The transnationalization of the issue was made especially clear in 2018, when Argentina was at the epicentre of similar protests and debates, as its Congress debated legalizing abortion. Argentinian advocates on opposed sides of the controversy took to the streets in massive protests, simplifying their positions into uniformly coloured bandanas or handkerchiefs (light blue for the 'pro-life' side and green for the 'pro-choice'). These handkerchiefs and the same corresponding colours were taken as a signifier throughout the rest of the continent. Today, from Mexico all the way to Chile, on '*Twitter*' and in the streets, bandanas identical to those shown in Argentina are used as a personal flag to signal a clear-cut position within the abortion debate.

Advocates on opposed groups also resort to the depiction of particular and differing types of 'characters', for example, victims of specific situations or practices, along with their messages, in order to maximize emotional impact and engage opinions and support. The controversies, especially in the context of this type of political polarization, often also involve de-legitimizing discourses about certain laws: '*this doesn't represent me/us as an individual/a community/a religious group/a nation*', '*this norm was imposed on us by spurious authorities/through a flawed procedure/by foreign actors and agendas*', etc. Although simplification is a common way of conveying messages in a protest, framings on this issue are often inaccurate, using inflammatory words or examples of extreme cases, in an attempt to get an emotional response followed by engagement in the issue. As happens often in other contentious topics, depicting the ideological opponent as a caricature of its most extreme representatives is a simplistic strategy, yet one commonly used by opposed groups of advocates in the abortion debate.

Paradoxically (because of how often the issue appears portrayed as 'black and white'), most of the activists concerned with abortion, who have some degree of expertise on the matter, have opinions falling somewhere in between absolute prohibition or absolute permissiveness, with only few vocal minorities actually standing on either of those extremes. Surveys on the issue across Latin America show that, when pressed to give a more detailed answer, most people have nuanced opinions, also within a range of possibilities.[36] Activists themselves seem to forget this nuance often, rooting their activism in an '*Us versus Them*', '*Team Good and Team Bad*', dichotomous vision of the issue.

The simplification of the debate into short '*tweets*', and effectively into two different colours on clothing accessories, would make the issue seem clear-cut, when in reality it is far from being so. Also, some still assume that 'pro-life' groups in Latin America comprise mostly conservative people of generational cohorts over 40 years of age, or that women traditionally have little agency or less active voices.[37] This is, however, inaccurate these days: across Latin America, churches and other traditional groups manage to mobilize large groups of young people in their anti-abortion protests, and women have a strong and growing presence in 'pro-life' advocacy groups.[38]

These opposed 'sides' of the debate indeed see themselves as two opposed, clear-cut sides of a debate. Despite the potential overlap that could exist between their worldviews – for example, being that much of the *'pro-life'* camp at least agrees with the *'pro-choicers'* in saying that the idea should *not* be to criminalize women in a punishment-focused framework, and often also agree that the state should provide support for vulnerable single mothers in order to avoid abortions – polarization online and offline makes it even harder to find compromise and common ground. This parting of ways is likely to intensify, as politics within the region become increasingly polarized and the potential points for common ground are forgotten. A better understanding of the case's nuances could help sweep off the layers of dust under which the 'pathways to dialogue' risk staying buried.

The Fickle Legal History: Constant *'Pendularity'* in the Legal Status of Abortion

The issue of abortion stands in contrast to other aspects of women's rights where there has been continuous historical progress, generally with no 'rolling back'. For instance, no contemporary nation-state that has granted women the right to vote has later suppressed it, at least not in a lasting or permanent manner (discounting exceptional cases of countries which may be experiencing extraordinary circumstances of civil war, occupation by foreign powers or by local fundamentalist groups, etc.). Nor has there been, in very general terms, an ongoing re-contestation of whether women should be legally allowed to seek a divorce, to work with equal pay, to attend higher education, etc.

Abortion, on the other hand, is a frequent matter of what I deem '*legislative oscillation*' or '*pendularity*', especially in the Americas. It is a frequent subject of political and public controversy in the region, and opposing groups display fundamentally irreconcilable viewpoints while engaging in cultural and legalistic narratives that are incompatible and at odds with one another. Proposals of legal reforms to liberalize, or to 'roll back', restrict, and re-criminalize abortion are relatively frequent – some which end up passing into law, and some not. Numerous policy changes regarding abortion in Latin America have happened in recent decades,[39] which is indicative of how relevant the topic stays within the region. To name some of the most extreme cases first: El Salvador had more permissive abortion laws until the late eighties, when the government eliminated all allowed exceptions, and enforced a total legal ban on abortion; Nicaragua implemented a full abortion ban only in 2006, with no exceptions.[40] To date, these two are among the very few countries worldwide, where abortion is prohibited with no exceptions.

The following countries have also had recent changes (or reform projects were presented) in their abortion related laws, between 2015 and 2021: the Dominican Republic in 2021 (from full ban to only allowing in cases of rape), Argentina in 2020 (legalizing until the 12th gestational week, after the unsuccessful attempt in 2018 which had sparked transnational protests), Ecuador in 2021 (permitting abortion in cases of sexual assault), and Colombia in 2022 (legalizing until the 24th gestational week). Chile showed exceptionally quick shifts after 2017 (ending the decades-long total ban, at the time one of the few in the world, firstly admitting the three '*causales*' in 2017 and then legalizing until the 14th gestational week in 2021).[41] Within Mexico, access to abortion was liberalized in Mexico City in 2007, which prompted backlash in other states (spearheaded by the Catholic Church), several of which ended up passing more restrictive abortion laws. Only beginning in 2019, other Mexican subnational states started to liberalize abortion laws (Oaxaca in 2019; Hidalgo, Veracruz, Yucatán and Coahuila in 2021), making for an incredibly mixed legal panorama of abortion restrictions within Mexico.[42]

If we go further back, we encounter more reforms: while Nicaragua fully banned abortion in 2006 with no exceptions, in the same year Colombia was decriminalizing only in the three common '*causales*', while Uruguay liberalized access in 2012 to become one of the most permissive countries in the region. That different Latin American countries can move into such opposite directions in a similar timeframe of the last two decades is remarkable. No matter the legal status of abortion in one Latin American country or the other, such status is almost certain to be constantly challenged in legal courts, as well as the court of public opinion.

In Mexico (where this is mostly an issue of subnational politics), when abortion was liberalized in the capital in 2007, the National Commission of Human Rights was in fact among those to challenge the decision at the Supreme Court.[43] Similar challenges are common throughout the region: in Nicaragua, the full ban instituted in 2006 was challenged in the Supreme Court in 2008, however to no avail.[44] The Inter-American Court on Human Rights (IACHR) has condemned absolute prohibitions like that of El Salvador, adding fuel to the debate as the ruling was domestically framed as "an infringement on national sovereignty".[45] On this background, advancements in any direction seem fragile and temporary.

Opposed groups of advocates create, re-create, enact, and contest *meanings*, often with clear results of legal and policy change. This has been the case in Mexico since the 1970s, and with much more intensity in the past two decades: beginning around the three years leading up to 2007, when certain legal reforms started to trigger a larger debate on abortion at the national level,[46] then reaching a critical turning point in April 2007 when abortion until the 12th gestational week was decriminalized in Mexico City (which in turn triggered opposing and backlash movements), and continuing until today.

I should remark a crucial point to keep well noted throughout this book: decriminalization is *not* the same as legalization. While the former refers to eliminating punishment for a certain act, the latter is understood in this context as a much wider-encompassing practice, which involves the state further regulating a procedure and/or providing access to it. In 2007 in Mexico City, abortion was initially *decriminalized*, but this was also accompanied throughout the years by a *legalization* process where public health institutions in Mexico City began to provide access to abortion, and local laws in the capital were amended to regulate who could offer the procedure and how. Since 2007 and until today, abortion can be obtained in Mexico City until the 12th gestational week, and the procedure is provided by both public and private healthcare institutions. This remark is applicable to other countries' respective legal systems.

Another important message to 'take home' from this brief mention of recent legal changes throughout Latin American countries (and one that risks being overlooked in discussions about international/transnational advocacy) is to '*watch for federalism*', in countries that have laws varying at the subnational level such as Mexico and Argentina. In these and other federal states, national laws set a basic common ground, but regulations at the subnational level are the final determining factor of what is accepted or prohibited, or of what policies are meaningful in practice – not only in legal principle. In such places, access to abortion or a lack thereof is largely determined by the *subnational* policies.

In the United States, we encounter this '*pendularity*' as well. It is frequent that Republican governments attempt to pass restrictions on abortion at the national and subnational levels (even before *Roe vs. Wade* was repealed in 2022, and more strongly so afterwards, along with 'trigger bans' designed to come into effect immediately with the repeal), while Democratic administrations attempt to facilitate access. Another notable aspect of abortion-related norms in the United States is the "Global Gag Rule"[47] or "Mexico City Policy",[48] a restriction on the provision of abortion services (or even abortion information) by institutions receiving US financial aid abroad.[49] The Global Gag Rule, almost as a matter of routine, is reinstated whenever a Republican government is in office and withdrawn when a Democrat governs in the White House.

In quite an exceptional way, abortion is a political flashpoint in the United States and other American (and some European)[50] countries, where it has become almost a political tradition that right-leaning governments attempt to restrict access while left-leaning governments aim to liberalize it, a constant 'pendulum' oscillating back and forth, above the ever-present "legitimacy gap": the frequent disjoint between moral discourse and achievable policy.

The Mexican Case and Three Crucial Contextual Factors

The Mexican debate, in its modern facet, can be said to begin with the "Paulina Case" ("*Caso Paulina*")[51] in the early 2000s. It concerned an underage girl from northern Mexico who had a pregnancy resulting from sexual assault and who was subsequently denied a legal abortion by authorities in the subnational state of Baja California. The case was eventually brought to the Inter-American Commission of Human Rights, in 2004. This event reignited the debate and the advocacy with renewed force, paving the way for crucial law reforms and ultimately leading to the decriminalization of abortion in the capital, in 2007.

Legislative backlash ensued throughout the subnational states after 2007. Since then and until 2021, almost every year saw at least one relevant legal reform concerning abortion – most of them at the level of the local state laws, and only occasionally at the federal level. This speaks to the controversial as well as polarizing nature of the issue, since the reforms go in different directions: some towards restriction and some towards liberalization. At the time of undertaking the research and analysis of data which ultimately became the basis for this book (up until late 2021); the subnational states of Oaxaca, Hidalgo, Baja California, Guerrero, Coahuila and Veracruz were the only ones besides Mexico City to have also decriminalized abortion until the 12th gestational week. All of them did so only quite recently, beginning with Oaxaca in 2019. Meanwhile, the rest of the *estados* tightened anti-abortion laws by passing Constitutional reforms enshrining the protection of life from the moment of conception (since each *estado* has its own local Constitution, as well as its local Criminal Code or *Código Penal*).

Two much more recent developments (by late 2023) will be referred to in the future as crucial milestones: with Mexico's Supreme Court ruling against the criminalization of abortion in 2021, and then in 2023 declaring that the Federal Criminal Code (*Código Penal Federal*) should not penalize abortion anymore and that *federal* healthcare institutions should offer the procedure. And while the Mexican federal laws apply to federal institutions (as opposed to the subnational, local-state-ruled institutions), at the moment of writing these lines, more than half of the subnational states still criminalize abortion in their local laws, which do not immediately lose validity by the Supreme Court's rulings. Such are the nuances and complexities of the Mexican federal legal system which I set to analyze throughout the book.

In the case of Mexico City and other subnational states, the use and negotiation of frameworks, meanings, and dimensions of the abortion debate were a relevant factor in the different outcomes of those ideological clashes.[52] Abortion was legalized in Mexico City in 2007 through a successful framing of the issue as one of *maternal mortality, health and rights*, by using, among others, the image of the poor and disempowered woman as an element of advocacy. In the ensuing backlash, several other Mexican states toughened their local anti-abortion laws after 2007, mostly by enshrining a protection of life 'from the moment of conception' in their local constitutions. In this case, the advocates identifying as 'pro-life' activists developed their own strategies, also through framing, meaning-making, and the contestation of concepts and principles – by presenting, naturally, the image of the 'murdered' unborn as the ultimate defenceless victim. Advocates in Mexico City (many of whom were politicians, taking up the issue of legalizing abortion despite potential costs to their political careers) relied on transnational advocacy networks, contacting global SRHR organizations or 'sister' institutions abroad, while opposing groups throughout the country also interacted with global 'pro-life' groups.[53]

Three contextual factors add nuance and complexity to the Mexican case as studied here. Firstly, an important constitutional reform was carried out in 2011, where international human rights treaties signed by Mexico are granted equal weight as a part of national law. This represents a major paradigm shift in Mexican legal tradition,[54] which up until that point only recognized (in the first 30 articles of the Federal Constitution) the existence not of human rights but of "Individual Guarantees" (*Garantías Individuales*), granted *by* the Mexican state *to* the individual Mexican national.

The newly adopted text recognizes those articles as "Human Rights and Their Guarantees" (*De Los Derechos Humanos y Sus Garantías*), recognizing that such rights are inherent to the human person (instead of 'granted by the state'), mentioning international treaties as an equally valid source of law as the Constitution, and upholding the *pro-persona principle* of the highest possible protection of rights. The source of such protection can be either the constitution itself or international legal documents signed by Mexico.

Secondly, Mexico is a federation where each administrative division (subnational state or '*estado*') creates its own legislation concerning abortion, since this issue falls under the umbrella of health laws and criminal codes, of which every *estado* has its own at the local level (although there is also a Federal Criminal Code and a General Health Law, setting a basic common ground). Each has its own local constitution, as well. This makes for a complex case where we find a large network of laws on varying levels of governance, and where the country's political system gives each subnational state some degree of autonomy over its own norms and policies. In the case of abortion-related laws, in a rather exceptional manner, each of the Mexican *estados* has created its own regulations (rather than merely following the 'legalistic tradition' of roughly copying Mexico City's laws with minor adaptations). These significant changes in abortion-related policy were triggered, for the most part, starting in 2007,[55] when Mexico City first decriminalized abortion within the first 12 weeks of pregnancy. This major legal change was built upon other legislative efforts carried out by advocates shortly before, in the couple of years leading up to 2007.

The third factor of interest is the plurality of the Mexican national state and the growing sociopolitical representation of this plurality.[56] This is reflected not only in a diversity of ethnic groups whose political voices have been growing slowly yet steadily; increased citizen participation in diverse NGOs and civil associations; and the existence of newer political parties as well as the growing influence of older, previously marginalized parties. All in all, civil society and other stakeholders (e.g. religious institutions) have had a rapidly growing role in shaping policy and representing citizens' interests. It should also be noted that this civil society is getting increasingly involved in *transnational advocacy*, where issues such as abortion transcend state boundaries, with activists on opposed sides of the debate seeking alliances abroad as well as using international legal texts to sustain their positions.

Three Distinct 'Advocacy Events': Mexico in Times of Sociopolitical Polarization

During 2018 and 2019, I carried out in-depth personal interviews with around 30 advocates for and against the legalization of abortion, engaging them on the general abortion debate, on their competing discourses in advocacy, on the contextual factors mentioned in the previous sub-section, and also on three specific 'sub-cases' or 'advocacy events'. These events can be understood as moments in time when the contestation reached points of high intensity: recent arenas which have strongly shown this contestation unfolding, with the two competing discourses through advocacy.

Expert advocates were carefully chosen: those who have had a known role in, for example, presenting a particular legislative reform, proposing a specific policy, acting as a link with 'sister' institutions in other countries or in global forums, drafting written communications, or sending messages to international institutions at times when the legality of abortion has been up for debate. A very clear example of such a global debate happened at the UN Office of the High Commissioner for Human Rights (OHCHR), with the creation of the "*Draft Comment No. 36 on the Right to Life*". The comment was published in its final form in 2018 as the *"General Comment No. 36 to the International Covenant on Civil and Political Rights (ICCPR) on the Right to Life"*,[57] following a period of time during which individuals as well as organizations could send their written comments to the OHCHR.

The three aforementioned 'sub-cases' are the following:

1) **The decriminalization of abortion (and its subsequent legalization) in Mexico City in 2007,** which built on events from three years prior such as the *"Caso Paulina"* and the passing of the "Robles Law" or "*Ley Robles*".[58] This decriminalization prompted political and social backlash, as well as opposing legislation in other Mexican subnational states. These opposing reforms at the subnational level went on throughout the following decade, the most recent having come to pass in 2021.
2) **The Constitutional Assembly of Mexico City in 2016–2017,** in the context of major administrative reform at the subnational state level. As the capital transitioned from being the 'Federal District' into another '*estado*' like those in the rest of the country (one now officially called 'Ciudad de México'), the legality of abortion in Mexico City was again contested by legislators and stakeholders when drafting this new Constitution, with some attempting to 'roll it back' while others wanted to codify 'a right to abortion' into the new text.
3) **The unfolding of a parallel debate beyond Mexican borders.** This refers, in general, to the transnational advocacy happening in recent times with regard to abortion and how Mexican advocates have connected to this transnational and global realm. Two concrete examples emerged, with impeccable timing, during the years of my research: on the one hand, the aforementioned global debate on abortion at the OHCHR in the years of 2017 and 2018 during the creation of the "*Draft Comment No. 36*", and on the other, the national abortion debate unfolding in Argentina in 2018, parallel to the Mexican debate and with clear exchanges between advocates of both nations. Because one can point out the precise timing of these transnational instances of global/transnational contestation, I have chosen to group them as a third event, representative of more general transnational/global exchanges.

These two latter international instances, the parallel national debate in Argentina and the 'open global forum' of sorts at the OHCHR, clearly showcased the *'transnationalisation'* of the advocacy and discourses, where Mexican advocates established links with a larger transnational and global arena. Within such transnationalization, we can find different modes of 'global engagement'. Mexican advocates for and against legal abortion have established links with 'sister' institutions or with allied movements abroad (especially the contact between Mexican and Argentinian advocates, when Argentina had its similar debate), or with their larger 'parent' institutions or organizations with similar goals (such as links between *Pro-Life International* and *Pro-Vida* in Mexico, or between Catholics for Choice and *Católicas por el Derecho a Decidir*). Thus, the exchanges between advocates at the domestic level and the global level are happening not only 'vertically' linking local advocates and international institutions but also 'laterally' between advocates in various countries.

In the global debate that happened at the OHCHR, multiple state representatives, associations, NGOs, and experts worldwide engaged in discussions (via oral and written statements) about the *"Draft Comment No. 36 on the Right to Life"*. Although the document didn't focus solely on abortion, it clearly was the most contentious and widely discussed point. The OHCHR received an almost equal number of comments 'for' and 'against' legal abortion from numerous sources globally – making it a clear case of global debate and of a "multilogue"[59] on a contested issue. In a much larger sense, cases like these two, showcasing transnational advocacy, are emblematic of the globalization of contested cases – what we could deem *'the globalization of polarization'* or *'discourse clashes going global'*.

The three 'instances' show concrete results in terms of advocates' law-making and policymaking goals, in Mexico and beyond its borders. Through them, one can point at Mexico's complex legal environment (its federal status giving room to a multitude of laws, placed at different levels of governance), as well as at the diversity of possible interpretations of law and norm. Meanwhile, the third instance also provides a snapshot of transnational advocacy and international dimension: how advocates interpret norms, ascribe meanings, and re-signify concepts, not only in an 'isolated' domestic bubble but globally as well.

The years 2018 and 2019 were a fortunate time to study activism on abortion in Mexico. These were intensely active years, of 'advocacy in action' surrounding contested norms. One of the very first hints that emerged while analyzing the data was that appealing to 'human rights' as an ideological spearhead, or trying to conjure them as an 'argumentative weapon', has not quite led to any workable solutions in the abortion debate. This is because opposed groups of advocates in the abortion debate have carefully constructed a defence of differently recognized individuals (the woman and the unborn) precisely by appealing to fundamental human rights. Opposed groups can (and often do) find human rights-based legal grounds, for defending their respective ideas. In the Mexican case, the intense advocacy carried out on both 'sides' of the debate has so far galvanized and solidified the opposing views, rather than fostering meaningful dialogue.

For as much media engagement, public protests, written statements, and other kinds of contestation practices have been carried out by opposed groups, little to no meaningful dialogue happens between or across them: advocates self-identify as 'for' or 'against', yet rarely acknowledge nuances or reach across to ideological opponents. They rather engage in a conversation with their own followers, each side mostly *'preaching to the choir'* in its own ideological echo chamber. They carry out "lawfare"[60] practices of pushing for legislative and policy changes, with opposed groups having achieved several such 'legislative victories' in recent years. Both positions are thus solidified and often emboldened into more radicalization, more polarization, and moving further away from potentially overlapping principles or from pathways to dialogue.

The Global Contentiousness of Abortion: International Human Rights Law and Local Policymaking

Analyzing current laws in various countries, as well as international legal documents on human rights like those previously mentioned, we find that there is no clear consensus on what the precise legal status of abortion should be (permitted completely, permitted with limits, banned completely, banned with exceptions . . .) or what should governments' role be in relation to abortion[61] (to criminalize and apply penalties, to only criminalize in principle or only some related aspects, to *not* criminalize and rather completely de-regulate, or to actively provide it as a part of family planning or other types of medical services).

This sociopolitical contentiousness of abortion is not an exclusively Latin American phenomenon – similar social movements and struggles around this issue are found in the United States[62] as well as in some European countries such as Poland and Ireland. One peculiarity however, which displays the results of diverse advocacy efforts within the Latin American region (and which explains how opposed advocates on this debate often find solid legal grounds on which to base their arguments), is the recognition of a right to life *"in general, from the moment of conception"* in Article 4 of the Inter-American Convention of Human Rights (also known as the *Pact of San José*), of which Mexico has been a signatory since 1981. This is one notable difference from the Universal Declaration of Human Rights, which does not mention "conception" or any other point, for that matter, at which protection of life should begin (other than that, both documents are very similar).

Although the Pact of San José does allow ample room for state-by-state interpretation of its articles (through its text and through the generally accepted procedural rules of this and other international instruments), the mere existence of such wording in Article 4 of the *Pact of San José* showcases the lack of consensus on different international institutions, about a specific point at which the obligation to protect life begins. It also showcases that the arguments for opposition to abortion, worldwide and in the Americas, do not originate exclusively from ideological positions based on religious principles, appeals to moral tradition, or blind conservatism (though such positions certainly do exist and are held by numerous, quite vocal advocates). Instead, they are often carefully constructed on international legal foundations, norms, and principles.

Not only the Pact of San José but also other international legal documents from both the United Nations and the Inter-American Human Rights Systems (Declarations, Pacts, Covenants, etc.) are interpreted and invoked by advocates on opposite sides of the debate as encouraging or opposing legal abortion.[63] I thus engage with the concept of *norm contestation* within the context of these colliding interpretations of international human rights and principles of justice, examining the Mexican case as an example of how advocates aim to fill the "legitimacy gap" of abortion norms through their discourses – and what can be done towards attaining dialogue, ultimately for the creation of on-the-ground policy and compromise.

Within the discourses put forth by advocates, this international dimension plays a relevant role. Advocates engage in increasingly transnational activism, as well as in a search for 'international legitimacy'. They appeal to international legal texts and human rights documents as supporting their own position while also contesting opposing texts. Yet adding this international dimension has not definitively 'solved' the debate, as texts stemming from the United Nations and Inter-American Human Rights Systems (Declarations, Pacts, Covenants, Programmes of Action, etc.) are interpreted and invoked by opposed groups of advocates as promoting or opposing legal abortion.[64] It seems instead that this transnational advocacy, and the practice of discursive engagement with this international dimension by opposed groups, has only helped to further solidify, encroach, and polarize each set of ideas, making the discourses to appear even more irreconcilable.

Abortion is also a multidimensional matter.[65,66] The debates about its legal status involve not only the rights of two differently recognized subjects,[67] as well as clashing perceptions of relevant rights, the right to life, to health, to private medical decisions regarding reproduction, but also other tangential yet relevant aspects such as disability rights,[68] sexual violence, and how to facilitate (or whether to even allow, according to some 'pro-life' advocates) an abortion following rape, or the rights of medical personnel to conscientious objection and to refuse to participate in certain practices. Though it is impossible to predict what may happen in future decades without getting into speculation, it is likely that scientific and technological advancements will continue to change the landscape of this debate.

Furthermore, the 'taboo' status of abortion in many cultural contexts is in itself a reason why deeper analyzes of some of these dimensions have been lacking. The complex and multidimensional nature of it (even if constraining it to the realm of human rights norms) calls for a framework through which to see this case, as well as to potentially use for other cases of a similar nature: polarized and *'pendular'*. My work explores the complexities of the abortion debate in Mexico as a story of advocacy and clashing discourses, while applying this analytical framework of *norm contestation* and a detailed norm typology for the 'competing discourses'.

Scholars have usually addressed the legality of abortion (and the advocacy, for and against, that surrounds it) as an issue of women's reproductive rights,[69] through a lens of gender studies and feminist movements' decades-long demands in favour of women,[70] or through a sociological one which sees access to abortion as one of the many dimensions of gender inequality and the legitimacy of women's individual choices.[71],[72] Medical and biological sciences are unlikely to provide final (or even just satisfactory) answers to philosophical matters such as the point at which sentience begins, nor are they likely to inform policymaking in a way that addresses pressing social issues. While abortion obviously is an important issue within gender studies and sociology, my work suggests looking at it as a contested normative issue within Political Sciences and International Relations, highlighting the clashing interpretations of human rights and the *competing principles* on human rights.

While philosophical ponderings on life, personhood, and abortion might never be fully resolved,[73] what is ultimately interesting for most advocates and for scholars on International Relations is the actual policy creation that unfolds due to the norm-generative process of *contestation.*

Analyzing Advocates' Discourses through Norm Contestation

Abortion norms and policies present a unique case for a theory of norm contestation, as well as exploring advocacy through discourse in a larger sense. It stands in contrast to other sociopolitical movements and historical shifts such as women's achievement of the right to vote. In these historical examples, one progressive discourse has remained 'victorious', so to speak, with no constant 'back and forth' in legislation granting or restricting women's access to a certain practice. Pro- and anti-legal abortion advocates use narratives and discourses which remain strong within large segments of society, which are fundamentally incompatible with one another, and which contest and challenge not only the existing normative order but also *each other* – as well as international legal texts.

Binaries, of course, can be problematic in their excessive simplification of complex issues; this includes analyzing *'pro'* and *'anti'* abortion discourses as two distinct conceptual entities. A 'binarization' of discourses can easily be interpreted as assigning essentialist and monolithic characteristics to large groups of people, reducing complex ideologies to the supposed 'black or white' of two sports teams. In practice, policies and solutions to the abortion debate can (and do) run through a spectrum of possibilities. One important objective of this book is precisely to question this supposed binary and to propose possibilities of a 'middle ground' that may constitute a *pathway to dialogue.*

It is fundamental to remember that potential solutions to this debate are multiple, diverse, and 'non-binary', even if activists themselves at times seem to forget it. They tend to depict opposed groups of advocates as a caricature of its most extreme representatives or to take opposing ideas to their most exaggerated extremes, while also galvanizing *and* simplifying their own opinions. The abortion debate in Argentina in 2018, where legalization up to 12 weeks' gestation was discussed (but rejected at the time), showed this polarization. Activists on opposed groups simplified their stance, down to the point of coloured handkerchiefs with brief slogans: blue for the 'pro-life' activists and green for the 'pro-choice', two supposedly distinct, mutually exclusive 'options' in stance and discourse.

Throughout my analytical work, I often do rely on this binary categorization for analytical purposes: if for the only reason that advocates on 'opposed sides' of the debate *effectively see themselves as two opposing sides of a debate*, with no possible 'middle ground'. As a result, the possible common solutions, the potential core concepts of agreement, tend to be forgotten. Analyzing them as such is a choice stemming from their own discourses, not a methodological choice made for the sake of simplicity, nor does it signal agreement on my part that the issue should be treated as binary. On the contrary, it is my intention that this endeavour becomes a useful addition to the debate, in that it can bring conceptual suggestions to remind activist leaders that they indeed stand on a spectrum (as it shows through their own elaborations, once they are pressed into fleshing out their more concrete propositions), where compromises might be possible.

Analyzing legal complexities is one thing; the real-world practice of carrying out effective and engaging advocacy is another. The activists themselves frame the problem and the discourses in binary manners because this makes for 'catchy' and simplified activism. Complex realities get reduced to slogans, to short phrases which can fit on a cardboard sign or a '*tweet*', and even to specific colours in clothing accessories which signify a position 'for' or 'against' in the debate. Be it in the extended interviews carried out for my research, in their public communications or in their media messages, it is often the case that the advocates themselves present information in this binarized way, and such polarization has conceptually shaped the abortion debate in Mexico. Once those advocates with expertise (medical or legal, for example) are further questioned, that is when the nuances in their proposals properly flourish, revealing a wider spectrum of possible policy measures concerning abortion.

It is my hope that the complexities discovered throughout this analysis of norms, discourses, and practices will help to showcase the non-binarity of the topic, as well as the large spectrum of possibilities in policy and practice – precisely in contrast to how they often see themselves and the debate at large. In subsequent chapters, I map out in detail: the norms that advocates have proactively proposed, as well as those that they have reacted against and opposed; the principles that they claim to defend; the laws and legal reforms that they have helped to create; the discursive shifts in the debate throughout time; and the international legal texts which they either quote as supportive of their discourse, or whose legitimacy they call into question.

It is likely that the incompatible viewpoints on abortion will stay incompatible, and the efforts to bridge the "*legitimacy gap*"[74] will likely be subjected to everlasting contestation. For it is precisely the *'contestedness'* and *'irreconcilable-ness'* of fundamental norms competing in debates over abortion, like the right to life versus a woman's right to her own self-determination, which has caused a frequent dead-end in the abortion debate. Expert advocates in Mexico, for and against legal abortion, aim to fill this *"legitimacy gap"* of abortion norms, often through the interpretation and framing of international norms. Having interviewed around 30 of them in depth, on how they work in aiming to change (or to maintain as valid) the laws regarding abortion (and only on rare occasions work towards building on-the-ground compromise), one objective of my work is, ultimately, to use this analysis to propose *'pathways to dialogue'* in this especially complex legal issue.

Possible Compromises and Pathways to Dialogue?

The fundamentally irreconcilable viewpoints on abortion are likely to stay irreconcilable too, as abortion presents a uniquely 'odd' case not only within Human Rights ontology but even within women's issues and women's rights in a narrower sense. The contestation of norms regarding abortion and its legal status, therefore, is likely to continue whatever those norms may be, whether they are strictly prohibitive of abortion, or whether they grant liberalized access – or anything in-between.

Even the middle-ground compromises achieved in some contexts (such as in Mexico City, where it was legalized until the 12th gestational week after advocates put forward arguments based on public health concerns)[75] are likely to still encounter everlasting questioning and reform attempts, often according to political sways. The very nature of abortion is legally and normatively odd, for it is possibly *the* unique case where two differentiated, recognizable holders of (at least potential) rights, the pregnant woman and the unborn, find such rights starkly at odds with each other . . . all within the physical body of one of them. This 'oddness' calls for a new approach in studying this complex problem.

I aim not to answer a question of which advocates stand to reason in *their* interpretation of international norms, but rather to provide a mapping of '*how*' they attempt to fill the everlasting "legitimacy gap" of abortion-related norms. And very importantly, a *'how-possible?'* that both discourses happen to remain so strong within large sectors of society. The book looks at the constructions of potential solutions, based on what advocates present for the creation of actual on-the-ground policy: how one might find middle grounds within the conflicting norms at stake or craft second-best solutions to what is still perceived as a most fundamental clash of rights and principles of justice.

My goal is to help the reader to gain fuller understanding of not only *'the abortion in Mexico story'* but also such pathways to dialogue on an issue that seems to see much clash and polarization – but little actual dialogue. *Understanding*, on my own part, before attempting to *explain*, proved to be an exercise of clarity on this issue that finds itself caught in public and political gridlock. Those varying, and often, *opposed* interpretations of norms will be studied as complex discourses, focusing on advocates and the various contested dimensions of the abortion debate, their framing of international norms, the global organizing principles put forward by institutions and by individual advocates, and their perceived policy solutions to this clash.

When the issue of abortion is addressed by the international agencies that often address it – that is, institutions which are rather focused on public health or demographics, such as the World Health Organization (WHO) or the United Nations Population Fund (UNFPA) respectively – such institutions tend to place their focus on medical aspects (such as the risks of unsafe abortion and its relation to maternal mortality),[76] rarely analyzing the role that advocacy and norm contestation play in the normative environment that surrounds abortion, or the clash in principles. Yet herein also lies an important clue, pointing at one of the earliest 'framework shifts' through which some advocates have aimed for compromise on abortion: the idea that it is a *public health* issue, rather than one of human rights.

This framework shift – and the agreement and disagreement in various contexts, on the idea that *'abortion is about public health, and health is about social justice'* – advanced the cause for legalizing abortion within several national and supra-national normative arenas but saw backlash or lack of success in others.[77] However, there are some groups which still do not accept the framing of 'access to abortion' as a matter of public health.[78]

An assessment of the potential principles that could serve as starting points to find this dialogue and this overlap points at various ideas. Firstly, a 'path back into the origins', of sorts, can be found in a revisiting of the concept of '*despenalización*' (decriminalization), one of the first demands on the part of Mexican feminists since much earlier decades,[79] as a starting point for a new pathway into mutual understanding. Decriminalizing is not the same as 'legalizing', and it certainly doesn't sufficiently address other problems of access, nor does it provide a wider spectrum of reproductive choices. A core agreement on 'de-criminalization' rather than 'legalization' thus presents its own sets of insufficiencies and, again, leaves many groups of advocates dissatisfied – notwithstanding the fact that it functions more easily as an abstract principle rather than as a legally codified reality. But the non-criminalization of women who go through abortions is an important point of agreement for groups of opposed advocates in Mexico.

Even if the fundamentally irreconcilable normative viewpoints are likely to stay irreconcilable due to the peculiarities of the case, some concepts that are still in early stages of development such as *'suspensive rights'* or *'potential rights'* might serve too as organizing principles in this case of contested norms – potentially also in other cases. I will delve deeper into these in further chapters. Newer ways of seeing this phenomenon may eventually lead to compromise and to reaching second-best agreements in policymaking.

Scholars and advocates working on other issue areas can gather insights from this endeavour: how advocacy movements aim to create efficient messages, build ties with transnational networks, and portray different kinds of contextual, individual, and legislative elements in a search for workable public policy – ideally for durable compromise as well. From the Mexican case, and from this topic which is arguably one of the most contested in today's normative environment, perhaps other principles (potentially global and applicable elsewhere) can be extracted. The abortion issue may well be an example of how to find 'pathways to dialogue' within a complex normative environment, on a highly contested issue where advocates have been previously encountering clashes, polarization, sociopolitical *'pendularity'*, and, in short, lack of agreement in policy and in practice.

Agreements on legal abortion have a 'temporary' feel to them and are subject to change at the next blow of opposing political winds – especially at subnational levels. This sustained conflict makes for one of the most interesting cases of a contestation that is ongoing and particularly difficult to resolve. Something to be said about this 'pendular' movement is that if focus is kept only on the extremes (full bans *versus* full permissiveness), we risk missing the movement of the pendulum across the 'grey areas' where the middle-ground solutions or second-best agreements may exist. Abortion regulation comes with this oscillation; yet keeping these 'grey areas' in mind is what might make for pathways to *agreement* and not only *dialogue*.

As I analyze how *'the devil is in the details'* (details such as how certain advocates in Mexico have attempted to enact legal changes by working with technical norms, or with somewhat obscure secondary laws), a counterpart to this phrase emerges. For the 'devil' may indeed be in the details, but *'the angels (of dialogue) are in the middle ground'*. Much legal and normative progress can be achieved, if at least temporarily, by diving into this detailed 'devil' of technical norms. However, true and meaningful dialogue between two seemingly irreconcilable groups rather lies in the middle ground of the intermediate: organizing principles that can be well recognized by opposing groups. Can compromise be reached in order to bridge this global legitimacy gap?

Notes

1 For clarification, the term "subnational states" refers to the 32 provinces into which the Mexican federation is divided.
2 The concept of *"lawfare"* as proposed by Rachel Sieder and her research team at the CMI Institute in Norway.
3 See Wiener, 2014.
4 Sieder *et al.*, 2014.
5 Wiener, 2014. The concept of the "legitimacy gap" is explained in subsequent chapters.
6 In the Spanish language (in which all the interviews were carried out), the most relevant translation of either word is *'activista'*, which is indeed what many interviewees self-declare to be. The only applicable translation of 'advocate' would be *'defensor (de)'*, which is also a label that some of the interviewees identify with. But *'defensor'*, as a self-standing word, is less connected to practices or processes of supporting causes and can carry a slightly more passive connotation than *'activista'*. Someone can declare themselves to be a *'defensor'* of something (e.g. a certain religious principle), without necessarily involving themselves much in practices of protest or contestation towards change.
7 Reilly, 2009, p. 35.
8 Heer and Grossbard-Shechtman, 1981.
9 Clapham, 2007, p. 148.
10 By 'consented abortion', I clarify the reference to any abortion willed or needed by the pregnant woman, so as to distinguish them from cases of *forced* abortions. The latter would present us with different legal considerations: both the woman and the unborn would easily be framed as the victims of one same invasive, violent practice.
11 The Catholic Church of medieval times, for example, did not refer to pre-birth life as beginning at 'conception', but rather at a point called *'quickening'*: when the foetus' movements could be felt.
12 Zúñiga Fajuri, 2011, p. 64.
13 Center for Reproductive Rights, 2021.
14 Peterfy, 1995.
15 Mangel, 1988.
16 The question of privacy was indeed one of the main conceptual cornerstones on which Roe versus Wade was passed in the United States, legalizing abortion. See Garrow, 2015.

17 See Saxton, 2013.
18 Hesketh *et al.*, 2011.
19 Potter, 2018.
20 UN WOMEN, 2017.
21 See Lamas, 2012.
22 Unless otherwise specified, throughout this book whenever the legal status of abortion in a particular country is quoted, the information has been provided by the Center for Reproductive Rights' *"Map of the World's Abortion Laws"* (most updated version, November 2021. See references).
23 Center for Reproductive Rights. World Map of Abortion Laws, 2021.
24 In Mexico, abortion laws fall under the umbrella of general health-related laws, and the prohibitions appear in the Criminal Codes, which are both decided on a state-by-state basis: each subnational state has its own Criminal Code and its own local Health Law. This means that each of the 32 Mexican states can decide on its own about the status of abortion, as well as the legally allowed exceptions, allowed time frames, specific punishments when it's illegally performed, etc.
25 See Ramos Muñoz and Villagrán Alarcón, 2019.
26 Interviewed Expert No. 24, See Annex 1.
27 Shah, Ahman and Ortayli. ICPD Beyond 2014 Expert Meeting, 2014.
28 Beltrán y Puga *et al.*, 2019.
29 Vázquez, 2006.
30 Pollitt, 2014.
31 Zúñiga Fajuri, 2011.
32 Blofield, 2006, p. 10.
33 Alarcón Loayza *et al.*, 2017.
34 Kane, 2008.
35 Seen in various images of public protests in Mexico City, Saltillo, Guanajuato and other Mexican regions.
36 Navarrete and Ramírez, 2021.
37 Morán Faúndes and Peñas Defago, 2016.
38 Gianella Malca *et al.*, 2017.
39 Kulczycki, 2011.
40 Human Rights Watch, 2017.
41 Center for Reproductive Rights, 2017.
42 As of November 2021.
43 Olivares *et al.*, 2007.
44 Human Rights Watch, 2017.
45 Deutsche Welle, 2021.
46 Juárez *et al.*, 2009.
47 Marie Stopes International, 2017.
48 So-called because of the ICPD Conference that took place in Mexico City in the eighties.
49 Pérez Hernández, 2017, p. 23.
50 Cook *et al.*, 2014.
51 Lamas, 2009, p. 165.
52 Alarcón Loayza *et al.*, 2017.
53 Joyce, 2013.
54 Carbonell and Salazar, 2011.
55 Lamas, 2009, p. 170.
56 Chávez Becker and González Ulloa, 2018, p. 50.
57 United Nations Office of the High Commissioner for Human Rights, Human Rights Committee, 2018.
58 Lamas, 2009, p. 154.
59 Wiener, 2014.

60 For more on "lawfare", see various works from Sieder *et al.* (2014–2017).
61 DiSalvo, 1991.
62 See Cohen *et al.*, 2021. At the time of editing this book in 2023, abortion legality in the United States has been rolled back, as the "Roe vs. Wade" ruling was overturned in 2022. Particularly worrisome are the developments in the state of Texas, since late 2021, which also pave the way to stark forms of abortion re-criminalization.
63 Mizrahi Nedvedovich and Zúñiga Tapia, 2017.
64 Cook *et al.*, 2014.
65 Goldberg, 2015, p. 2.
66 Cook *et al.*, 2014.
67 Pollitt, 2014.
68 Saxton, 2013.
69 Finer and Fine, 2013.
70 Marecek *et al.*, 2017.
71 Blofield, 2006.
72 Lamas, 2009.
73 Faúndes and Barzelatto, 2006.
74 Wiener, 2014.
75 Juárez *et al.*, 2009, p. 8.
76 Guttmacher Institute and World Health Organization, 2012.
77 Finer and Fine, 2013, p. 586.
78 Balbontín, 2016.
79 Lamas, 2009, p. 155.

References

Alarcón Loayza, N., Bartolini Esparza, M., Contreras Díaz, A.J., Mizrahi Nedvedovich, C., Ortiz Trujillo, D., Pérez Hernández, C., and Zúñiga Tapia, F.R. (2017). *Aborto: La Política de un Estado Claudicante*. Series: Todas y Todos Valemos en México. Mexico City: Consejo Editorial de la Cámara de Diputados, LXIII Legislatura.

Balbontín, A. (2016). *Minister of Health Provides Key: Abortion is Not a Public Health Issue*. Chile: El Demócrata. https://www.eldemocrata.cl/opinion/minsal-da-la-clave-aborto-no-es-tema-de-salud-publica/

Beltrán y Puga, A., Machado, M., and Peñas Defago, A. (2019). "Derechos Sexuales y Reproductivos de las Mujeres en América Latina a Debate." *Discrepancias; Encartes*, 2(3), 231–243.

Blofield, M. (2006). *The Politics of Moral Sin: Abortion and Divorce in Spain, Chile and Argentina*. Routledge.

Carbonell, M., and Salazar, P. (2011). *La Reforma Constitucional de Derechos Humanos: Un Nuevo Paradigma*. México: UNAM Instituto de Investigaciones Jurídicas.

Center for Reproductive Rights. (2017). "Chile Makes History." www.reproductiverights.org/feature/chile-makes-history. Accessed August 23, 2017.

Center for Reproductive Rights. (2021). "The World's Abortion Laws: Map." http://worldabortionlaws.com/map/. Accessed November 2021.

Chávez Becker, C., and González Ulloa, P. (2018). *Las organizaciones de la sociedad civil en México: hacia una reforma de la LFFAROSC*. México: Senado de la República, Instituto Belisario Domínguez.

Clapham, A. (2007). *Human Rights: A Very Short Introduction*. Oxford University Press.

Cohen, I.G., Adashi, E.Y., and Gostin, L.O. (2021). "The Supreme Court, the Texas Abortion Law (SB8), and the Beginning of the End of Roe v Wade?" *Journal of the American Medical Association (JAMA)*, 326(15), 1473–1474.

Cook, R.J., Erdmann, J.N., and Dickens, B.M. (2014). *Abortion Law in Transnational Perspective: Cases and Controversies*. University of Pennsylvania Press.

Deutsche Welle. (2021). "Corte IDH aborda la criminalización del aborto en El Salvador." March 11. www.dw.com/es/corteidh-aborda-la-criminalizaci%C3%B3n-del-aborto-en-el-salvador/a-56833283. Accessed May 2021.

DiSalvo, C.R. (1991). "Abortion and Consensus: The Futility of Speech, the Power of Disobedience." *Washington and Lee Law Review*, 48, 219.

Faúndes, A., and Barzelatto, J. (2006). *The Human Drama of Abortion: A Global Search for Consensus*. Vanderbilt University Press.

Finer, L., and Fine, J.B. (2013). "Abortion Law Around the World: Progress and Pushback." *American Journal of Public Health*, 103(4), 585–589.

Garrow, D.J. (2015). "Liberty and Sexuality: The Right to Privacy and the Making of Roe v. Wade." *Open Road Media.*

Gianella Malca, C., Sieder, R., Peñas, A., Machado, M.R. de A. (2017). "A New Conservative Social Movement? Latin America's Regional Strategies to Restrict Abortion Rights." Chr. Michelsen Institute; CMI Brief; 16; 5; 06-2017; 1-5. https://ri.conicet.gov.ar/handle/11336/79530.

Goldberg, S.B. (2015). "Multidimensional Advocacy as Applied: Marriage Equality and Reproductive Rights." *Columbia Journal of Gender and Law*, 29(1).

Guttmacher Institute and World Health Organization. (2012). "Abortion in Brief." Joint Publication by Guttmacher Institute and the World Health Organization. January 2012. www.who.int/reproductivehealth/publications/unsafe_abortion/induced_abortion_2012.pdf?ua=1.

Heer, D.M., and Grossbard-Shechtman, A. (1981). "The Impact of the Female Marriage Squeeze and the Contraceptive Revolution on Sex Roles and the Women's Liberation Movement in the United States, 1960 to 1975." *Journal of Marriage and the Family*, 43(1), 49–65.

Hesketh, T., Lu, L., and Xing, Z.W. (2011). "The Consequences of Son Preference and Sex-Selective Abortion in China and Other Asian Countries." *CMAJ*, 183(12), 1374–1377.

Human Rights Watch. (2017), "Nicaragua: Abortion Ban Threatens Health and Lives", July 31. www.hrw.org/news/2017/07/31/nicaragua-abortion-ban-threatens-health-and-lives. Accessed May 28, 2021.

Juárez, F., Singh, S., García, S.G., and Díaz Olivarrieta, C. (2009). "Estimaciones del aborto inducido en México: ¿qué ha cambiado entre 1990 y 2006?." *Perspectivas Internacionales en Salud Sexual y Reproductiva*, Special Issue of 2009, 4–14.

Joyce, K. (2013). "Mexico's Abortion Wars, American-Style." *The Nation*, September 16. www.thenation.com/article/mexicos-abortion-wars-american-style/. Accessed November 2021.

Kane, G. (2008). "Abortion Law Reform in Latin America: Lessons for Advocacy." *Gender & Development*, 16(2), 361–375.

Kulczycki, A. (2011). "Abortion in Latin America: Changes in Practice, Growing Conflict, and Recent Policy Developments." *Studies in Family Planning*, 42(3), 199–220.

Lamas, M. (2009). "La Despenalización del Aborto en México." *Nueva Sociedad*, (220), 154–172.

Lamas, M. (2012). "Mujeres, aborto e Iglesia católica." *Revista de El Colegio de San Luis*, 2(3), 42–67.

Mangel, C.P. (1988). "Legal Abortion: The Impending Obsolescence of the Trimester Framework." *American Journal of Law and Medicine*, 14(1), 69–108.

Marecek, J., Macleod, C., and Hoggart, L. (2017). "Abortion in Legal, Social, and Healthcare Contexts." *Feminism & Psychology*, 27(1), 4–14.

Marie Stopes International. (2017). "Re-enactment of the Mexico City Policy." *Reproductive Choices News*, January 2017. www.msichoices.org/news/2017/1/re-enactment-of-the-mexico-city-policy/#. Accessed May 2021.

Mizrahi Nedvedovich, C., and Zúñiga Tapia, F.R. (2017). "Las recomendaciones de los organismos internacionales como mecanismos de presión política." In *Aborto: La Política de un Estado Claudicante*. Todas y Todos Valemos en México, 53–67. Mexico City: Consejo Editorial de la Cámara de Diputados, LXIII Legislatura.

Morán Faúndes, J.M., and Peñas Defago, M.A. (2016). "Strategies of Self-Proclaimed Pro-Life Groups: Effect of New Religious Actors on Sexual Policies." *Latin American Perspectives*, 208(43: 3), 144–162.

Navarrete, D., and Ramírez, V.H. (2021). "¿Qué opinan las personas sobre el aborto en México?" *Animal Político*, January 13. www.animalpolitico.com/blog-invitado/que-opinan-las-personas-sobre-el-aborto-en-mexico/. Accessed June 2021.

Olivares, E., Muñoz, A., and Sevin, M. (2007). "Rechaza Carpizo impugnación de CNDH a la reforma sobre aborto." *La Jornada*, May 28. www.jornada.com.mx/2007/05/28/index.php?section=capital&article=038n1cap. Accessed June 2021.

Pérez Hernández, C. (2017). "Antecedentes del Aborto en México." In *Aborto: La Política de un Estado Claudicante*, edited by Pérez Hernández, *et al*. Mexico City: Consejo Editorial de la Cámara de Diputados, LXIII Legislatura.

Peterfy, A. (1995). "Foetal Viability as a Threshold to Personhood. A Legal Analysis." *The Journal of Legal Medicine*, 16(4), 607–636.

Pollitt, K. (2014). *Pro. Reclaiming Abortion Rights*. New York: Picador.

Potter, R.B. (2018). *The Abortion Debate. Reaction to the Modern Women's Movement, 1963 to the Present*. Routledge.

Ramos Muñoz, N., and Villagrán Alarcón, C. (2019). "Del papel a la práctica: Las problemáticas que enfrenta el aborto en tres causales." *Repositorio.uchile.cl*

Reilly, N. (2009). *Women's Human Rights: Seeking Gender Justice in a Globalized Age*. Polity Press.

Saxton, M. (2013). "Disability Rights and Selective Abortion." In *The Disability Studies Reader*, edited by L. J. Davis, 87–99. Routledge.

Sieder, R., Gianella, C., Gloppen, S., Gargarella, R., Bergallo, P., Gonzales, A.C., Peñas, A., de Assis Machado, M. R. R., and Ely Yamin, A. (2014–2017). "Abortion Rights Lawfare in Latin America." Research Project at CMI Chr. Michelsen Institute, Norway. Norwegian Research Council. www.cmi.no/projects/1841-abortion-rights-lawfare-in-latin-america.

United Nations Entity for Gender Equality and the Empowerment of Women/Entidad de la ONU para la Igualdad de Género y el Empoderamiento de la Mujer (UN WOMEN/ONU Mujeres. (2017). "El progreso de las mujeres en América Latina y el Caribe 2017. Transformar las economías para realizar los derechos." www2.unwomen.org/-/media/field%20office%20americas/documentos/publicaciones/2017/07/un16017_web.pdf?la=es&vs=4654

United Nations Office of the High Commissioner for Human Rights, Human Rights Committee. (2018). "General Comment no. 36, Article 6 (Right to Life)." CCPR/C/GC/35, 3 September 2019. https://www.refworld.org/docid/5e5e75e04.html

Vázquez, R. (2006). "Algo más sobre el aborto." *Debate Feminista*, 34, 19–32.

Wiener, A. (2014). *A Theory of Contestation*. Springer.

Zúñiga Fajuri, A. (2011). "Aborto y Derechos Humanos." *Revista de Derecho Valdivia*, 24(2).

2 The Mexican Case

An Abortion Storyline

In this chapter, I begin the deeper analysis of Mexico as a study case regarding the recent history of abortion advocacy and the laws that advocates have affected. This chapter and the next constitute the section containing most of the information gathered during fieldwork in 2018 and 2019. This time spent in Mexico (the capital City as well as a few visits to three Mexican subnational states: San Luis Potosí, Coahuila, and Aguascalientes) provided experience and material for a more solid analysis of their messages, discourses, interpretations of meanings, and contestation modes.

Twenty-six expert advocates in total were interviewed (see Annex 1 for a detailed list of the interviewees). I reached out particularly to advocates who (1) are experts on a specific field, such as medicine or law, or experts on the abortion-related advocacy itself and/or (2) have had a role in policymaking on the issue, for example, presenting a particular legislative reform, proposing a specific policy, acting as a link with 'sister' institutions in other countries or in global forums, representing Mexico in an international debate, or sending written communications to international institutions where the legality of abortion has been debated – as happened at the UN Office of the High Commissioner for Human Rights (OHCHR) with the creation of the Draft Comment No. 36 on the Right to Life, and the truly global debate that it represented. Not all of these advocates are continuously active on the specific issue of abortion; rather some of them have been mobilized into action specifically at points in time when particular events occurred.

At the time of designing the plans for the first round of fieldwork (summer of 2018), it was of special interest to try to reach out to politicians and parliamentarians, as the recently elected government (with a newly elected, left-leaning administration headed by Andrés Manuel López Obrador) allegedly represented a progressive approach to gender equality and women's rights. There was also renewed interest in the issue of abortion following the similar debate in Argentina, with many of such transnational exchanges resonating in social media.

A second rich source of primary and secondary information was the attendance to two protests and one conference: first a massive 'pro-life' march in Mexico City in September 2018, mobilized by a coalition of NGOs coordinated by the *Frente Nacional por la Familia* (National Front for the Family); secondly a small

DOI:10.4324/9781032642338-2

pro-legal abortion protest in the state of Coahuila in 2019, organized by several local feminist groups; and thirdly a an anti-abortion conference by Jorge Serrano Limón, one of the most prominent figures in Mexico's 'pro-life' movements since the late 1980s, at the catholic Universidad San Pablo, in San Luis Potosí.

Almost all of the interviewed advocates, as well as many organizers or participants to the marches and the conference, provided written material and documentation of their advocacy. This became a rich trove of primary material which includes short books authored by the interviewees, reports, written communications with other advocates, images used for protests or to convey messages on social media, printed flyers and posters, 'props' or objects used as symbols during protests, invitations to events online or in-person, and copies of proposed law reforms. Some of this material is peculiar, and it has been of interest to include detailed descriptions of it, as it is quite illustrative of certain aspects of advocacy.

Timeline and Crucial Legal Shifts

Abortion was uniformly illegal throughout the country until 2007 (when Mexico City decriminalized and legalized it), appearing as a crime in the Federal Criminal Code as well as in every subnational Criminal Code.[1] Within the framework of Mexico's federal system, this means that each subnational state (until the present day) decides on the legality status of abortion, about its own specific exceptions to abortion prohibition, as well as its specific penalties for cases of abortion. All subnational states in the country admit to at least one such exception.[2] The only exception which is uniformly admitted throughout the entire country is the exception in cases of rape, though most states admit also the other two most common *'causales'* (as mentioned in Chapter 1): risk to the mother's life and foetal unviability.

Whenever advocates target the Mexican laws that are related to abortion in some way, be it to defend its illegality or to try to legalize it, they almost always target the same documents: the Federal and subnational Criminal Codes (which detail if and in which cases shall abortion be considered a crime, and the penalties that it carries); the General Health Law and subnational Health Laws (which only regulate abortion as a medical practice in the cases where it has been legalized); and the Federal and subnational Constitutions (mostly when 'pro-life' groups target the articles on the 'right to life', to try to amend them into declaring life to be protected 'from the moment of conception').

It was the pivotal year of 2007 that marked the starting point at which abortion was decriminalized and later legalized in Mexico City until the 12th week of pregnancy, with no restrictions as to the woman's particular reasons. The capital thus became the first subnational state[3] to legalize abortion with a 'model of gestational limits', instead of a 'model of exceptions' as existed in the rest of the states. This defining event came after several years of advocacy by defenders of women's reproductive health and rights.[4]

For the purposes of this reform, the term 'abortion' as a punishable act was redefined in Mexico City's Criminal Code to mean "*interruption of a pregnancy after the twelfth gestational week*"[5]; therefore, causing that all the penalties mentioned for abortion would only be applicable after that point. At the same time, the other '*causales*' were still retained in Mexico City's Criminal Code, thus also keeping the non-punishable nature of abortion in the cases of rape, risk to the woman's health, or unviability of the foetus. The main rationale presented by pro-legalization advocates in order to advance these reforms was that (as many international and research organizations point out[6]) unsafe illegal abortion is almost impossible to eradicate, and it puts women at risk of injury or death – this risk being disproportionally higher for poorer women with unequal access to sexual education, contraceptives, and proper medical care.

After this amendment to the Criminal Code of Mexico City, what followed were amendments to Mexico City's Health Law[7] and its related Regulations (*Reglamentos*) to regulate the practice in those cases in which abortion is now admitted. Therefore, the reform approved by Mexico City's Legislative Assembly also came with a mandate to reform the health-related laws, in order to provide the public service to women requesting a legal abortion.[8] Once those reforms were in place, from that point forward, all local laws in Mexico City which mention services or provisions related to abortion before the 12th week now refer to the procedure as "Legal Interruption of Pregnancy" (*Interrupción Legal del Embarazo,* or *ILE).*

It is important to remark that this is why I refer to abortion in Mexico City as having been both *decriminalized* (through what was essentially a legal redefinition) and *legalized*, since the reforms also gave place to new constitutive norms[9] in order to provide access to the practice. These redefinitions and re-framings were, at the time (and continue to be), heavily challenged and contested by so-called pro-life advocates. Large sectors of the population view them as illegitimate, arbitrary, and fundamentally unfair.

Before the year 2000, there had only been scarce attempts towards relaxing some of the anti-abortion measures and prohibitions in some subnational states, but such attempts were an anomaly and almost always unsuccessful – only succeeding sometimes in lowering the prison sentences for women convicted of abortion. Advocates in the state of Chiapas tried, in the decade of the 1990s, to add more exceptions to prohibition, suggesting reasons of family planning (once a woman already had a number of children) or economic hardship in cases of single mothers as exceptions. The initiative did not prosper due to opposed advocacy by 'pro-life' groups and the conservative-leaning PAN political party (*Partido Acción Nacional*), who put forward arguments about foetuses' capacities to hear sound from early in gestation.[10]

Historically left-leaning political parties like PRD (*Partido de la Revolución Democrática*) and PT (*Partido del Trabajo*) have been favourable to the cause of decriminalizing abortion since the mid-1990s, following the recommendations of international conferences such as ICPD Cairo and Beijing (1994 and 1995, respectively), where abortion was put forward as a global issue for women's health and the prevention of maternal mortality.[11] However, both parties remain a political minority outside of Mexico City – even more minoritarian after the 2018 presidential election, when leftist candidate López Obrador won and his recently founded *Morena* party (*Movimiento Regeneración Nacional*) became the main leftist political force in the country. PRD is now on the verge of disappearing, and PT has always been a rather fringe, minority party throughout the entire country, one that never had a significant presence in any subnational state save one or two, and only holding control of a few municipalities nationwide. In present days, *Morena* is the party mainly supporting abortion liberalization.

Previous to 2007, however, a few crucial stepping stones had been laid out, which paved the way for eventual legalization in the capital. One of them was the *Caso Paulina,* concerning an underage girl who got pregnant following sexual assault in the state of Baja California, in 1999. After local state government denied the victim the possibility of an abortion (even though it would have been a clearly admitted exception to prohibition, following sexual assault), pro-legalization advocates took the case to the Inter-American Commission on Human Rights. It was only partially resolved years later with an "amicable agreement"[12] between the Mexican government and the victim in the early 2000s, with some financial compensations (*Paulina* never got an abortion).

While the case resolution itself was not revolutionary (mostly in the vein that the Mexican state had indeed violated *Paulina's* rights by denying an abortion in a case of sexual assault), it had a strong media coverage and, at a time when Mexico was experiencing a growth in the participation of civil society on many issues, it placed abortion firmly on the agenda of many feminist groups.[13] It was emblematic and helped to change public perceptions of the abortion issue.[14] It also, however, mobilized intense 'pro-life' advocacy.

Two other important stepping stones pre-2007 were, firstly, the creation of the reform known as "Ley Robles" in the year 2000 (so called because the main proponent was the well-known politician Rosario Robles).[15] This was a reform to the Criminal Code of Mexico City, lowering the penalties for abortion and adding new exceptions to prohibition.

The second came in 2004, a change which was buried deep within legal technicalities, but one that renowned academic Marta Lamas (expert on feminist movements in Mexico and feminist advocate herself) identifies as a crucial step towards eventual decriminalization.[16] It also concerned the Criminal Code of Mexico City: while abortion was still illegal then, a change was made where the exceptions to abortion prohibition (the so-called *causales*) changed from being identified as "causes for the extinction of penalty" (*"causas de extinción de la acción penal"* or *"acciones de no punibilidad"*) into being now called "causes for exclusion of responsibility" (*"excluyentes de responsabilidad"*).[17]

It was indeed such a seemingly minor, 'technical' detail that only a few legal experts at the time detected what the reform meant or identified it as the major change of legal paradigm about abortion that it was. Some conservative parliamentarians even championed the reform because it also included a provision on "conscientious objection" for medical personnel (defending their right to refuse abortions), desired by conservative advocates.[18] Not only Marta Lamas but also some of the advocates interviewed for this book talk about this change as a highly technical but crucial reform. Briefly explained, it re-conceptualized the exceptions to abortion prohibition, from being *"a reason why the crime is not punishable"* into *"a reason why the crime does not exist in the first place"*.[19] This change allowed not only to eliminate criminalization of any woman who aborts and any personnel assisting her but it also opened the legal 'door' for adding or considering more "causes for exclusion of responsibility", such as a higher number of gestational weeks.

This change in paradigm also partially rids women of the stigma related to having an abortion (at least in the legal sense), a stigma which would still exist if one was defined as having committed a crime where the punishment gets 'legally dropped' – as happened with the previously existing paradigm. Other expert advocates who are academics themselves, mention how this subtle yet profound difference in the legal terms was a major (yet very unrecognized) cause for a paradigm shift regarding abortion in Mexican law.[20]

Of course, these legal technicalities do not immediately change a country's cultural views. They also don't change the stance of advocacy groups deeply invested in seeing abortion be considered as 'murder' regardless of a law's wording, nor the stance of groups invested in declaring it 'a woman's right' rather than just a mere 'non-crime' (or opinions held by the public at large agreeing with either position, or with anything in-between). Most advocates are rather unbothered with these sorts of technicalities, appealing instead to broader moral principles such as 'protecting life from conception' or 'a right to bodily autonomy'. This 'legal technicality', however, comes as an interesting display of how a relevant legal change was achieved through the 'devil' that is in the legal details, changes that are seemingly very small but that slowly begin to change the legal landscape concerning a certain practice . . . and which, over the course of time, may influence an eventual (albeit slow) cultural change.

However, the way in which abortion was eventually legalized in 2007 in the Mexican capital was not exactly through the 'would-have-been-obvious' legal route of simply setting the 12-week timeframe as one 'exclusionary cause of responsibility' but rather through a bolder political move – a complete redefinition of what 'abortion' meant. In the reform initially approved in April 2007, abortion was not yet quite 'legalized': it was *redefined*, that is, given a new legal meaning altogether. One might call it *'decriminalization through redefinition'*. The amended Criminal Code of Mexico City now declared abortion to be as much of a punishable crime as it was before, but 'abortion' now meant *"interruption of a pregnancy after the twelfth gestational week"*.[21]

Penalties are still in place for 'abortion': it simply means something different now, in Mexico City laws, than it did pre-2007. Legalization *did* follow after April 2007, in the sense of the constitutive norms that regulated access to the 'Legal Interruption of Pregnancy', but these norms came later than the initial *redefinition*. This *'re-definitory'* reform is still today referred to, by many 'pro-life' advocates, as somewhat of a "legal somersault",[22] depicted by them as a somewhat arbitrary political manoeuvre by "playing around with concepts and meanings".[23]

On a similar note about reforms carried out via 'technicalities' or, in this case, through a second-tier kind of law, special attention will be given in later sections to another recent change which concerned the so-called NOM0046, a technical norm of federal scope. "NOM" stands for *"Norma Oficial Mexicana"* (Official Mexican Norms), these are official written norms which set standards and regulations on various matters: typically the technical regulations for diverse industries, for medical practice, or protocols to be followed by authorities if a crime occurs – which is the case here concerned. NOM0046 became the subject of intense and quite unusual controversy in 2016, when it was reformed to grant much easier access to abortion, through the public healthcare system, in cases of rape.[24] This reform to NOM0046 was strongly challenged by 'pro-life' advocates, in several different manners including the presentation of a controversy to the Mexican Supreme Court – calling it 'unconstitutional', 'legal overreach', as well as an override of parental authority (since underage girls can get abortions under this new normativity). The Supreme Court, however, upheld the reform.

What followed throughout the country after 2007 was a convoluted 'game of political backlash' where, for every step advanced in the capital, other Mexican states (where 'pro-life' groups and the Catholic Church had a stronger influence) moved in the opposite direction, with more local legislations toughening anti-abortion laws by recognizing the right to life from the moment of conception in the local Constitutions (each subnational state in Mexico has its own local Constitution, as well as its own Criminal Code).[25] Mexico has seen, for many years now, a heated political and public debate on abortion, with advocates, NGOs, and civil society actors presenting their arguments for and against legalization, some focusing on public health claims, others on moral arguments, religious norms, or human rights and women's rights.[26]

It is an emotionally charged issue, with differing (and often contradictory) conceptualizations as well as policy agendas, acting as a clear example of *"lawfare"* as explained by Sieder and her research team – a strategic use of rights and litigation in battles over abortion rights,[27] *"by actors of different breeds to advance contested political and social goals"*.[28] Contested and contradictory concepts lie at the very core of the debate, often fundamentally irreconcilable in their differences and worldviews, and the controversy is displayed not only through protests and messages in social media but also through a 'crossfire' of attempted legal reforms – some successful and some not.

In an article detailing this history of Mexico's legal landscape of abortion, Pérez Hernández[29] lays out a useful timeline of the most important events. Though he focuses it on the specific laws that were changed in relevant years, for the structuring of my analysis, it is useful to take this information and rather present it as a table (Table 2.1) detailing the main 'victories' by each of the opposing advocacy groups in the debate. Seeing the information in this side-by-side manner is helpful, not only because the advocates for and against legal abortion indeed see themselves as two opposed sides but also because very few of these reforms could be called 'neutral' – they have most often been advanced and pushed forward by one

Table 2.1 Timeline of Legal Changes Affecting Abortion throughout Mexico, from 1981 until 2023

Year	*Reform favourable to the 'pro-life' side*	*Reform favourable to the 'pro-legalization' side*
1981	Mexico ratifies the American Convention of Human Rights (Pact of San José), which protects life *"in general, from the moment of conception"*.	Mexico also placed a reservation to that very article, enshrining the federal nature of the country, where each subnational state can define its own matters about the beginning of legally protected life.
1994	The local Constitution of Chihuahua is the first one to be amended to "protect life from the moment of conception", as well as the first to abolish the death penalty (the relation between the two, according to some advocates' discourses, will be further explained).	
1995		Publication of NOM007: the Secretariat of Health lays out a definition of 'abortion', for the purposes of setting medical standards, using clinical criteria to medically define 'abortion' (*'aborto'*) in order to distinguish it from a 'late miscarriage'[30] (*see endnote for important linguistic distinction*). 'Abortion' is then medically defined to be the *"Expulsion of the product of conception, of less than 500 grams in weight or until 20 weeks gestation"*. This was rather inconsequential for the abortion debate at the time, but author Pérez Hernández as well as 'pro-life' advocates/authors Bartolini and Alarcón[31] denounce it as being a norm that *"redefined abortion at the margins of the rest of the law"*, and for allegedly *"setting a precedent of using NOMs to override the legislative competencies of Congresses, and to redefine abortion at will"*.
1999		The *"Caso Paulina"* is brought to the Inter-American Commission on Human Rights. As a consequence, Mexico revises its NOM about domestic violence, to strengthen the regulations permitting abortion in cases of sexual violence.
2000	Several parliamentarians sue against the *"Ley Robles"* to the Mexican Supreme Court. The Court upholds the legality of the *"Ley Robles"* but also "recognizes the fundamental character of the right to life".	Approval of the "Robles Law" (*Ley Robles*): reforms are made to the Criminal Code of Mexico City, lowering the sentences for abortion and adding more exceptions to prohibition (*'causales'*).

(*Continued*)

Table 2.1 (Continued)

Year	*Reform favourable to the 'pro-life' side*	*Reform favourable to the 'pro-legalization' side*
2002		After the Supreme Court had upheld the "Ley Robles", the Secretariat of Health in Mexico City publishes medical standards for abortion (reframing it as "legal interruption of pregnancy"), for the legally admitted exceptions to prohibition (*'causales'*).
2004		Changes to the Criminal Code of Mexico City: changing the "causes for the extinction of punishment" into "causes for the exclusion of responsibility".
2005	Constitutional reform abolishes the death penalty in Mexico, by eliminating its explicit mention anywhere in the Constitution – except for a paragraph in Article 22, forbidding Congress to pass any laws that may sanction the death penalty as a punishment. Some 'pro-life' advocates argue that this, by inference *in contrario sensu*, means that life is unconditionally protected from the moment of conception.	Pro-legalization advocates argue that the death penalty is another topic altogether and that the Constitution does not specify that protection to life should be absolute and universal, nor that it is applicable to foetuses. Neither the death penalty nor the right to life from conception is explicitly detailed in the Mexican Constitution.
2007		Abortion is decriminalized in Mexico City, through its conceptual re-definition in the local Criminal Code as "the interruption of pregnancy happening after the 12th gestational week". Subsequently, the local Health Law was modified too, legalizing abortion by outlining procedural regulations and access, where it is no longer called abortion but "Legal Interruption of Pregnancy".
2008	The National Human Rights Commission and the Attorney General sue against the legalization of abortion in Mexico City, denouncing the reform to the Supreme Court as 'unconstitutional'.	The Supreme Court upholds the legalization of abortion in Mexico City as valid; declaring that each subnational state can decide on their own about local laws regarding abortion.
2009	Many subnational states begin reforms to their Constitutions, to protect "life from the moment of conception" (about 18 subnational states to date).	NOM0046 is created: it deals with the matter of protocols for institutional attention towards victims of sexual assault, stating that emergency contraception must be provided to them, up until 120 hours after the assault (at this point, the NOM did not yet declare that access to abortion should also be provided to the victims).

(*Continued*)

Table 2.1 (Continued)

Year	*Reform favourable to the 'pro-life' side*	*Reform favourable to the 'pro-legalization' side*
2011	Major Constitutional reform, concerning human rights: international human rights treaties signed by Mexico are now considered part of national law, on par with the Mexican Constitution and other domestic laws. Protection of human rights shall be progressive and grant all persons the highest possible protection of rights.	
2013		Creation of the General Law on Victims of Crime (*Ley General de Víctimas*), which recognizes interruption of pregnancy as an emergency medical service: access should be granted to all victims of sexual assault (as it is an admitted exception to abortion bans in all subnational states, as well as in the Federal Criminal Code).
2016		NOM0046 is reformed. The previous version only granted victims of sexual assault access to emergency contraceptives; after the reform, it now grants the victims also access to abortion (building on what was stated in the *"Ley General de Víctimas"* from three years prior). Crucially, it also eliminates any need to prove that the assault happened or to report it to any authorities at all. Abortion is to be authorized following a written declaration by the victim, that the pregnancy is a result of sexual assault. Underage girls can also access abortion in this case without parental consent, from the age of 12.
2018	'Pro-life' advocates especially from the minority political party PES (*Partido Encuentro Social*) get a reform passed, known as the "Law of Conscientious Objection". It is not quite a new law, but rather the addition of a paragraph to Article 10 of the General Health Law, permitting doctors to refuse to practice abortions in public hospitals if they are 'conscientious objectors' – but with an obligation to refer the patient to non-objecting personnel. (A similar provision on conscientious objection existed already in Mexico City's Health Law, after abortion was legalized in 2007.)	

(*Continued*)

Table 2.1 (Continued)

Year	*Reform favourable to the 'pro-life' side*	*Reform favourable to the 'pro-legalization' side*
2019		The state of Oaxaca decriminalizes abortion in the same manner as Mexico City did in 2007: through legal redefinition of abortion as "interruption of pregnancy after the twelfth week". It thus became the second subnational state to do so, after 12 years of abortion being illegal in every other state besides the capital.
2021		The states of Hidalgo, Veracruz, Baja California, Coahuila and Colima decriminalize abortion, through the same legal redefinition as Mexico City and Oaxaca. After the case presented in the state of Coahuila, *the Supreme Court of Mexico declares any criminalization of abortion to be unconstitutional*, based on a defence of women's rights. This does not constitute a law in itself, but the Court's jurisprudence is undoubtedly one of the strongest precedents that can be set, and paves the way for nation-wide decriminalization, possibly legalization as well. The Court also invalidates the 2018 reform on "*Objeción de Conciencia*", declaring that doctors' conscientious objection should not stand in the way of a woman seeking abortion.
2023		In a second landmark ruling, the Mexican Supreme Court declares that penalties for abortion should be removed from the *Federal* Criminal Code and that Federal healthcare institutions should offer the procedure to women who request it.

Source: Based on Pérez Hernández 2017; expanded by author using fieldwork data.

of the pro- or anti-abortion advocacy groups and are still today very much interpreted by activists as either favourable or unfavourable to their stance. Rarely has any of these changes been uncontested, since the reforms tend to come precisely as a result of contestation either proactive (when their 'side' proposes the change) or reactive (when they are protesting against it). Pérez' timeline only covers until year 2016, and I supplement it with the latest important events from 2016 until 2023 – as also informed by my fieldwork in Mexico.

With this 'panoramic view' of how advocates for and against abortion have fought their "lawfare" in Mexico, one can start to identify the many potential authorities involved in creating and enacting these reforms: not just Congresses but also judges, health authorities, crime persecuting authorities, among others, as well as the many legal and technical minutiae which can play a part. With the Supreme Court declaring criminalization of abortion to be unconstitutional in 2021, the strongest possible precedent has been set, for eventual decriminalization throughout the country. However, the case still remains (and will probably remain so for years to come) that advocates on opposed sides of the debate continue to have irreconcilable viewpoints and that 'pro-life' advocates will continue to challenge the Supreme Court's decisions. It also stands that, under the federal system, each subnational state has its own Criminal Code, and thus the 'pulls and pushes' of advocacy will still be needed for the achievement of the concrete, legally codified reforms in those subnational documents.

In Mexico and elsewhere, contestation in the abortion debate is likely to persist for three main reasons: the strongly controversial nature of the issue where both discourses remain strong, the primal collision of rights and principles that abortion entails, but also the nature of contestation itself – as a source rather than a detractor of legal legitimacy. Fundamental viewpoints are likely to stay irreconcilable. In the case of Mexico, the topic remains very local in a legislative sense, while at the same time, the advocacy is seeing increasing transnationalism.

Advocacy through Print: Notable Documentation Provided by Advocates

Next in importance to the extended interviews themselves are all the written materials that were obtained because the interviewees directly provided access through copies or photographs. These documents were, in almost every case, created and willingly shared by them. They comprise short books or manuscripts authored by them, flyers about their advocacy activities or handed out during protests, law reform proposals, written statements and annual reports by the NGOs that they associate with, constitutional challenges presented to local judges and to the Supreme Court, communications with other advocates, invitations to conferences or protests, or communications that they sent to international organizations and global forums (such as pieces sent to the OHCHR at the time of debating the aforementioned *"Draft Comment No. 36, on the Right to Life"*). Almost every interviewed advocate, for and against legal abortion, provided at least one piece of documentation, which greatly enriched fieldwork research and provided proof of their activity as well as records of their main messages.

I will not detail all the documentation provided by advocates here – the previous paragraph gives a general idea of the main gist of many such documents. (For the comprehensive list of all materials that advocates provided, see Annex 2.) Instead, I will detail only those which were remarkable in some way, because of how illustrative they are of the pro- and anti-legal abortion advocacy as has been carried out in Mexico. These remarkable materials reflect much of the current framing and messaging in Mexico's contemporary abortion debates, and they are richly informative in and of themselves. They are quite telling not only about abortion as a topic in itself but also about the *advocacy* itself: the strategies, the *hows*, even the use at times of information pieces that were clearly deceptive by design, fully meant to be deceptive as a deliberate part of advocacy efforts.

What sets all these pieces apart from any advocacy documentation available online is how advocates thoroughly expressed their direct ties with the material that they were providing: the pieces were, for example, law reform proposals that they themselves were drafting and furthering (regardless if they were ultimately passed into law or not), a book on the issue which was co-authored by an interviewed advocate, annual reports from their organization, printed publicity about events they would host or about services offered, screenshots of personal communications with other advocates (transnational communications, at times). The fact that the advocates themselves provided these materials (and the vast majority did so unprompted, of their own initiative) speaks of the importance that the pieces have to them, in their own activism. Thus, I analyze them as important carriers of their messages, interpretations, and meanings.

1. **The book "*Aborto: La Política de un Estado Claudicante*" ("*Abortion: the Policy of an Abdicating State*", 2017).** This is an edited volume by several academics and legal experts who lean towards a critical view of abortion legalization in Mexico City. The interviewee/advocate that I met with is co-author of two chapters. It examines the constitutional and legal underpinnings of the abortion-related reforms, challenging the notion that legalization improved maternal health outcomes (since protection of women's health had been the initial reasoning for abortion decriminalization in Mexico City, to supposedly prevent mortality and morbidity resulting from unsafe abortions). The book posits that a mere provision of abortion services did not translate necessarily into better such outcomes for women there: rates of maternal deaths in Mexico City did remain higher than in some of the subnational states where abortion stayed illegal. Authors showcase the complex and multi-faceted reality of women's reproductive health, contesting the notion that a mere provision of abortion services would, in and of itself, reduce general rates of maternal mortality.

   The book is heavily referenced throughout my research; as it provides not only a great deal of factual information about the history of abortion norms in Mexico and what changed since legalization in 2007, but also a trove of information about common messages used by 'pro-life' advocates who are legal experts, and who carry out their advocacy from an academic angle: through law, as well as through what they deem to be *'bioethics principles'*.

It gives deep insight into how Mexican 'pro-life' expert advocates interpret international law, UN and OAS human rights documents, as well as their own advocacy. The book was mentioned often by several of the interviewed 'pro-life' advocates; showing that this piece is well known amongst them and commonly referenced in their activism. Some chapter authors have ties with the *Early Institute,* a Mexican think tank that creates policy-oriented research on many issues related to the protection of childhood and families: preventing drug addiction in young people, protecting children from sexual abuse, advocating for better policies of parental leave at the workplace, or protecting women from exploitative surrogacy practices, among other topics.

Concerning their abortion-related research, the authors build their arguments on a basis of 'bioethics', to advocate against abortion. The title itself, *"Abortion: the Policy of a Claudicating State"*, uses this rather uncommon word, *"claudicante",* of which the most exact translation into English is *'to abdicate'* in the sense of 'opting out of a responsibility'. Therefore, the title carries the implication (further voiced throughout the book's pages) that by adopting a policy of providing access to abortion, the Mexican State has illegitimately "given up" its obligations towards "true protection of women's health and rights".

2. **Annual report booklet "Católicas por el Derecho a Decidir, 20 años" (*20 Years of 'Catholics for the Right to Decide'*).** Published by the NGO of the same name, the booklet was provided by one interviewee and it features a summary of the organization's activities in the past 20 years. On the issue of abortion, 'Catholics for the Right to Decide' is a truly remarkable organization, as they defend legal abortion and decidedly present one of the most curious cases of 'intersectionality' between Catholicism and modern feminism.

   The booklet provides interesting reasonings, based on a peculiar interpretation of catholic theology, of the legitimacy of abortion as a woman's choice. They draw justifications from catholic theology for why abortion can and should be a legitimate choice for women, including catholic women: for example, pointing out at the divine forgiveness and understanding for any action, or at the catholic "liberty of conscience" which can make any personal decision a morally respectable one as long as it was made "through liberty of conscience". It also heavily uses symbology and imagery that refers to, for example, the Virgin Mary (a sacred, venerated figure for Mexican catholics) having been offered *'motherhood as a choice'*.

Also gifted by the advocate was a USB memory stick containing their animated publicity series "*Catolicadas*"; and 20 postcards featuring various advocacy messages. Some cards present cartoon characters representing catholic nuns, along with messages defending inclusion of LGBTQ+ people in church life, diversity in sexual orientation, or the liberty of conscience and free choice in sexuality – including abortion as a choice for women. Others represent what catholics call "votive offerings" (usually messages giving thanks for a divine favour, or once a religious vow has been fulfilled), including the allegedly real short testimonies of women who give thanks to God or the Virgin Mary, for having been able to access a necessary or wanted abortion. Another few depict hand-drawn scenes of rural and small-town life, with short phrases about how these women reconcile their abortion experiences with their catholic faith, teachings and theology.

Although official catholic leadership strongly rejects this organization (and a majority of catholics considers them to be an illegitimate or 'spurious' organization), they are still a large NGO with significant international presence. They advocate on human rights, and the embracing of subjects within international human rights that are controversial to catholics (as they also promote the sociopolitical equality of LGBTQ+ persons), through their own vision of catholic theology, even while clearly running in opposition to official catholic stance. Their interpretation is one that aims to establish dialogue between traditional Catholicism and progressive movements.

3. **A printed flyer created by the "Centres of Support for Women" (*Centros de Apoyo a la Mujer*, or CAMs).** Copies of this flyer are distributed across the city of San Luis Potosí and presumably many other places. The CAMs are a network created by Jorge Serrano Limón, the founder of the *"Pro-Vida"* NGO group in Mexico – *"Pro-Vida"* has been active since the late 1970s and has ties to the USA-based "Pro-Life International" group, one of the oldest anti-abortion advocacy organizations worldwide. These CAMs have the goal of dissuading women from having abortions by providing them with some temporary support measures.

   The flyer is remarkable because it can objectively be described as misleading. It does not feature the logo of the CAMs or "Pro-Vida", but rather that of another organization called "DeSÍde" (which has been featured in several news articles, warning that it is "a façade" and "a fake centre of clinical practice"). This word "DeSÍde" is a mix of the Spanish word for 'decide' (same as in English) and 'sí' ('yes'); giving the impression that their information is about the 'decision' or 'choice' to have an abortion (as supporters of legal abortion often refer to 'the right to choose'), but while subtly conveying the 'sí' that 'pro-life' advocates often use as a short signifier for an anti-abortion stance: *'say yes to life'*.

Under the logo, the letters "ILE" appear, normally used in Mexico to refer to the "Legal Interruption of Pregnancy" *(Interrupción Legal del Embarazo)*. The information is vague, promising "*an immediate solution, on the same day*" to "*women who have decided to interrupt their pregnancy*". It also says: "*because you deserve to decide freely*", promising *"free counseling"*, and a telephone number. The advocate who provided the flyer openly agreed that its purpose is to mislead women into thinking that it advertises abortion services. It is clearly constructed in a way that it appears to point to an abortion provider' services, meant to allure women who will then be counselled to decide against abortion (cost-free and on the same day, one can presume) and to seek alternative support with them.

These and other openly misleading strategies are justified by them as legitimate, *"because they ultimately save lives"*. News articles have denounced these misleading flyers and the deceitful abortion-related campaign. The articles document this as an extensive practice in Mexico: misleading propaganda, as well as 'pro-life' centres masquerading as 'clinics for women's health' or posing only vaguely as 'Centres on the Interruption of Pregnancy' across the country and especially throughout Mexico City.[32]

4. **A printed invitation to the public conference by Jorge Serrano Limón, prominent 'pro-life' activist** (I personally attended the conference, in the city of San Luis Potosí). The invitation features a photo of Serrano Limón giving a speech, as well as an image of a foetus in-utero, however with the message: *"The woman is at risk"* (*"La Mujer está en Peligro"*), as well as the phrase *"We are living through an unprecedented attack on the human being inside the womb"*. It's remarkable as a piece of advocacy for its depiction of legal abortion as a "danger" to women as well as the conspiratorial tone of the message: the "unprecedented attack" of what many 'pro-life' advocates deem to be a global 'pro-abortion' effort 'against the natural family'.
5. One 'pro-life' advocate shared a printed copy of a **response given by the Mexican government (by INAI, the government agency specializing on transparency and the provision of official information to citizens), to an official request for information.** In this response, the INAI shares the data as of 30 June 2018, of exactly how many individuals were imprisoned for the crime of abortion per subnational state. The advocate's idea, by sharing this, was to prove that it is an 'extremely small number': official registry shows that, at that time, a total of 156 individuals were in prison for abortion-related crimes; and out of the 156, a total of 151 were men rather than women.[33]

This rather surprising fact could be explained in several ways. Some of those men might be doctors or other medical personnel who performed abortions (in the Mexican Criminal Codes, penalties for abortion are harsher for the medical personnel performing them, than for the pregnant woman); some others could be men who forced a woman to undergo an abortion (forced abortion being a crime in every local Criminal Code in Mexico, and subject to much harsher penalties than abortions consented by the woman); or men who were otherwise complicit to illegal abortions. Another possible explanation is that if a man commits violence against a woman and causes a miscarriage, in the Spanish language this is also called *'un aborto'* (abortion); and thus the crime is classified in the same data group as those abortions willed and consented by the woman.

The advocacy goal here was to show that news headlines or reports about the supposed 'imprisonment of thousands of women for abortion' are misleading, and that the media often reports the numbers for abortion-related *complaints*; conflating those numbers with the actual *prison convictions*. This could indeed be observed in several news articles, which do conflate both numbers in a way that appears as misleading. The presentation of these official statistics, by the 'pro-life' advocates, is meant to weaken pro-legalization arguments about the unfairness of the criminalization, stigmatization and imprisonment of women who abort. It is meant to convey the message that *"very few women are ever given prison sentences for abortion (and actually many more men are); criminalization is rarely happening to women who abort"*. Paraphrasing the words of the advocate I interviewed: keeping abortion illegal makes sense because, while prohibition discourages *some* abortions, the ones actually performed rarely result in women being legally persecuted.

It is curious that they would choose to turn this data into an anti-decriminalization point in any case; and even more so, that they would try to use it as a reason to keep abortion illegal in written laws as they stand. Firstly, an important weakness of this argument is the fact that, as long as abortions are illegal, it is difficult to accurately tell how many are being performed, making it hard to estimate if the ratio of persecutions to illegal abortions is 'low' or 'high' for the sake of discussion – independently if the incarcerated individuals are men or women.

The second weakness is that, if the idea is that the penalties for abortion are rarely ever carried out anyways, then this argument hinges on a basic principle of impunity and of *non-implementation* of the existing laws, while conceding that they generally do not wish to see women imprisoned for abortions. Several advocates indicated that they believed a financial penalty, and a mandated period of community service, should be 'adequate punishment' for abortion. Opposed advocates could just as easily use the same data and the same argument about this impunity in practice, to advocate in favour of decriminalization (if indeed the sentences are being almost non-existent anyways); or by arguing that even *one* woman imprisoned for abortion (or one man, for that matter) 'is one too many'.

The use of this data also doesn't address the issue of *social* stigmatization at all: in the views of pro-legalization advocates, abortion should be a legitimate choice or even 'a right', and therefore even a social stigma for women who abort is unfair – let alone a criminal sentencing, whether carried out or not.

6. One advocate shared a **screenshot of a "tweet" where a person shares an invitation to a women-only talk in the city of Mazatlán, Sinaloa, on the topic of "Myths about Abortion" and "how to safely abort at home"**. While this shows the involvement from many parts of civil society on the topic of abortion, the message also raises alarm among advocates on opposed sides of the debate, since any procedure for "home abortion" can carry important medical risks to the woman.

   Some advocates online can be found, who speak in favour of this 'self-managed abortion at home', discussing points about personal privacy and why choose to go through the abortion experience alone in a home setting – bearing some similarities to people who advocate for the right to choose an unassisted home birth. I didn't personally find any pro-legalization advocates who endorse this practice due to potential medical risks, but clearly it is becoming another controversial (*contested*) point among 'pro-choice' advocates, who build on an argument about the right to privacy and to 'self-manage' biomedical procedures.

7. **Invitation to a lecture by Argentinian 'pro-life' advocate and medical doctor Chinda Brandolino, titled "Globalization of Abortion: the Culture of Death"** (*La Globalización del Aborto: la Cultura de la Muerte*), to take place in the Mexican state of Sonora. This provides an example of transnational advocacy, where activists reach across nation-state barriers to transmit messages and information. It also shows 'pro-life' advocates' views of abortion as a global conspiracy of sorts, in favour of 'death', the supposed 'destruction of the family', etc. It is one among several examples of direct transnational communications, between advocates who are sending messages to their counterparts beyond borders (for other such materials, by advocates both for and against legal abortion, see Annex 2).

8. One interviewed pro-legalization advocate shared an image of a **public "tweet" by academic, legal expert and prominent pro-legalization advocate Estefanía Vela, where she praises the decriminalization of abortion in Oaxaca in 2019,** commenting that eliminating penalties in the Criminal Code does not come in contradiction with a local Constitution "protecting life from the moment of conception". Vela also writes that the local Constitution need not be reformed for this change in the Criminal Code to be valid; also stating that denying women access to abortion

violates their human rights; quoting CEDAW as well as the *Artavia Murillo vs. Costa Rica* case at the Inter-American Court on Human Rights (about the personhood of embryos or lack thereof; this case is often used by pro-legalization advocates to support legal abortion).

Other materials of great interest, for the analysis of clashing messages and suggested concepts, were not given directly by the interviewed advocates but personally gathered or recorded while in Mexico: promotional items obtained during public protests, photographic evidence of advocacy messages, other publicity items, or publicly available documents found at the time of carrying out the research. I analyze them also as important "footprints" in the advocacy process. As with the previous section, I am only detailing those that are remarkable for some reason (the comprehensive list can be found in Annex 2).

1. Various publicity materials were gathered at the in-person attendance of the 'pro-life' protest called "Blue Wave" (*Ola Celeste*) that took place on October 20, 2018, organized by a coalition of civil society organizations, chiefly among them the *Frente Nacional por la Familia*. The main protest took place in Mexico City (and this was the one that I personally attended), but other parallel protests happened on the same day in almost every capital city of all Mexican subnational states. Gathered by myself or gifted by attendants were:

   a. Seventy-one photographs taken during the protest, mostly capturing the messages written on signs and carried by the attendees. (Some of these photographs, or parts of them, are featured at the end of this chapter.) Many of the signs feature, along with the written statements and messages, pictures of babies a few months old, visually conflating the idea of an embryo with that of a born, full-term child of a few months' age. Some other signs (although only a few) contained gruesome imagery that allegedly comes from abortion procedures. Some online sources denounce the supposed fake or misleading nature of these images, alleging that they are rather images stemming from the miscarriages of very advanced pregnancies, or from stillbirths, or from abortions that had to happen in exceptional circumstances or through very uncommon procedures. Allegedly, the depictions are then constructed in such a way as to make all abortions seem much more gruesome than they really are.
   b. Handkerchiefs in a light blue colour, with the printed message "Salvemos Las Dos Vidas" (*Let Us Save Both Lives*), identical to those used by 'pro-life' Argentinian protesters. These handkerchiefs as a 'pro-life' symbol originated in Argentina; in fact, the light blue colour was taken from the Argentinian flag. The colour was appropriated as part of the symbolism of the Argentinian 'pro-life' movement, framing the 'pro-life' message as a nationally unified claim. The blue handkerchief as a 'pro-life' symbol has now been taken up

by 'pro-life' advocates and movements all throughout Latin America, in a very successful creation of a transnational symbol and signifier.

c. A compact disc containing the USA-produced, 'pro-life' short documentary film: *"A Silent Scream"*. The documentary contains alleged testimonies of doctors claiming that they used to be pro-abortion but later regretted it and spoke against it, as well as gruesome footage and imagery allegedly taken from procedures of abortion. It is a very well-known and widely circulated piece among 'pro-life' advocates, in the United States as well as in Latin America. In the same way as in previous point 'a', some sources denounce the supposed fake or misleading nature of such images, selecting pictures of exceptional cases or exceptional abortion methods, in order to make procedures of abortions seem more gruesome than they are.
d. 'Pro-life' advocates were handing out small, chalkstone-made models of an embryo, allegedly 'real size' at about 10 weeks' gestation, gifted along with religious paraphernalia and postcards to sign for "pledging to the protection of all the unborn". These chalkstone models have been a feature in 'pro-life' protests for many years and can be understood to be a physical symbology – a tangible signifier of a victim of rights violation.
e. A pamphlet called *"Ama la Vida por Mí"* (Love Life for Me) with medical information about in utero development, some parts of it outdated (quoting medical studies from around the 1960s) or misleading. It contains alleged testimonies of women who had abortions (unquoted and with almost no identifying information). Much of the information that it contains on abortion procedures is misleading, as it states that abortions are carried out through gruesome means involving sharp tools (supposedly a procedure called *"curetaje"* in Spanish, using a *"cureta"* or sharp medical knife) or through *"saline injections to the foetus' head"*. However, clinics in Mexico City report that all legal abortions are carried out either with drugs (pills containing Misoprostol and Mifepristone) or through a procedure of manual intra-uterine aspiration (known as AMEU).[34]

The pamphlet also warns of severe medical risks during or after abortion, alleging that clinics "rarely can perform it safely" and a testimony of a woman who allegedly aborted at five months gestation, a point at which it is no longer legal in most countries barring extraordinary circumstances (but this is not mentioned as being the case), and who describes the procedure as a traumatic and regrettable event. Photos and copies of the same pamphlet can be found online, websites refer to it being used also in Argentina, during their own 'pro-life' protests in 2018.

The gruesome procedures described in the pamphlet were more common for illegal abortions in the past, but they are highly risky and involve significant rates of injury or death for women. Nowadays, given that much safer methods are available, the procedures described in the pamphlet would rarely be used for legal abortions, although we cannot know with certainty whether some *illegal* abortions are still carried out in those ways.

2. During the pro-legalization protest event called *"Tendedero Feminista"* ("Feminist Clothesline") attended in September 2019 in Saltillo, Coahuila, the following materials were gathered:

   a. Twenty photographs taken during the event, mostly capturing the messages written on signs and carried by attendees – most signs were hanging from an extended "clothesline" of sorts, hence the name of the protest. Many of the messages featured alleged testimonies of women who aborted, or who were sexually abused and wanted to interrupt pregnancies resulting from violence; these are however unverified and with little to no identifying information. Others explain why the illegality of abortion puts women at risk.
   b. Green handkerchiefs with 'pro-choice' messages, the most common one being roughly translated from Spanish as "Education to Decide, Contraceptives to Avoid Abortion, Legal Abortion to Avoid Deaths" (*Educación para Decidir, Anticonceptivos para No Abortar, Aborto para No Morir*). But other green handkerchiefs have different messages, such as "Legal Abortion Now!", "It Will Be Law", "Legal, Safe and Free Abortion", or interestingly, "The Three Causes Are Not Enough" (*Las Tres Causales No Bastan*).
   c. Fifteen images found online, most of them taken by other people during other public protests for and against legal abortion, in Mexico and other countries (Argentina, Spain). Very similar messages to those seen in Mexico appear, furthered by advocates on opposed sides of the debate. Pictures can also be found online of identical publicity and paraphernalia as that gathered in the Mexican protests: pictures of an identical chalkstone model of a human embryo (including photos of prominent 'pro-life' activist Jorge Serrano Limón holding one of them), pictures of the same green and blue handkerchiefs signifying the opposed 'sides' of the debate, pictures of the same pamphlet "*Ama la Vida Por Mí*", and pictures of the publicity poster for the American 'pro-life' documentary film "*A Silent Scream*". This is worth mentioning because it serves as proof of both the transnational nature of this debate and the common messages used across borders.

To be considered in a brief category of their own are the seven communications sent by Mexican advocates to the global forum that happened at the United Nations Office of the High Commissioner for Human Rights (OHCHR), when discussions were taking place for the drafting of what eventually became the "General Comment No. 36 to the International Covenant on Civil and Political Rights (ICCPR) on the Right to Life". This was a unique and highly illustrative instance of a true global *multilogue* and of global contestation taking place in it.

During some time comprising parts of the years 2017 and 2018, comments could be sent by governments, national and international NGOs, civil associations, or simply by individuals and citizens who wanted to share opinions and expertise about the drafting of the General Comment. The piece drew attention and controversy, mainly because of two topics: the mentions about euthanasia and its possible regulations, as well as one article mentioning abortion and its regulations, in turn. Seven comments were sent from Mexican organizations. And in two cases, the persons authoring or directly participating in the creation of these communications were interviewed for this book.

1. Text by the NGO "Mexican Commission on Human Rights" *(Comisión Mexicana de Derechos Humanos)*. Although it does not adopt a position directly against abortion, it discusses the General Comment mentioning abortion in terms of national sovereignty, commenting that states have the national sovereignty to decide on the most adequate and progressive implementation of human rights, that a 'right to abortion' is not recognized by the ICCPR, and that nation-states cannot be forced to comply with a provision to grant access to abortion.
2. Text by the Center on Advanced Social Research (*Centro de Investigación Social Avanzada*), based in the state of Querétaro. They comment against the legalization of abortion, especially through a framework of possible discrimination against (unborn) persons with disabilities.
3. Text by the coalition of NGOs "The Family Network", (*La Red Familia*). Interviewed advocate No. 6 (see Annex 1) participated in drafting this communication. This is however a curious piece, because even though *La Red Familia* is a very openly anti-abortion advocacy network, and although interviewee No. 6 was also very clear during the interview about their anti-abortion stance and activities, this piece does not mention abortion at all. Nor does it directly argue against abortion as an international obligation. It rather provides extensive commentary about the importance of human rights and the related international treaties, about the fundamental principle of *Pacta Sunt Servanda*, and in a similar vein to the communications sent by the *Comisión Mexicana de Derechos Humanos*, it specifies that General Comments are only non-binding suggestions or observations by experts, and that there is no imposition on nation-states to implement anything that goes against its own internal human rights provisions.
4. Joint text by the Center for Studies and Integral Training for Women (*Centro de Estudios y Formación Integral de la Mujer*) and the Early Institute. Interviewed advocate No. 10 participated in creating this communication. The piece argues against abortion, on what is deemed 'bioethical principles'.
5. Joint text by the Aguirre, Azuela, Chávez, Jauregui Pro-Human Rights Foundation (*Fundación Aguirre, Azuela, Chávez, Jáuregui, Pro Derechos Humanos A.C.*); the Mexican National Academy on Bioethics (*Academia Nacional Mexicana de Bioética*); the Autonomous University of Puebla (*Universidad Popular Autónoma Del Estado De Puebla UPAEP*); and one researcher from the Universidad Anáhuac. The piece opposes abortion legalization, mentioning the Inter-American Convention on Human Rights (Pact of San José) as a legal basis in its argumentation.

6. A text by the Institute of Analysis of Family Policy in Mexico (*Instituto de Análisis de Política Familiar en México*), whose director is the same person directing the NGO "National Front for Families" (*Frente Nacional por la Familia*), one of the most prominent NGOs advocating against abortion and against homosexual marriage in Mexico. The piece argues against legal abortion; however, the argument is more constructed on technicalities about the legal overreach that it represents if the OHCHR pressures states into legalizing abortion.
7. A text by the Mexican representatives of CitizenGo, which is a transnational citizen organization advocating against abortion (among other topics). This piece also advocates against the legality of abortion as a legitimate (or legal) choice.

Through all that was gathered in the field (expert interviews and extensive documentation), the complex framing of the issue of abortion is shown through the ideas that advocates propose and those that they oppose, the concepts that they suggest and those that they react against or consider inadequate or illegitimate, all of which constitutes ways in which they have engaged in norm contestation about abortion. We also can observe clues and indicators of transnational advocacy: their links with the global and with allies abroad. This serves to gain a much richer and clearer insight into how advocates on opposed sides of the debate have negotiated meanings, frameworks, and concepts, and how such negotiations have ultimately influenced (or failed to influence) policy and legislation changes. Activists have engaged, for many years now, in meaning-making and meaning-negotiation, as well as the contestation of various concepts through their efforts.

Being a Researcher: Part of the Research Itself

Any serious piece of social science research should of course strive for self-awareness on the researcher's own positionality with regard to the field (understood as the entire context, comprised by the place, the people approached, language, cultural context, etc.); ethics of the methods used; potential limitations of the research and methods; possible biases or preexisting assumptions; and any other considerations of factors that have moulded the research as it is, for better and for worse. In this exercise (as much as for the content itself of this book), the aim is first to *understand* rather than (or at least before) attempting to *explain*. Some of my earlier analytical attempts were perhaps aimed at trying, a tad arrogantly, to 'solve' the debate. It became clear over time that not only might this debate be fundamentally 'unsolvable' but also that my lone efforts cannot possibly do that – and perhaps should not attempt to either, focusing instead on *understanding first,* and on suggesting pathways for dialogue.

Continuing a reflection on positionality, much can be commented about making aims towards 'objectivity' in research. In some academic environments, the idea prevails that the researcher should attempt to keep a measure of 'neutrality' or 'objectivity' towards that which is being studied.[35] However, other recent and more constructivist strands of academia point out that this is a nearly impossible endeavour, for the researcher rarely approaches the object of study through a '*blank slate*' eye of complete unawareness or neutrality[36] – not only we are always influenced by preexisting notions and conceptions but also we look at the world through the glass of a specific cultural context, a specific education or training that inevitably carries some ideological baggage of one sort or another, a language, and the limitations of time and place.

The questions that one asks in the field, or the very approaches that one uses in a search for information, can carry implicit biases which, if they cannot be erased, should still be kept in an eye of conscious awareness. Some academics therefore speak against this illusion of supposed 'neutrality'; however, it was still my effort during the creation of this book to approach what are (self-)identified as 'both sides' of a debate with an aim towards understanding them, in their nuance and complexity – as can be expected from the worldviews of complex individuals that happen to carry competing proposals. The effort of approaching advocates both *for* and *against* the liberalization of abortion, in order to gather viewpoints from opposing sides, helps to attain a richer vision of what the contestation, construction, and negotiation of concepts has meant for opposed groups on this debate in Mexico.

My analysis does lay down an analytical framework of 'for' and 'against' legal abortion which can be pointed out as 'binary'. Any binary view of discourses or narratives can be problematic, and although these potentially problematic aspects of a 'binarization' have to be accepted and kept in constant awareness, the choice is an analytical one stemming from the fact that this is a study of norm contestation by groups of advocates who have themselves constructed their worldviews as a binary. Due to the nature of norm contestation, which often entails reacting *against* something or presenting a competing proposal to an existing premise, the way in which activists carry out their contestation on any topic tends to make for situations where they construct their arguments in a manner that is, if not always 'binary', often *relational* or *oppositional*.

That many advocates on a variety of issues speak of themselves as 'anti' or 'pro-something' activists is an example of this frequently oppositional stance. The very fact that pro- and anti-abortion advocates in Mexico, Argentina, the United States and other places effectively see themselves as two camps (often reduced and simplified into two colours) is and should remain worrisome and problematic, perhaps studied as part of a larger tendency towards polarization and binarity in current politics in general: where many debates are simplified into being 'left- or right-wing', 'liberal or conservative', 'progressive or traditional', 'capitalist or socialist', etc.

The loss of nuance on many fronts, with people effectively seeing themselves as a part of 'two camps' being carried further and further into extremes, makes for fewer middle-ground workable solutions – instead giving way to the impression of having been excluded from a debate, or pushed aside in order to make way for the imposition of an illegitimate solution – as many Mexican advocates indeed report feeling like. The final aim of this analytical choice, to temporarily 'agree' with the advocates themselves on seeing the issue through their constructed binary 'looking glass', can hopefully be helpful in the end, to bring the nuance and middle-ground solutions back into the debate.

Before carrying out interviews, ethical considerations were taken into account, carefully considering whether any advocates or their activities could be put at risk because of being interviewed. This was not found to be the case for any of them, and their privacy is being protected through the use of only a number and initials to identify them (see Annex 1). Their previous consent for recording and for being (anonymously) quoted in this research was asked and respected at all times. When dealing with a sensitive issue like the one here studied, it should not be ignored that women from very conservative and traditional Latin American societies, particularly those who have had an abortion (whether the procedure was legal or illegal), tend to not be vocal at all and, in many cases, have not informed their families about their procedures, since they could risk rejection, ostracism, or even overt aggression.

Because of this, advocacy organizations themselves sometimes have problems gathering reliable data, or reaching the very women who might need them the most. However, my research did not directly address women who were in this position. No persons were contacted for reasons of them having been involved directly in a case of abortion, neither as a patient nor as medical personnel, nor any other role carrying involvement in it (noting that the sexes of the interviewees have not been disclosed but the ratio is of a roughly equal distribution of men and women advocates). It is my suggestion that any future effort to directly interview such women must be carried out carefully, especially as to not put them (and the researcher) in situations of personal risk. A similar social risk might exist for some of the activists who advocate for the legalization of abortion, in certain regions of Latin America.

Other considerations about positionality have also been given conscious thought, such as my own personal character as a researcher in this field at that time. Being a Mexican woman, as well as an academic and in my early to mid-thirties, it was important to hold self-awareness of "*How do the experts and interviewees see me?*". . . For instance, some 'pro-life' advocates can at times be wary of researchers and academics. However, the fact of being a Mexican national (and thus able to communicate with all advocates in Spanish, their native language), as well as being a woman, may have had an effect of eliciting somewhat more trust in most or a lot of the interviewees, most of which agreed to longer interviews where they spoke freely and seemingly with great authenticity.

It must be acknowledged, however, that only later in the process of coding and analyzing the data, as well as exchanging with other academics in Hamburg on issues of positionality (and having very interesting exchanges about the academic's role as an advocate, or vice versa), I realized that during fieldwork I may have also fallen into 'the objectivity trap' mentioned earlier. While I was on the field, in an attempt to gain what I thought would be 'easier access to advocates on opposed sides of the debate', I made it very clear in my written communications to them that

Figure 2.1 Green and blue handkerchiefs side by side, used across Latin America in abortion-related protests. The green handkerchief used by pro-legal abortion advocates has the message: "*Educación Para Decidir, Anticonceptivos Para No Abortar, Aborto Legal Para No Morir*" ("Education to Decide, Contraceptives to Avoid Abortion, Legal Abortion To Avoid Death"). The blue handkerchief, used by 'pro-life' activists across Latin America, usually has the message *"We Save Both Lives"* or as seen here *"United for Both Lives"*.

Source: Photograph by Facundo Nahuel Hernández, Argentina, 2024. Permission to use photograph authorized in writing by Facundo Nahuel Hernández.

I was *"interviewing advocates both for and against in the abortion debate, as an academic who studies the issue"*.

This was informed by my perception that I would perhaps gain easier access to advocates on opposed sides of the debate if they absolutely did *not* perceive me as a part of any of the involved groups. My attempt to take this 'distance' from the subject (i.e. from the advocacy), was probably a discursive device intended to gain access to the field as a supposedly 'neutral observer', something I believe we

Figure 2.2 Sticker handed out at pro-abortion street protest in Saltillo, in the green colour that has signified pro-legal abortion movements in Latin America, with the message *"Motherhood will be wanted, or it will not be"*.

Source: Picture by author at pro-abortion protest in Saltillo, 2019.

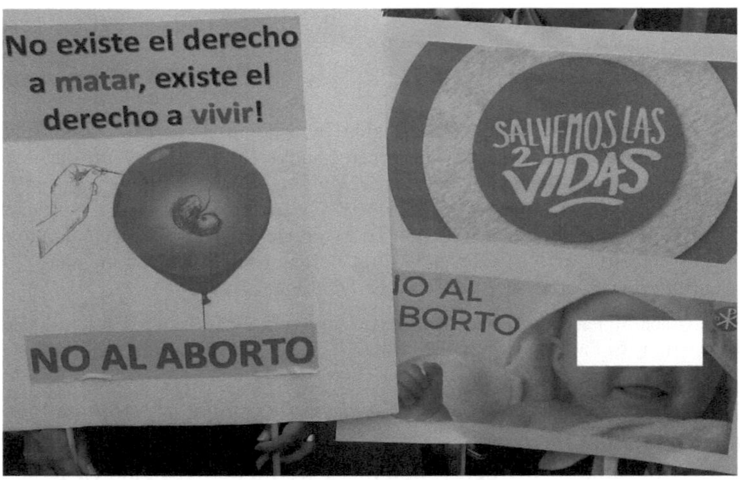

Figure 2.3 Posters with messages at 'pro-life' protest in Mexico City: *"There is no right to kill, there is a right to life. No To Abortion"* and *"Let Us Save Both Lives"*. Images of infants a few months old are often used, conflating embryos with full-term babies.

Source: Picture by author at 'pro-life' protest in Mexico City, 2018.

Figure 2.4 Poster seen at 'pro-life' protest in Mexico City. *"Your Rights . . . And Mine?"*.

Source: Picture by author at 'pro-life' protest in Mexico City, 2018.

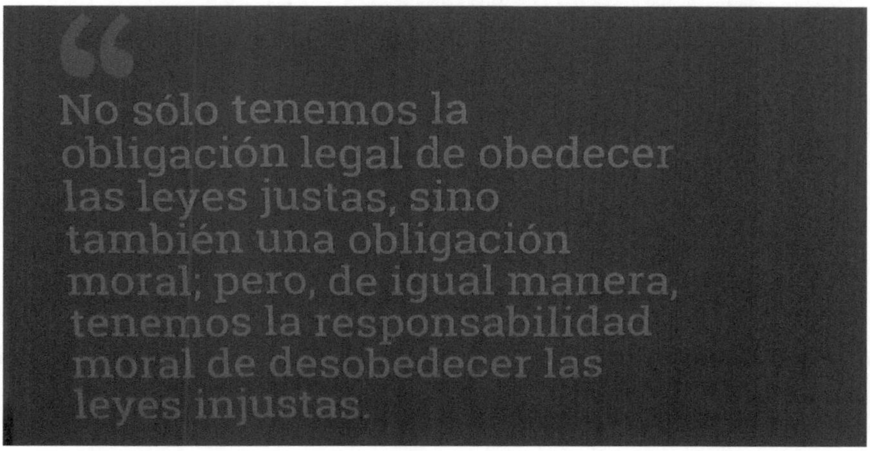

Figure 2.5 Message on 'pro-life' poster at protest in Mexico City. *"We not only have the legal obligation to obey fair laws, but also the moral obligation to do so; in an equal manner we have the moral responsibility to disobey unfair laws"*.

Source: Picture by author at 'pro-life' protest in Mexico City, 2018.

Figure 2.6 Handed out during 'pro-life' protest in Mexico City: a chalkstone model of a human embryo, real-life size at around 9–10 weeks' gestation.

Source: Picture by author at 'pro-life' protest in Mexico City, 2018.

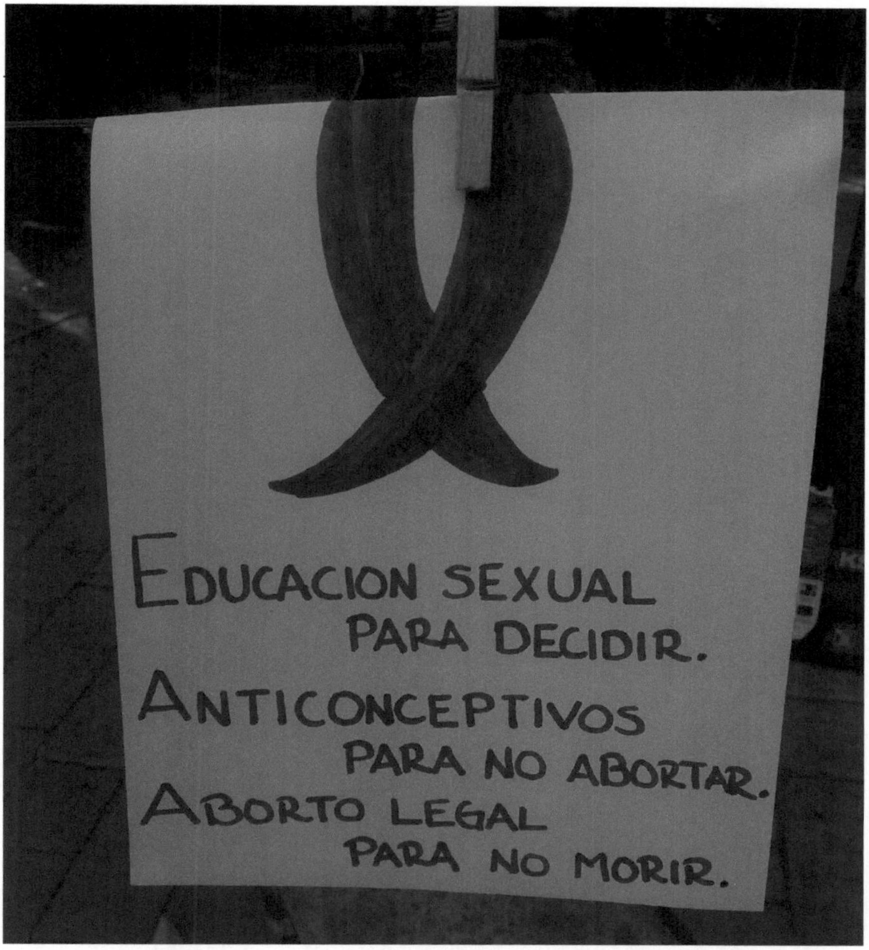

Figure 2.7 Message at pro-abortion protest in Saltillo, along with a depiction of the green handkerchief that signifies a pro-legal abortion stance: *"Sexual Education to Decide, Contraceptives to Avoid Abortion, Legal Abortion to Avoid Death"*.

Source: Picture by author at pro-abortion protest in Saltillo, 2019.

can never be in this debate. The paradigm of supposed 'objectivity' was informing these attempts at distancing myself, and the results of my attempts to access the advocates might have gone differently (for better or for worse) if I had shown any ideological leanings while on the field.

Not only was I at times 'playing this card' of supposed academic neutrality but I also have come to realize that I was also trying to take even more distance from the topic (of abortion advocacy *in Mexico*) by clarifying to the advocates that,

Figure 2.8 Monument to the Mother in Mexico City, with the two plaques that could be seen until recent years at the base: the plaque on top saying, *"To Her Who Loved Us Before Knowing Us"*, and the plaque at the bottom, added by feminist advocacy movements in the 1990s: *"Because Her Motherhood Was Consented"*. The latter plaque was not re-added after the Monument was rebuilt following the 2017 earthquake in Mexico City, which destroyed the statue.

Source: Photo by John Mitchell, 2009. Rights purchased from John Mitchell, through Alamy.com

Figure 2.9 Message at pro-abortion protest in Saltillo: *"Light up your voice: share your story to eliminate silence and help more women to raise their voices about their abortion experiences"*.

Source: Picture by author at pro-abortion protest in Saltillo, 2019.

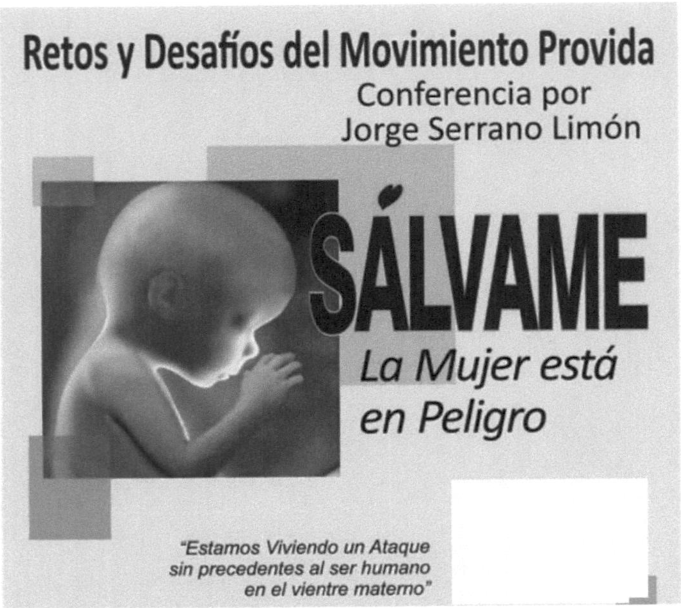

Figure 2.10 Invitation to the conference by Jorge Serrano Limón in San Luis Potosí, 2019. *"Challenges of the Pro-Life Movement. Conference by Jorge Serrano Limón. 'Save Me!'. . . The Woman is at Risk. We are living through an unprecedented attack towards the human being in the womb"*. Shared with author in printed format, as well as widely on social media, 2019.

Source: Permission to use authorized in writing by the Universidad San Pablo in the city of San Luis Potosí, the institution which organized the Conference.

although I am of Mexican origin, I was carrying out doctoral research in Germany. In this way, perhaps at times subconsciously, I was trying to further signal 'un-involvement' in the debate and in the Mexican activism – with the idea, valid or not, that this might open more doors in accessing the activists who may be wary of members from a perceived 'opposite team' within the country. And while it is true that I do not attach to myself the label of 'activist' in this Mexican debate (as I have not carried out activities aimed at furthering a specific policy change there), it would be disingenuous to claim ideological purity or 'neutrality'.

Nowadays, the idea is emerging in further literature that the scholar can be an activist, and the activist a scholar. While one can (and should) make a constant effort to be self-conscious about the need to approach study subjects with a scientific mind, the two identities don't necessarily have to exist separately or as a mutually exclusionary choice. And in our modern world where sociopolitical and ideological influence can often come from places of questionable scientific legitimacy, or through economic and political agendas disguising as 'fact', perhaps it

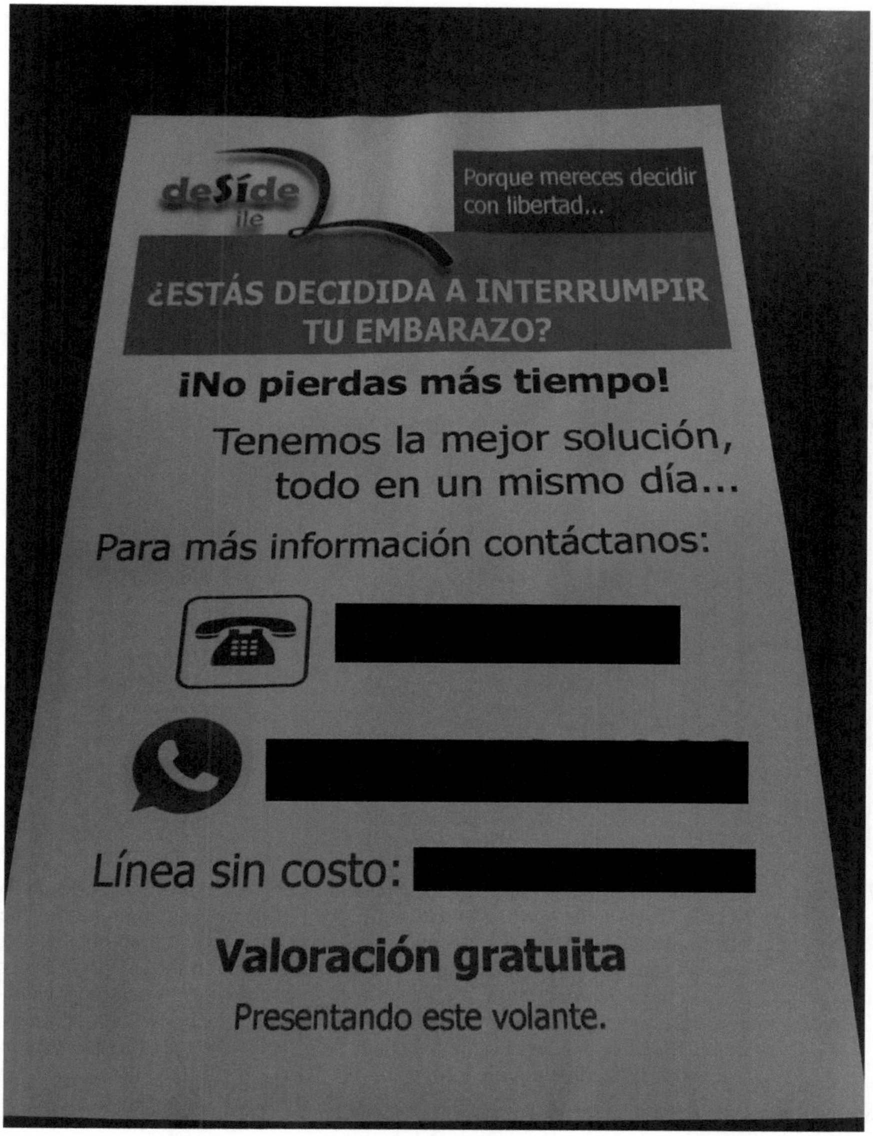

Figure 2.11 Photo of flyer gifted in the field by 'pro-life' advocate. It is meant to present, rather deceitfully, as an abortion service, when in reality it is meant to channel women into organizations which will discourage them from abortion and offer alternative support. *"Because you deserve to decide freely . . . Have you decided to interrupt your pregnancy? Don't waste more time! We have the best solution, all on the same day . . . For more information, contact us . . .".*

Source: Photo taken by author in San Luis Potosí, 2019. Permission to use authorized in writing by the "Centros de Ayuda para la Mujer Latinoamericana".

Figure 2.12 Cover of the Annual Report by the Mexican NGO "Catholics for the Right to Decide" (*Católicas por el Derecho a Decidir*). It depicts the main hall of the Virgin of Guadalupe Basilica, a cherished place for Mexican Catholics, along with a message of religious gratitude by the organization to the Virgin Mary of Guadalupe, reconciling Catholicism with their activities in favour of women's right to access abortion. Gifted to author during interview with advocate from *Católicas*, publicly available in their Website as well (painting by Alfredo Vilchis, as quoted within the Report).

Source: Permission to use authorized in writing by "Catholics for the Right to Decide", Mexico.

stands to reason even more that the scholar can, and often should, speak from a position that admittedly stands nowhere 'neutral'.

Future research in the matter of abortion will surely be needed, as the topic most likely will continue to change – not only as the issue's *'pendularity'* continues, as our conceptions of human rights continue to change and evolve, but also as biomedical sciences and technology themselves advance and certainly bring new considerations. Any future research dealing with the intersection between technology,

Figure 2.13 Example of promotional postcard by the Mexican NGO "Catholics for the Right to Decide" (*Católicas por el Derecho a Decidir*), depicting character of a nun wearing the green handkerchief that signifies a pro-abortion stance, and the message: "You will not stop being a catholic if you make decisions using liberty of conscience".

Source: Gifted to author by advocate from *Católicas*, publicly available in their website as well.

normativity, and the protection of public health as well as the rights of all individuals is sure to bring groundbreaking new developments in public philosophy and political science, as well as situate itself at the frontiers of our understandings of life, rights, and health.

Notes

1 In Mexico, there is one overarching Constitution, one overarching General Health Law, and one overarching Federal Criminal Code. However, each subnational state has its own local versions of each: a state-level Constitution, a state-level Health Law, as

well as its own subnational Criminal Code. This is a rarity even among other federal nations, which tend to have only one single, unified Criminal Code. In this manner, each Mexican state is given much political and legislative leeway on many issues, provided that the subnational laws do not contradict the general bases laid out by the federal documents.

2 Mizrahi Nedvedovich and Zúñiga Tapia, 2017, pp. 59–60.
3 Mexico City is, both geographically and administratively, a subnational state on its own.
4 Lamas, 2009.
5 Mexican Government, Criminal Code of Mexico City, 2002. Last amended February 2021.
6 World Health Organization, Media Centre, 2017. *Preventing Unsafe Abortion.* Fact Sheet.
7 Every subnational state also has its own local Health Law, but these only mention abortion for the purposes of medically regulating the cases where it is approved as legal.
8 National Institute of Women, Mexico (INMUJERES), 2009.
9 A 'constitutive' norm is here understood as one which creates ('*constitutes*') the space for newer laws, regulations, procedural rulebooks, etc., which would not exist previous to that initial normative reform.
10 Pérez Hernández, 2017, p. 23.
11 Pérez Hernández, 2017, p. 24.
12 Organization of American States. Inter-American Commission on Human Rights (2007). Informe No. 21–07.
13 Bartolini Esparza and Alarcón Loayza, 2017.
14 Pérez Hernández, 2017, p. 24.
15 Lamas, 2009.
16 Lamas, 2009, p. 158.
17 Bartolini Esparza and Alarcón Loayza, pp. 35–36.
18 Lamas, 2009, p. 163.
19 Fieldwork data: Interviewee No. 10 (see Annex 1).
20 Bartolini Esparza and Alarcón Loayza, p. 35–36.
21 Mexican Government, Criminal Code of Mexico City, 2002. Last amended February 2021.
22 Fieldwork data: Interviewee No. 24.
23 Fieldwork data: Interviewee No. 7.
24 Comisión Nacional de los Derechos Humanos, 2016.
25 Malkin, 2010.
26 Juárez *et al.*, 2009.
27 Sieder *et al.*, Norwegian Research Council, 2014–2017.
28 Gloppen, 2018, p. 6.
29 Pérez Hernández, 2017, pp. 28–29.
30 Although the distinction between these two concepts could seem clear enough in the English language; in Spanish the word, *'aborto'* is used for both abortions and miscarriages. It thus becomes very important, in legal semantics, to separate the two: when it is an involuntary *'aborto'* (a miscarriage) *versus* a voluntary one ('abortion' as understood in English). In general, the fact that one same word is used in Spanish to refer to both things can create great confusion, even potential legal trouble for an individual, as it always requires the clarification of whether an *'aborto'* was voluntary or involuntary.
31 Bartolini and Alarcón, 2017, p. 32.
32 See Marie Stopes Mexico, 2021.
33 Name of the official document: Executive Secretariat of the National System for Public Safety, National Registry of Penitentiary Information, June 30, 2018 (*Secretariado Ejecutivo del Sistema Nacional de Seguridad Pública, Registro Nacional de Información Penitenciaria, 30 Junio 2018*).

34 See Marie Stopes Mexico, 2021.
35 Anthropological studies tend to be more aware of this impossibility of neutrality, and of the importance of also analyzing the relationship between the observer and the observed: see Duneier and Back, 2006.
36 See also Hill, 1997.

References

Bartolini Esparza, M., and Alarcón Loayza, N. (2017). "Análisis de las Normas y Sentencias Relacionadas con el Aborto en México Durante los Últimos 25 Años." In *Aborto: La Política de un Estado Claudicante*. Todas y Todos Valemos en México, 31–51. Mexico City: Consejo Editorial de la Cámara de Diputados, LXIII Legislatura.

Comisión Nacional de los Derechos Humanos (CNDH). (2016). "NOM-046-SSA2-2005. Violencia Familiar, Sexual Y Contra Las Mujeres. Criterios Para La Prevención Y Atención." In *Marco Normativo CNDH*. www.cndh.org.mx/sites/all/doc/Programas/VIH/LeyesNormas-Reglamentos/NormaOficialMexicana/NOM-046-SSA2-2005_ViolenciaFamiliarSexual.pdf. Accessed November 2021.

Duneier, M., and Back, L. (2006). "Voices from the Sidewalk: Ethnography and Writing Race." *Ethnic and Racial Studies*, 29(3), 543–565.

Gloppen, S. (2018). "Conceptualizing Lawfare: A Typology & Theoretical Framework." Center on Law and Social Transformation, Norway. www.academia.edu/35608212/Conceptualizing_Lawfare_A_Typology_and_Theoretical Framwork. Accessed July 2020.

Hill, A.G. (1997). "Truth Lies in the Eye of the Beholder: The Nature of Evidence in Demography and Anthropology." *Anthropological Demography*, 223–247.

Juárez, F., Singh, S., García, S.G., and Díaz Olivarrieta, C. (2009). "Estimaciones del aborto inducido en México: ¿qué ha cambiado entre 1990 y 2006?." *Perspectivas Internacionales en Salud Sexual y Reproductiva*, Special Issue of 2009, 4–14.

Lamas, M. (2009). "La Despenalización del Aborto en México." *Nueva Sociedad*, (220), 154–172.

Malkin, E. (2010). "Many States in Mexico Crack Down on Abortion." *The New York Times, Americas*, September 22. http://www.nytimes.com/2010/09/23/world/americas/23mexico.html?_r=0

Marie Stopes Mexico. (2021). "Clínicas de aborto falsas. ¡Cuidado!." https://mariestopes.org.mx/clinicas-de-aborto-falsas/. Accessed November 2021.

Mexican Government. (2002). "Código Penal para el Distrito Federal" (Criminal Code of Mexico City). https://paot.org.mx/centro/codigos/df/pdf/2021/COD_PENAL_DF_26_02_2021.pdf. Accessed February 2021.

Mizrahi Nedvedovich, C., and Zúñiga Tapia, F.R. (2017). "Las recomendaciones de los organismos internacionales como mecanismos de presión política." In *Aborto: La Política de un Estado Claudicante*. Todas y Todos Valemos en México, 53–67. Mexico City: Consejo Editorial de la Cámara de Diputados, LXIII Legislatura.

National Institute of Women, Mexico (Instituto Nacional de las Mujeres, INMUJERES). (2009). "Answers to the Questionnaire Sent to Governments by the United Nations Division for the Advancement of Women, on the Application of the Beijing Platform of Action (1995) and Results Obtained by the Twenty-Third Extraordinary Period of Sessions of the General Assembly (2000)." http://www.cepal.org/mujer/noticias/paginas/8/36338/Mexico.pdf.

Organization of American States. Inter-American Commission on Human Rights. (2007). "Informe No. 21–07" (Caso Paulina, México). https://www.cidh.oas.org/annualrep/2007sp/mexico161.02sp.htm.

Pérez Hernández, C. (2017). "Antecedentes del Aborto en México." In *Aborto: La Política de un Estado Claudicante*, edited by Pérez Hernández, *et al*. Mexico City: Consejo Editorial de la Cámara de Diputados, LXIII Legislatura.

Sieder, R., Gianella, C., Gloppen, S., Gargarella, R., Bergallo, P., Gonzales, A.C., Peñas, A., de Assis Machado, M. R. R., and Ely Yamin, A. (2014–2017). "Abortion Rights Lawfare in Latin America." Research Project at CMI Chr. Michelsen Institute, Norway. Norwegian Research Council. https://www.cmi.no/projects/1841-abortion-rights-lawfare-in-latin-america. Accessed August 26, 2020.

World Health Organization, Media Centre. (2017). "Preventing Unsafe Abortion." Fact Sheet. http://www.who.int/mediacentre/factsheets/fs388/en/

3 Norm Contestation, Advocacy, and Abortion as the "Odd" Human Rights Case

What is then "*norm contestation*" and why does it serve as an analytical tool for the abortion debate?. . . Wiener defines *contestation* in International Relations as a "*social practice [that] entails objection to specific issues that matter to people*".[1] It "*involves the range of social practices which discursively express disapproval of norms*".[2] Norms are understood to be both "structuring" and "socially constructed", a view that allows for examination of the role of norms beyond state behaviour.[3]

'Norm' relates to that which is *'normal'*, conventional: that which is or ought to be '*the normality*' or normalized behaviour. In relation to groups and their practices, norms *"describe collective expectations for the proper behaviour of actors with a given identity"*.[4] In this sense, in any given society, a 'norm' can be any practice which is either understood to organically stem from 'natural' human behaviours or those behaviours which are conventional and should be accepted. There is a dimension of 'social-constructed-ness' of norms too, in order to distinguish socially acceptable behaviour from that which simply 'exists in nature'. Written law often balances between a certain *'naturalness'* and a *'constructed-ness'*: the artificial yet desirable social contract, a certain rationality that would not be found in 'the undisturbed natural world'.

The legalistic definition of 'norms' relates to written law. 'Norm' is sometimes understood as synonymous with 'law'; it should be especially remarked that this is the case in the Spanish language, more strongly than the English language. In the linguistic context of Mexico, the word 'norm' carries a stronger association to 'written law'.[5] Norms are however not quite the same as written laws: the latter are taken to be a representation of that which ought to be considered 'normal behaviour' (meaning 'acceptable') but also 'normal courses of action' to take when a transgression has occurred. We cannot understand norms outside their particular social context – nor as foreign to the agent interacting with them through *practice*.

Practice is *observable behaviour*, and it tends to show the enacting or implementation of a norm, or the lack thereof when a transgression is committed (when acting outside what is 'normal'). Written laws are typically generated by established practice but aim at *regulating* practice, too. Practice can also stem from certain regulating norms: those understood as 'constitutive norms'.[6] Norms stem from practice but can also make practices possible. Thus they can be both structuring and

DOI:10.4324/9781032642338-3

constitutive; socially constructed and socially construct*ing*; the result of practice and a source of it. Practice becomes norm, and vice versa.

Norm contestation is the practice of challenging the *statu quo* or specific changes (suggested or enacted) to it. In democratic states with a presence of civil society, citizens can question and critically engage with the rules and norms governing them, an ongoing process. Advocates on all sorts of social issues get increasingly involved in the process of creating norms, or questioning the legitimacy of the normative *statu quo*. Our ideas on the meaning of concepts such as *justice*, *rights*, *obligations* or *morality* evolve over time. The possibility to contest norms is a basic constitutive and regulatory element of legitimate governance. It is a process with the power to define and re-create meanings – rules can properly work only when it is possible to contest them. Contestation "*both indicates and generates legitimacy*"[7] of norms, linking them to a community that changes over time, its norms moving along with it: diverse actors *"dispute the validity, meaning or application of norms"*.[8]

To contest or challenge a norm can mean diverse types of actions, be they in a more discursive sense of challenging an idea or practice through speech or writing, or through a behaviour that aims to transmit a message of disagreement with the legitimacy of a norm (civil disobedience or failure to comply). Wiener delves into categorical distinctions of contestation: discursive and behavioural, proactive and reactive, which are fitting for the analysis of the issue here presented. Laws and norms are not fixed in time but rather, as expressed by Finnemore and Sikkink, they display transformations and often a "life cycle",[9] the legitimacy of any law or norm is upheld by a constant process of challenge, and contestation is a part of ongoing conversations about norms, practices, and the ways in which they influence each other. This touches upon the distinction between *legality* and *legitimacy*, which of course bears great importance. A law can be without widely accepted legitimacy in a particular society, or conversely, a widely accepted (legitimized) social practice may be deemed illegal.

While advocates or stakeholders on social issues often want to seek for 'immutable' principles, norms are in fact fluid and subject to change – their legitimacy contested as part of the process of global governance. Abortion, and *what* its legal status ought to be, has been a contentious and contested topic by excellence, across many societies, Mexico being only one example within numerous others, in Latin America[10] and across the globe.

Abortion as a practice is still not accepted as legitimate *nor* legal in many societies and is taken to need normative regulation (from laws banning it outright, or regulating it as a medical procedure, setting limits to its legality, etc.). Yet since 'norms lie in the practice', it can still be a common occurrence even if illegal. If we are to see a connection between 'norms' as *'someone's idea of what should be acceptable'*, and the realities of what people actually do, a much more reflexive question is then, *"Whose practices count?"*[11]... Whose voices tend to be heard, or who has access to contestation as a practice in itself? And who does not, for reasons of historical social marginalization?

Contestation can be also conceived as a meta-organizing principle of governance: the fact that norms can be subject to challenge, questioning, evolution, change (or outright rejection) signifies that those norms are 'alive' and to be taken with some measure of seriousness. Changes in norms indicate that contestation took place. One could argue that norms truly exist only when they can be challenged and that allowing for these challenges themselves (as well as constructing adequate spaces for them) is vital to democratic societies – in itself a principle to be taken in high regard.[12]

Contestation as a form of 'meaning-making'[13] thus enriches the analysis of advocacy in the abortion debate, helping to understand the ways in which groups or communities understand and contest the idea of abortion being 'a right' for women or 'a health-related right'. The way in which activists on women's rights have constructed access to abortion as a 'right to choose' stands in stark contrast to how the self-proclaimed 'pro-life' advocates portray abortion as 'murder'. Who does each group perceive, in each case, as a *'victim'* or a *'transgressor'*?. . . The subjective nature of these meanings regarding abortion and rights makes for a fascinating study on norms and legitimacy.

Discursive and Behavioural Contestation

The difference between a *"discursive"* and a *"behavioural"* contestation[14] can be clearer in some issue areas than in others. "Contestation" comes through diverse modes of practice. In the case of abortion (and related laws), as a strongly controversial issue placed at the forefront of many advocacy efforts, we find activists who engage in (and encourage others into) a variety of actions including public protests, social media engagement, sharing written statements, organizing conferences and events, as well as drafting law reform proposals either as independent citizens or as established political actors. A first distinction between "discursive" versus "behavioural" contestation is useful in beginning to 'sort out' these many avenues of action and practice. Again it should be clarified that the distinction is not always clear-cut, and many practices clearly involve both things: a certain behaviour accompanied with a message or statement.

Discursive refers to the expression, in verbal or written form, of a certain viewpoint. It can be of a constitutive nature: proposing newer meanings of previous concepts or suggesting the creation of a new law or regulation. New practice can stem from discourse: for example, how the historically recent 'human rights' discourse gives way to new practices of peer-reviewing states' behaviour.

Behavioural contestation can take various forms, a clear example being the deliberate failure to implement or comply with a law or rule, because of a perception of illegitimacy or unfairness. The mere 'breaking of a rule' does not imply contestation *per se*, and of course, committing a crime is most often *not* done with purposes of protest, nor sending a political 'message' or statement, nor is it done with aims of social change. It can be viewed as contestation if done with, for lack of a better term, 'a reasoned purpose and message': because a law is seen as unfair or lacking legitimacy. In fairness, it isn't always easy to distinguish cases when an individual or institution is failing to implement a rule, or actively breaking a law, because of some 'reasoned purpose'. Such an intent must be expressed at some point – discursively.

Lines separating "discursive" and "behavioural" contestation are decidedly blurry. In some issue areas, it might be difficult to distinguish one from the other. Although discursive contestation can sometimes be 'only discursive', behavioural contestation, on the other hand, is most often *accompanied by* some sort of discourse, especially considering the previous idea that a reasoned *purpose* should be distinguishable when an agent deliberately fails to implement a law or engages in civil disobedience. Furthermore, the act of uttering a discourse can be construed as 'a behaviour' in itself.

I use the distinction between the two as one analytical tool of the "norm contestation" framework, even if distinction isn't always clear. For many advocates and activists, their entire 'practice' (or 'behaviour', if we will) is centred on uttering and repeating a certain discourse. I refer to 'discursive' contestation when I detect that an advocate or institution's abortion-related activity is focused rather on contesting, suggesting or interpreting meanings and principles. I use 'behavioural' contestation, on the other hand, when they engage in proposals of action focused on the written laws (e.g. the attempts to change the text of the local constitution or to design a new women's rights law), or when there is a clearer disobedience of a law on ideological grounds – failing to implement in order to make a statement, disobeying for the purpose of sending a message. Whereas 'discursive contestation' is thus focused more strongly on meanings and principles, 'behavioural contestation' has a focus on written law: be it creating law, changing it, rejecting it, or outright disobeying it.

Proactive and Reactive Contestation

Proactive contestation is that which comes from a more 'original' or 'self-standing' point, whereas *reactive* contestation happens as a response towards something else,[15] such as opposition to a particular event, law, or practice. Advocates' messages and actions are analyzed first on the dimension introduced in the former subsection; whether they could be considered more "discursive" or "behavioural". As a second step, they are then analyzed on whether they could be called "proactive" or "reactive". Examples of more "proactive" ways of advocacy would be when the person or institution either suggests a new meaning or interpretation of a concept (when it is "discursive" contestation), or attempts to reform or create a written law (when we talk about "behavioural" contestation). A "reactive" kind of advocacy could then be, in the former "discursive" categorization, contesting or protesting against someone else's interpretation of meanings or concepts, and in the "behavioural" case, when disobeying or failing to implement a certain law, because of a perception that it is illegitimate.

Here, too, the distinguishing lines become admittedly blurred. It is almost impossible to find instances of contestation, even those coming across as strongly proactive, which can be considered one hundred per cent original. Contestation almost always comes as response towards something else, speaking towards a *statu quo* which 'ought to change'. It can be seen as a long chain of historical debate, argument, and counterargument, rekindled when new information comes along, about what 'justice' ought to be. Claims of originality are hard to make: messages and actions related to the abortion debate usually come as a response to something else, just as they do in any other issue area.

Abortion goes far back in history – its criminalization in many contexts likely came as a result of new worldviews (religious or philosophical, for instance) deeming it worthy of punishment. Newer interpretations of women's rights or human rights have then reacted to the criminal and social penalization of abortion, proposing that it should be accepted or, at the very least, decriminalized as a practice. For the past few decades activists, lawmakers and other stakeholders have been in a constant cycle of 'reacting' to one another's ideas, actions, interpretations and law reform proposals.

Though this viewpoint would make it seem like every message and action on abortion is a "reactive" mode of contestation (and has been for a long time), it is still analytically useful to make a distinction and to attempt to trace a line, blurry as it may be, between when an advocate seems to be more or less suggesting a 'newer' conceptual interpretation rather than reacting to someone else's, or when activists are trying to create a new law (or to reform an existing one) versus 'merely' protesting an existing law by criticizing, disobeying, or purposefully failing to implement it.

Types of Norms and the "Legitimacy Gap"

The realm of international norms presents inherent cultural diversity, as well as different understandings of *norms* and what is desirable in a society: contestation and challenge to norms and principles are to be expected in a global arena. Wiener presents a typology of norms where we encounter three different Types,[16] especially useful in international law. Type 1 norms concern the most universally accepted global principles. Concepts and ideas such as *'democracy'*, *'rule of law'*, or *'sovereignty'* are examples of Type 1 norms, often situated at such an abstract level of the international legal order that they almost fall into the category of broad ideals, subject to widely varying interpretations at the local arena. Type 2 norms are located "one level below", in the form of *organizing principles*, and it is here that the "legitimacy gap" is found. Type 3 norms, located at the micro level of normative organization, generally concern standards, procedures, and regulations of a very narrow moral reach, often with the highest level of implementation-related (i.e. *reactive* as well as *behavioural*) contestation. Throughout the book, the three types of norms are referred to, in short, as T1, T2, and T3.

Type 2 norms are the connective tissue between Types 1 and 3, in more than one sense. To understand this, it is useful to clarify what "organizing principles" are. They are core assumptions, central reference points, from which other ideas can be classified – or 'organized'. Examples of organizing principles are concepts such as "common but differentiated responsibilities" (used in environmental protection issues)[17]; "responsibility to protect"[18]; or "equal sovereignty".[19] These are not 'end goals' in themselves, or self-standing principles of justice; but rather parameters around which to 'fit' or 'arrange' a course of action when an individual or state's behaviour is controversial, challenged or disagreed with.

These principles provide room for analysis as well as case-by-case contextualization. They are an 'intermediary type of norm', the bridge connecting larger moral claims and principles to the actual, on-the-ground practical enactment of norms. They are developed through the practice of policymaking, as a result of interaction and a norm-generative practice.[20] It is also here that we find the *legitimacy gap*: a 'space' existing between abstract ideals and the reality of practice; or said differently, between Type 1 (T1) and Type 3 (T3) norms. They constitute the *'how'* to implement norms, connecting the *'why'* (larger principles) to those complex realities on the ground.

In contrast to the more 'idealistic' moral character of Type 1 norms, Type 3 can be described as concerning 'standards', 'procedural regulation' or 'efficiency'. While T1 norms are moral claims often developed through centuries of political philosophy, T3 would be the aforementioned 'practical enactments', at the 'micro' level of normative organization. It stands to reason that a higher level of behavioural contestation would be found at this third level of normativity. By the time that a certain practice is to be regulated through detailed, T3 procedural laws, the bedrock of T1 norms on which it rests is formed by already well-established principles, often dating back centuries of philosophical and political history: concepts such as human rights (even in its narrower subsets like women's rights), individual liberties, the rule of law, etc.

Again, it should be remembered that this doesn't signify clear-cut lines. None exist which make a sharp distinction between discursive or behavioural, proactive or reactive contestation, nor between normative 'Types' themselves: they often blend together in what looks more like a scale or spectrum. Table 3.1 visually lays out the Types of norms.

I consider one variation from this table (taking also Wiener's later work into account; where the *discursive*, *behavioural*, *proactive* and *reactive* modes of contestation are more deeply developed). The 'degree of contestation' for the different Types of norms would not merely be considered 'high' or 'low', but instead this would depend on the 'mode' of contestation most often found for each given Type. So, for example, T1 norms are less 'behaviourally contested', and more

Table 3.1 Three Norm Types and the Legitimacy Gap in International Relations (Wiener, 2014)

Type	*Norms*	*Moral reach*	*Degree of contestation*
Type 1	Fundamental Norms	Broad	Low
Type 2	Organizing Principles	*Legitimacy Gap*	
Type 3	Standardized Procedures	Narrow	High

'discursively contested', while the opposite would tend to be true for T3 norms: higher degree of 'behavioural contestation', lower degree of 'discursive contestation'. (Later chapters will develop such an expansion to this table and related ideas).

It is still the case that T1 norms are broadly accepted, fundamental principles that tend to be less contested in general – for similar reasons as to why almost every country in the world at least claims to embrace concepts like 'democracy' or 'human rights'. But this does not mean that T1 norms are simply 'less contested' writ large; it rather means that the contestation of such principles often relates to discursive ways of proactively suggesting newer interpretations of their meanings: the *'how to'* implement the broad principle, or the *'what it means to us as a culture/group/people/organization'*.

These possibilities for interpretative contestation, focusing on the meanings and the *'hows'*, is the very element where *organizing principles* help to make sense of differing interpretations and to connect 'the principle' to 'the practice'. For instance, even some countries with totalitarian governments still claim to embrace the T1 principle of 'democracy' by supposedly representing a 'will of the people', but their embraced T2 organizing principles would not be connected in the same sense to concepts of, for example, multiparty systems or checks-and-balances on authority. And their T3 standardized procedures would not include the regulation of free and fair elections, nor the procedures to organize (constitute) a system of voters and vote counts. It stands to reason that a detailed analysis of *modes* of contestation (rather than *'degrees'*), helps make sense of *'how'* each of type of norm tends to be contested.

The core interest of this analytical framework lies in the *legitimacy gap* and the *organizing principles*, both situated at the 'middle' level (i.e. Type 2). At the domestic and policymaking level, in the case of abortion-related norms, what matters is the link between principle and applied normative change. There often is agreement about the need to uphold a public good (e.g. '*individual health*', *'right to life'* or *'right to individual choice'*), while acknowledging the existence of room for varying interpretations, as well as the ultimate need to compromise on viable solutions and principles accepted by the involved parties.

Accepted organizing principles can act as the link between those abstract principles and the regulations at the micro level: for instance, the legal details that clarify if abortion is to be permitted or punished, in which cases, and how, or the standards of adequate medical care for pregnant women or for women who have had an abortion. It is at this *'meso'*-level, between T1 ('larger principle') and T3 ('regulation'), that the real, on-the-ground policies and agreements attempt to find plausible, commonly accepted solutions and compromise, in order to bridge the *legitimacy gap*. On this issue, we might speak of another *"legitimacy gap"* that exists not only at the "Type 2" or "meso-" level of norms[21] but indeed also between both sets of ontologies: pro- and against legal abortion, each with a discourse forwarded by advocates.

Contestation as a process of norm-making, re-making, and *meaning-making* requires constant engagement: it is where we find clashing, balancing, bargaining with meanings, in attempts to bridge the legitimacy gap. The process involves translating and interpreting between groups with often opposed worldviews, walking around the legitimacy gap and attempting to bridge it with the best (or second-best) possible solutions. The harder questions lay here as well: What should the boundaries be, of a 'right to life' or a 'right to choose'? What role should the state play in balancing a woman's right to personal and private decisions over her own life, and the rights of her children or those of an unborn child? Should states adopt a non-intervention ('non-criminalization') policy with regard to abortion, or play an active role in either prohibiting or providing it? Should they create *constitutive* or *regulatory* norms? That is, creating conditions for a practice to exist, or constraining an established practice?

I ground this norm contestation framework within a social sphere of advocacy: analyzing the *process* of advocacy and the *results* at the local level, as well as the legal sphere of norms, the nature of such norms, the norm-making processes, and how conflicts about a norm are played out in a specific national or international context. This generation of normative meaning, and its relationship to the advocates 'on the ground', provides richer and dual insights: 'bottom-up' as well as 'top-down'. All in all, this analytical endeavour enriches our understanding of 'how norms work', through an empirical case where it has been especially difficult to attain productive dialogue, common ground, and workable organizing principles.

Any attempt at classification in a social science study invites challenges as to its potentially problematic nature. Lines separating or dividing concepts into discrete 'types' should not be taken to be clear-cut categorization but, instead, an analytical tool to invite further analysis or as a 'new way to look at an old problem'. This is applicable throughout the entirety of this book: 'clear lines' separating the Types of norms themselves are not to be assumed; rather to see the typology as a spectrum, a fluid *'continuum of law'* along which specific norms or written laws can be situated. Types are not 'neat boxes' for which we need to 'decide what goes where'; rather they are best seen as broadly placed markers along this continuum, useful tools to support a thinking process about the nature of certain principles and written agreements; similarly to the thinking tool on 'proactive/reactive' or 'discursive/behavioural' contestation. It serves us well to realize that every normative issue, or every type of potential conflict, is one where we find all three types of principles, standards, and ideas.

Type 2 can be seen as connective tissue, as well as an analytical space allowing for the contestation of one practice, one right, one principle, etc.; or also for the collision of different rights and norms. I propose a view into ways in which both sides of this debate may find commonalities and pathways to dialogue at this 'meso' scale. It is at this normative 'middle ground' that opposed expectations or clashing principles may, though need not always, meet in at least some agreements. A study of the contestation in this particular topic has shown that some advocates aim to place the issue of the legality of abortion as a matter of *health* rather than *human rights*, and turning this idea into a *global organizing principle*.

Dimensions in a Continuum of Law

Analysis of the "norm typology" shows several dimensions along which norms, principles, and written laws may be analyzed. For this analysis, two such dimensions are relevant: "Complexity" and "Moral Reach". I build on the concepts laid out by Wiener's[22] norm-typological analysis and map out these dimensions as intersecting along a Cartesian plane:

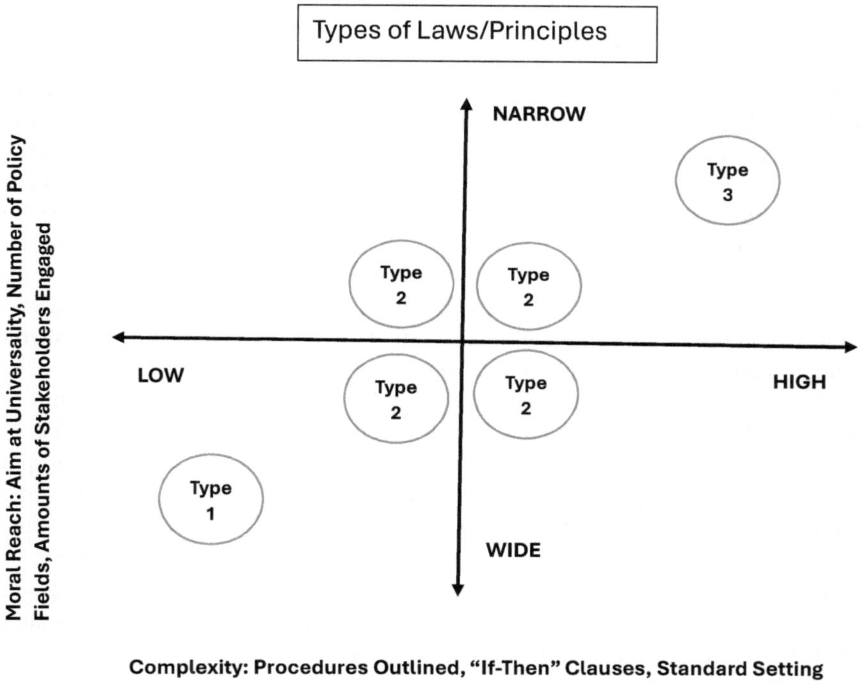

Figure 3.1 Dimensions of norms, along a 'continuum of law'.

Source: Author's creation, expanding on Wiener (2014).

Such a schematization is useful for separately thinking of these two dimensions, reflecting on *what* it means to call a certain norm "Type 1" or any other, and *why*. An intersection of both dimensions then follows, telling more about norms and laws themselves: what a particular norm or law *means*, *to whom,* and gathering clues about the intended scope, reach, or objective that it is created with.

Dimension of Complexity

This first dimension is especially applicable as related to *written* norms and laws. A 'more complex' norm or law would be one entailing procedures which a certain stakeholder is expected to follow – one that accounts for more contextual variations by providing conditional 'if' clauses ('if this precondition happens, a specific outcome should follow, as opposed to that in case of a different precondition') as well as one setting standards for desired outcomes in a behaviour, institution, industry, etc. A 'less complex' law involves less such specificities but often calls for the creation of, or refers to other, written laws or documents – whereas a 'complex' law tends to encompass enough self-containing detail in its text.

Dimension of Moral Reach

The second important dimension concerns 'moral reach'. This dimension particularly should be reflected upon as applicable to IR as a discipline. Within the legal systems of modern nation-states, certain principles are understood to be much more all-encompassing, or differently said, they are taken to be the bedrock on which many more principles rest, with some secondary principles only existing insofar as they are coherent with the larger bedrock principle. These fundamental principles can then be said to have a 'wider' moral reach: they have an aim at *universality*, where any law that would fall outside of it, or exist in clear contradiction to it, would be rejected as illegitimate. National sovereignty, democracy, inherent human dignity, or inalienable human rights are principles so fundamental – even taken for granted when drafting or creating other secondary norms – that they are presumed to be universal, and their reach encompasses numerous legal fields.

It refers as well to the number of policy areas that the law or norm touches upon, and the number of stakeholders that it concerns. An example of a legal document with the widest possible moral reach is the Universal Declaration on Human Rights (the aim at universality made clear on its very name), where each of the articles can well concern an entirely different field of law (criminal law, electoral law, gender equality, education, etc.). It is also a document on which virtually any politician or civil society advocate can claim a moral basis, for an incredibly wide spectrum of policy areas, concerning just about any stakeholder in a state's political life. On the opposite end, a technical norm concerning regulations for the food industry, or a local law dealing with insurance companies, has a narrow moral reach, concerning only a specific legal subfield as well as few stakeholders.

. . . And an Intersection Relating to Norm Typology

For analytical exercises using this chart (Figure 3.1), one can select certain norms, principles, international documents, or articles within a legal text. Because of how easy it is to situate within the chart, we can think once more of the Universal Declaration of Human Rights (UDHR): the basis of our modern understanding of internationally recognized human rights. We can situate it well into the bottom left corner of the chart: the leftmost side for very low complexity, and on the lower part for wide moral reach – perhaps no other legal text could be situated further down or further left than the UDHR. It is a quite abstract, general document providing the most ample room for national-, cultural-, and context-relevant interpretation.

To relate the chart back to the norm typology previously explained, it is relatively straightforward to situate normative "Type 1" as corresponding to the left and lower quadrant of the chart in general terms – more as if by 'rule of thumb' rather than as a marker of sharp distinguishing lines between any 'categories'. This matches an understanding of T1 norms as less complex and having a wider moral reach. Type 3, in contrast, can be situated at the right and upper quadrant, where we find norms and laws of higher complexity but narrower moral reach. They also tend to have a narrower scope in other dimensions than the ones here analyzed: relating perhaps to geographical spaces or periods of time.

Type 2 norms, situated 'in the middle' in more than one sense (and more than just the visual dimensions here seen), as well as bearing the controversies and clashes of the *legitimacy gap*, are thus placed towards the centre of the chart. This central area thus represents also the conceptual point where we find "organizing principles", as tools for situating other norms and principles. As indicated, this exercise represents the situating of labels within what is a spectrum of principles and laws. There is no sharp point (nor at the X and Y axes of the chart) marking a clear, discrete distinction between categories. If anything, the fact that T2 is situated at the centre of the chart is a reminder that this is where all of the lines strongly *blur* – rather than 'meet' or 'cross' neatly with one another, as would be the conventional understanding of a Cartesian plane with a 'zero' at its centre.

The most important point about this Cartesian graph and its usefulness is to understand that the information it provides is *relational* in nature – comparative, for lack of a better term, when accounting for the framework of thought about laws and norms placed along a spectrum or continuum. It is useful when seen in terms of: 'This norm is highly complex/morally encompassing, *compared to what?*'. . . hence the frequent use in previous subsections of terms such as 'more' or 'less', in reference to the dimensions. I take laws and norms and place them on a continuum. Simply calling a law 'complex' doesn't tell much; it rather becomes more useful to think of, for example, the UDHR as being *'less'* complex than Mexico's Federal Criminal Code, or as having a *'wider'* moral reach than the Convention on the Rights of Persons with Disabilities. These thought exercises provide us with a more useful frame of reference with which to analyze norms and laws.

What can be made of the 'emptier' sections in the upper left and lower right quadrants of the chart, further off-centre? Their parts that are still closer to the centre exist within the realm of T2 norms, closer to a 'centrist' position in terms of moral reach and complexity. But their farther-off sections are unlabelled because laws existing in those areas seem rare to find: it is uncommon to find laws of a very low complexity yet a very narrow moral reach at the same time or, in turn, laws of a high complexity yet at the same time a wide moral reach (if anything, much less common than found in modern legal realms). For any laws or norms existing in those areas, it could be said that by virtue of having a very narrow moral reach regardless of the low complexity (in the former case), or a very high complexity regardless of the wide moral reach (in the latter), it is more useful to see them as T3 norms for this chart's intents and purposes. Only by analyzing very concrete cases of such laws could we place them within the spectrum – even if roughly, their contextual details providing more answers.

Transnational and Global Advocacy

I lean on Keck and Sikkink's research on *transnational advocacy* networks, and their relevant definitions, in their view towards international and global norms.[23] A *transnational* advocacy network includes those actors working on an issue across state boundaries, who are bound together by shared values, a common discourse, and dense exchanges of information and services. Given the focus on *contestation* as a practice and an activity that takes various forms, even the 'mere' uttering of a statement by an advocate is here understood as a manner of contestation. In the context of norm contestation for social change, the advocate's role is multifaceted and multidimensional.[24] By engaging in this process, they are not only a contester but also a generator of meaning, an interpreter of norms through a specific framework or 'lens', often also a 'translator' or "*vernacularizer*"[25] of messages for a particular group.

Throughout the book I refer to 'the international dimension' of the issue of abortion (international laws that relate to it), though there is a distinction to make between *'transnational'* and *'global'* advocacy, instead of just calling both 'international'. While 'internationalization' is understood to be the interaction and exchange between states, *"transnationalization"* is a term that transcends the conceptual boundaries of the state and is more often used (as by Keck and Sikkink)[26] in strands of thought that move beyond the paradigm of the nation-state as the only stakeholder in international matters (or the most relevant). *International* organizations are increasingly becoming spaces open to participation of civil society groups, NGOs, private businesses, or prominent individuals: more *'global'* in that regard and not focusing solely on state governments. Analyzing *advocacy* in its modern forms, it is thus more useful to focus on the definitions of 'transnational' as well as 'global'.

The next useful distinction is between *"global"*[27] and *"transnational"*[28] advocacy. *Global* happens at the more abstract realms of international institutions, for instance, International Organizations, where principles and policies are usually enshrined in '*soft law*' that states can choose to adopt as it is, adapt to their own environment, or sometimes 'water down' to the point where its relevance is reduced. Mizrahi and Zúñiga explain 'soft law' as *"legal phenomena that are characterized by their non-binding nature, which however are not without legal effects, or other judicially relevant effects"*.[29] In a geopolitical environment where civil society has gained stronger presence and can pressure their own national governments for specific reforms, soft law is often a powerful tool, setting standards and parameters that governments are encouraged to comply with. *Global* advocacy can theoretically exist without necessarily referring to nation-states, focusing purely on issue areas; however, this is still rare, as the state-centric paradigm remains strong. *Transnational* advocacy, on the other hand, focuses on exchanges of information between local advocates and their allies situated in other countries, or in international organizations and networks.

Most interviewed advocates were shown to operate within a strong framework of the nation-state, despite their awareness of the international system and their interactions with it. They are, for this reason, more accurately portrayed as 'transnational' rather than 'global' advocates. Most of their advocacy efforts, however, have goals and objectives aiming towards changes in their national (or even only subnational) laws and contexts in Mexico. While *global* advocacy groups and networks do exist, in this sense they are still rare. *Transnational* advocacy networks and *transnational* advocates, on the other hand, are now much more common, in that they may indeed have frequent and active exchanges with International Organizations and with global networks, although the core of their advocacy is still aimed mostly at policies in their communities, subnational areas, nation-states, or regions.

Activists tend to operate in networks, *"distinguished largely by the centrality of principled ideas or values in motivating their formation"*.[30] Since many networks of advocates for social changes are now transnational, they blur the boundaries between a state's relations to its own nationals and the links that both the citizens and the states have to the international system – transforming the practice of national sovereignty. They are also sometimes referred as *"political or policy entrepreneurs"*,[31] mobilizing resources like information and membership. Actors in transnational advocacy networks are not only individuals, but they may also include international and domestic NGOs, research organizations, local social movements, media, churches, intellectuals, intergovernmental organizations, and parts of the executive or parliamentary branches of governments.[32]

With new platforms such as social media, civil society today has a stronger position in reaching out to the general public, making moral and emotional appeals, and contesting and negotiating meanings in order to aim for policies to change (or to remain unchanged): identifying victims, framing rights and obligations, pointing at duty bearers – who can become violators should they fail to comply, garnering the communication power of celebrities or important religious figures, contacting allies abroad, supporting aggrieved activists, voicing the testimonies of beneficiaries, and holding governments accountable in what Lister and Lee call the "*court of public opinion*".[33]

These portrayals are often shaped by the interactions between local advocates, transnational advocacy networks, and advocates in international and global institutions. Local advocates can be influenced by global advocacy groups and vice versa. Studying an interaction between established norms, and the advocates who seek to change them, as well as the ways advocates and norms influence each other, enriches this view with a grassroots, bottom-up approach rather than focusing solely on norms at the abstract or *'meta'* scale of the international arena. Advocacy can have a crucial influence in 'bringing issues to the table', garnering widespread attention and support.

Advocates interact with norms by engaging with and contesting meanings-in-use of concepts such as 'right to choose', 'right to life', etc., as well as the meanings of relevant written law. These concepts and laws carry different moral meanings for opposed groups of advocates, and depending on *how* a normative meaning is defined, the proposed norms and legal reforms change – often clashing with one another. In Mexico, advocates who contest human rights concepts and norms in the case of abortion, through well-constructed discourses, have had a clear impact on policy change. They create, recreate, and challenge meanings, with clear policy goals.

Their discourses also focus on a certain *framing* of messages: a particular angle through which to present information, including choices of specific wordings as well as accompanying images, testimonies from chosen points of view, or certain emotional tones used to better fit a particular narrative. It is a particular construction of interests and identities, instrumentalized for the advancement of an idea – often appealing to emotion. Construction of meanings is instrumentalized for an end purpose. Opposing sides of a debate present their information in a carefully crafted manner, and they can – and often do[34] – frame one same event or incident in very different ways, aiming to appeal to different types of individuals, or to different constituencies along a political spectrum. An individual or being can be framed as either a *victim* or a *threat to* something, or a transgressor of some norm; one specific event may also be interpreted as having very different meanings.

Societies ascribe meaning to behaviours, to rights, to advocacy, to health, to the identification of 'victims' in a particular case, and even to 'life' itself as a characteristic inherent to human beings. The way in which advocates construct their advocacy is also subjected to negotiated understandings of what it means to be a *rights holder*, or who is a *victim* in a particular case, or what instances should be perceived as 'violations of rights', *who* has violated those rights, *when* and *how* one can lose or forfeit a right . . . among many other concepts carrying meanings which can change and evolve over time. Even our understandings of *who* has the right to engage in advocacy in the first place (with the prerogative to speak in another's name or to portray other people), or *who* is to be portrayed in a certain advocacy message, is all subjectively constructed.

In the case of the legal abortion debate, such differences are strongly noticeable, not only in the case of Mexico but also globally at large. Opposing sides in the abortion debate refer to even the concept of abortion itself as either *'a right'* or *'a murder'*, indeed not a subtle difference nor a simple variation in nuance or degree. They also interpret quite differently *who* is a victim, or a transgressor, or a holder of *which* most relevant rights, and they give very different meanings to concepts like women's rights, progressivity in human rights (a crucial legal concept in Mexico after the human rights-related constitutional reform of 2011), the role of the State, or public health. This discourse framing was shown in detail in the interviews themselves. These were carried out in person in Mexico and analyzed in how messages have been framed to create two competing discourses. Their activism creates *meanings-in-use*, through narrative devices and the framing of a message.

Stone also writes about the formation of policy agendas through the framing of "*causal stories*": in her viewpoint, problems or difficulties themselves do not have the power to influence policy changes; it is rather *causal stories* that do.[35] She argues that in order to campaign on an issue, for the ultimate formation of a policy agenda, it must be converted into a narrative 'causal story' that establishes bearers of responsibility or guilt, or at least a potential agent of change.[36] As advocates on certain social issues connect with one another, in their goal to push for social changes, they engage discursively in this framing of their information, ideas. and strategies, and in what Keck and Sikkink call "symbolic politics": *"the ability to call upon symbols, actions or stories that make sense of a situation, or claim for an audience that is frequently far away"*.[37]

Framing Human Rights in Abortion Advocacy

The most relevant Declarations, Covenants, Pacts, Conventions, and other treaties (binding and nonbinding) of both the United Nations System and the Inter-American Human Rights System will be broadly referred to as 'International Human Rights Law' and are another cornerstone of this book. I engage with 'human rights' as a concept, specifically within the context of two notable and inter-related observations. The first is the historical path of human rights as a constantly broadening concept. The earliest conceptions of 'the rights of man' or 'citizen rights' were indeed confined not only to men but also to very specific types of men: owners of land or property, men of a certain national and ethnic background and of a certain age, etc. The history of 'human rights' can be taken to both begin and culminate in the fundamental notion (now taken as the political-philosophical departing point) that *human rights are inalienable to every human being by virtue of their humanity*.

But the history of how humankind arrived at that point (and how we continue advancing into newer, modernized understandings of rights) has been a history of expansion and inclusion.[38] This 'expansion and inclusion' has happened along more than one dimension: on the one hand, it extends into ever more groups of people each of them made distinct because of specific aspects of vulnerability or by particular histories of oppression (women, children, the disabled, indigenous peoples, people of African descent, etc.), and many of such groups are now represented in international rights law by a specific Declaration, Convention, or similar document. On the other hand, the expansion has also translated into the recognition of more and more varied kinds of rights: the so-called third generation human rights include such seemingly modern concepts as the right to a healthy environment,[39] to self-determination within group and collective rights, or to participation in cultural heritage.[40]

Yet this conceptual expansion (which in a strict sense is taken to signify social and humanitarian progress) also comes with the risk of a complete loss of meaning, clarity, or 'legal teeth' for the very concept of *'human rights'*. If every desirable feature of human life is everyone's 'human right', the concept becomes nebulous at best and meaningless in any court of law, at worst, it may as well backfire into becoming a tool for the defence of anti-social and undesirable behaviours or practices.

Clapham illustrates the point that "*almost everyone now emphasizes their point of view in terms of an assertion or denial of rights. Indeed, for some in the West, it seems we have already entered an era when rights talk is becoming banal*".[41] He recalls Kundera's words in what can be interpreted as both a critique of contemporary human rights thought, yet also an admission of how far we have come in terms of humanitarian justice: "*. . . But because people in the West are not threatened by concentration camps and are free to write and say what they want, the more the fight for human rights gains in popularity and the more it loses in concrete content, becoming a kind of universal stance of everyone towards everything, a kind of energy that turns all human desires into rights*".[42]

This does not render the concept meaningless: in analyzing transnational advocacy networks, Keck and Sikkink refer to *"certain discourses like that of human rights, (which) provide a language for negotiation. They permit also different negotiations to take place within the networks"*.[43] Human rights ideas provide the vocabulary to argue about whose interests should prevail and why and how to achieve certain ends in the context of conflict; however, they do not really "*resolve the tension between competing interests and visions of how the world should be*"[44] – less so when the concept becomes endlessly expansive.

When Rights Clash: Collisions and Irreconcilability

The second observation, connected to the previous one, is that as the realm of 'human rights' expands to include a constantly increasing amount of identitarian groups and of rights themselves (potentially losing the concept's significance in law), we are more and more likely to encounter cases of 'collisions' or 'clashes' of rights, groups, and interpretations. Clapham again illustrates a common example of such collisions: the conflict between an individual's right to privacy and other people's right to personal security – for example in the context of anti-terrorist policy.[45] Except for the internationally accepted ban on torture (and the understanding that *'to be free from torture'* is a fundamental human right), no other right is understood to be 'absolute': there is always some degree of bounded-ness, limitation, and potential conflict with the rights of another individual. The right to be free from torture is absolute in a way that not even 'the right to life' is: every modern society identifies, in its legal system, at least one instance where an individual or the state can take a human life – though these tend to be rather extreme cases like self-defence, violent attacks against the police or armed forces, etc.

If all (but one) internationally recognized human rights are bounded by some limitations, yet at the same time there are an ever-growing number of recognizable groups that bear an ever-growing number of rights, we are bound to find *more* potential conflicts between those rights. We can expect more contestation of rights-related norms: for the application of human rights law *"is almost always contested, with both parties to a dispute demanding that human rights law be applied in their favour"*.[46] Parties to such disputes often allude to some overriding principle, such as democracy, freedom, etc., without this allusion really resolving tensions between the different rights of different people.

Advocates indeed do as much in their abortion-related advocacy: interpret and frame internationally accepted human rights in the furthering of their pro- or anti-legal abortion discourses. The 'saturation'[47] of the human rights discourse very much appears in this case, with opposed sides of the debate building their narratives on (what they at least perceive to be) legally accepted human rights norms and principles. Abortion presents, within contemporary human rights debates, one of the most fundamental cases of 'collisions of rights' – and a very odd one as well. One that, because of its peculiarities, is nearly impossible to compare to any such thing as *'a similar case'*. It is the only case where two differentiated, recognizable holders of (at least potential) rights exist within one physical body and may at times have their rights conflicting.

Connecting this idea to the matter of *legitimacy (are these laws or norms truly compliant with human rights, to ultimately bring justice to our society?)* bridges the international legal realm to the subject of this book. *Human rights* and the norms related to them are 'kept alive' through practices of engagement with them, questioning them, and seeing them evolve in a contemporary society. It is advocates who engage in this process of norm contestation (often transnationally), framing issues and putting them on domestic and global agendas in a pursuit of justice.

Notes

1 Wiener, 2014, p. 1.
2 Wiener, 2014, p. 1.
3 Wiener, 2014, p. 27.
4 Keck and Sikkink, 1999, p. 90.
5 All the extended interviews were carried out in the Spanish language: they were set in Mexico and the subjects are Mexican activists, all of them native Spanish speakers. Spanish is also the working language of most of the documents, written laws, communications and statements analyzed in this book.
6 Bulygin, 1992, p. 201.
7 Wiener, 2014, p. 6.
8 Wolff and Zimmermann, 2016, p. 518.
9 Finnemore and Sikkink, 1998.
10 Gloppen, 2021.
11 In paraphrasing: Wiener, 2019.
12 Wiener, 2014, p. 15.
13 Wiener, 2014.
14 Similarly to how it was described by True and Wiener, 2019.
15 See also for "proactive" and "reactive" contestation as described by True and Wiener, 2019.
16 Wiener, 2014.
17 See Williams and Montes, 2016.
18 See Stahn, 2017.
19 See Sjursen, 2013.
20 Wiener, 2014, p. 36.
21 For more on the "legitimacy gap" as well as the normative typology and "levels", see Wiener, 2014.
22 See Wiener, 2014.
23 Keck and Sikkink, 1998.
24 Fayoyin, 2013.
25 See Merry and Levitt's works on "vernacularization of women's rights", 2017.
26 Keck and Sikkink, 1999.
27 Bryer and Magrath, 1999.
28 Keck and Sikkink, 1999.
29 Mizrahi Nedvedovich and Zúñiga Tapia, 2017, p. 62.

30 Keck and Sikkink, 1999, p. 89.
31 Mintrom, 1997.
32 Keck and Sikkink, 1999, pp. 91–92.
33 Lister and Lee, 2013, p. 84.
34 Corner and Hahn, 2010.
35 Stone, 1989, p. 282.
36 Stone, 1989.
37 Keck and Sikkink, 1999, p. 95.
38 See Elliott, 2008.
39 Gormley, 1990.
40 There is even contemporary discussion among environmentalists and philosophers on whether animals have 'rights', and what exactly can such 'rights' mean when referring to non-human subjects.
41 Clapham, 2007, p. 14.
42 Clapham, 2007, p. 17, quoting Kundera.
43 Keck and Sikkink, 1999, p. 100.
44 Clapham, 2007: preface.
45 Clapham, 2007.
46 Clapham, 2007, p. 1.
47 See Jiménez, 2014.

References

Bryer, D., and Magrath, J. (1999). "New Dimensions of Global Advocacy." *Nonprofit and Voluntary Sector Quarterly*, 28(1_suppl), 168–177.

Bulygin, E. (1992). "On Norms of Competence." *Law and Philosophy*, 11(3), 201–216.

Clapham, A. (2007). *Human Rights: A Very Short Introduction*. Oxford University Press.

Corner, A., and Hahn, U. (2010). "Message Framing, Normative Advocacy and Persuasive Success." *Argumentation*, 24(2), 153–163.

Elliott, M.A. (2008). *A Cult of the Individual for a Global Society: The Development and Worldwide Expansion of Human Rights Ideology*. Emory University.

Fayoyin, A. (2013). "Advocacy as a Strategy for Social Change: A Qualitative Analysis of the Perceptions of UN and Non-UN Development Workers." *Journal of Social Sciences*, 35(2), 181–193.

Finnemore, M., and Sikkink, K. (1998). "International Norm Dynamics and Political Change." *International Organization*, 52(4), 887–917. http://www.jstor.org/stable/2601361

Gloppen, S. (2021). "Conceptualizing Abortion Lawfare." *Revista Direito GV*, 17.

Gormley, W.P. (1990). "The Legal Obligation of the International Community to Guarantee a Pure and Decent Environment: The Expansion of Human Rights Norms." *Georgetown Environmental Law Review*, 3, 85.

Jiménez, M.P. (2014). "Human Rights Activism in Times of Cognitive Saturation: Talking About Tools." *Sur – International Journal on Human Rights*, 20, 419.

Keck, M.E., and Sikkink, K. (1998). *Activists Beyond Borders*. Cornell University Press.

Keck, M.E., and Sikkink, K. (1999). "Transnational Advocacy Networks in International and Regional Politics." *International Social Science Journal*, 51(159), 89–101.

Lister, G., and Lee, K. (2013). "The Process and Practice of Negotiation." In *Global Health Diplomacy: Concepts, Issues, Actors, Instruments, Fora and Cases*, 73–87. New York: Springer Science + Business Media New York.

Merry, S.E., and Levitt, P. (2017). "The Vernacularization of Women's Human Rights." *Human Rights Futures*, 213–236.

Mintrom, M. (1997). "Policy Entrepreneurs and the Diffusion of Innovation." *American Journal of Political Science*, 738–770.

Mizrahi Nedvedovich, C., and Zúñiga Tapia, F.R. (2017). "Las recomendaciones de los organismos internacionales como mecanismos de presión política." In *Aborto: La Política de un Estado Claudicante*. Todas y Todos Valemos en México, 53–67. Mexico City: Consejo Editorial de la Cámara de Diputados, LXIII Legislatura.
Sjursen, H. (2013). *The EU's Common Foreign and Security Policy: The Quest for Democracy*. Routledge.
Stahn, C. (2017). "Responsibility to Protect: Political Rhetoric or Emerging Legal Norm?" In *Globalization and Common Responsibilities of States*, 147–168. Routledge.
Stone, D. (1989). "Causal Stories and the Formation of Policy Agendas." *Political Science Quarterly*, 104, 281–300.
True, J., and Wiener, A. (2019). "Everyone Wants (a) Peace: The Dynamics of Rhetoric and Practice on 'Women, Peace and Security'." *International Affairs*, 95(3), 553–574.
Wiener, A. (2014). *A Theory of Contestation*. Springer.
Wiener, A. (2019). "Stakeholder Access to Norm Validation: Whose Practices Count in Global International Relations?" In *Contesting Global Environmental Knowledge, Norms, and Governance*, 127–143. Routledge.
Williams, M., and Montes, M.F. (2016). "Common but Differentiated Responsibilities: Which Way Forward?" *Development*, 59, 114–120.
Wolff, J., and Zimmermann, L. (2016). "Between Banyans and Battle Scenes: Liberal Norms, Contestation, and the Limits of Critique." *Review of International Studies*, 42(3), 513–534.

4 The Mexican Case

A Tale of Two Discourses

This chapter continues the analysis of the Mexican case as one of norm contestation and by referring to the norm typology outlined earlier – a detailed journey throughout the discursive pieces that showcase advocates' main concepts and ideas. This discursive evidence displays the concepts, meanings, norms and principles which are being contested and proposed by opposing sides of the abortion debate: the way in which they *contest, interpret, propose,* and *refute* a variety of ideas. I look at the different ontologies and their opposed worldviews through their eyes – and through the lens of norm contestation.

Herein lies the most empirically detailed part of my research. I map out the diverse types of contestations carried by advocates in the Mexican case, the norms being suggested, the changes being advocated for, as well as the clashing meanings-in-use given to a variety of concepts. This national dimension comprises the more substantial bulk of the primary information, continuing the path laid out in Chapter 2: through expert interviews in 2018 and 2019, attendance to two public protest events and one conference, as well as extensive documentation originating mostly from Mexican institutions and NGOs. It is here that the focus of the analysis is placed on mapping out a *normative, national dimension,* expressed and contested through the encountered discourses as presented and framed by advocates.

The ways in which Mexican activists have achieved specific goals of law reform tell a story about the types of laws that were targeted in each case, and very importantly, *why*. For instance, activists on the pro-legalization side of the debate have at times achieved their own advocacy successes in ways which are often convoluted, diving deep into the technicalities of secondary and tertiary norms. This was the case with the law recognized as NOM0046,[1] a more 'technical' kind of norm, which became instrumentalized in order to attain one step forward in the legalization of abortion in cases of rape, at the federal level. It will be explained in detail, how this and other secondary norms and laws were reformed, often through very subtle changes which in practice achieved concrete goals of changing the legal situation of abortion cases.

Moments of Relevance: The Crucial Recent Scenarios

Various moments of relevance stand out greatly in the 'storyline' of how abortion laws have progressed in Mexico, which I as well as the interviewed advocates

DOI:10.4324/9781032642338-4

identify as particularly relevant 'arenas' or 'scenarios' where the debate gained great public attention. I explore these as seen through the eyes of the advocates involved in them, as I had the chance to interview experts who directly participated in these moments of relevance. These can be seen as arenas where norms have been contested, at the constitutive as well as the implementing stage.[2]

Year 2007: Legalization in the Capital . . .

Although the interviewed advocates have been aware of the abortion debate (and also have a defined 'stance' within it) since before 2007, most of them identify that year as the pivotal point.[3] For many, this is also the point that called them into much stronger mobilization, especially those identifying as 'pro-life'.[4] In April of that year, the Legislative Assembly in Mexico City (spearheaded by representatives from the PRD, a left-leaning political party) decriminalized abortion until the 12th gestational week. It was done through a redefinition of 'abortion' itself as a concept in the Criminal Code of the capital city, going from "the interruption of a pregnancy at any moment of gestation" into "the interruption of a pregnancy after the twelfth week of gestation".[5]

The objective of the redefinition was to permit the 'switch' from a legal *"model of exceptions"* (where abortion was illegal but with some exceptions, cases which were exempt from prosecution: still the predominant model in the rest of the Mexican states) into a *"model of gestational limits"* that reformed the legal meaning of abortion itself. In this new model, abortion is penalized after that point, but not before, as it 'wouldn't be an abortion'.[6] The preexisting exceptions were however still maintained: thus abortion is also mentioned as having "Causes for Exclusion of Responsibility" (*Excluyentes de Responsabilidad*) in cases of rape, foetal unviability, or risks to the mother's life. Mexico City has thus adopted a 'mixed model' where the dominant consideration is the gestational limit in weeks. The three *'causales'* are understood to be rather exceptional cases where the crime is considered to 'not have happened'.

The reform came through an uncommon and unforeseen legal manoeuvre: *conceptual redefinition.* So, if we are to view 'abortion decriminalization' in a technically exact sense, initially abortion was not exactly *decriminalized* in Mexico City, but rather *re-defined* as "the interruption of pregnancy that takes place after the twelfth week of gestation".[7] The now-admitted practice taking place before the 13th week was re-conceptualized as "Legal Interruption of Pregnancy" *(Interrupción Legal del Embarazo* or *ILE*).[8] Many interviewed experts identifying as 'pro-life' contest this, speaking of this redefinition in terms that suggest illegitimacy, referring to it as "arbitrary"[9] or a "true legal somersault".[10]

Some 'pro-life' advocates and prominent political figures took this claim of illegitimacy to the Mexican Supreme Court, presenting a challenge in the form of a Constitutional Controversy (*Controversia Constitucional*).[11] Notoriously, the main proponents of this Constitutional Controversy were José Luis Soberanes, then director of the National Human Rights Commission (*Comisión Nacional de los Derechos Humanos, CNDH*), and the country's general prosecutor Eduardo

Medina Mora. This is telling of how controversial the reform was at the time, and still today. The Supreme Court upheld Mexico City's reform, declaring it constitutionally legitimate on the grounds that subnational states had the autonomy to decide on the changes to their own Criminal Codes and that this change did not go against the Mexican Constitution.

The 2007 reform set the precedent for subsequent changes in other regulations in Mexico City, such as the local Health Law, which was later amended into referring to legal abortion as "Legal Interruption of Pregnancy" and setting the regulations for providing the service to women in Mexico City, through both public and private health services.[12] The same reframing, in favour of the concept of "ILE", would later be included in newer regulations such as the General Law on Crime Victims (*Ley General de Víctimas*),[13] created in 2013. Even if decriminalization was initially achieved through conceptual redefinition, the Mexico City reform then became a proper abortion 'legalization' in a functional sense: it allowed for regulation and access, becoming a *constitutive reform* that created standards for practice, rather than a mere elimination of penalties.

Several contextual reasons explain the feasibility of the Mexico City reform: the capital's long history as a liberal and left-leaning hub (in many other issue areas such as, more recently, homosexual marriage and LGBTQ+ rights, Mexico City can be defined as an 'oasis' of social liberalism in an otherwise conservative country), stronger presence of left-leaning advocacy groups, and decades of small incremental changes in public perceptions favouring the legalization of abortion. Also influential was the media presence of two events and their corresponding advocacy: the first was the "*Paulina*" case, eventually taken to the Inter-American Commission on Human Rights (IACHR), concerning an underage girl who had a pregnancy resulting from rape and was denied an abortion by local authorities in Baja California.[14]

The second event was a heavily publicized corruption scandal concerning Jorge Serrano Limón, one of the most prominent 'pro-life' advocates in Mexico, and his organization, the National Pro-Life Committee *(Comité Nacional Pro-Vida)*.[15] Serrano Limón was accused of embezzlement and was imprisoned for a brief time, with the much-publicized process of his maligning having come hand in hand with the (also heavily publicized) sexual abuse scandals of the Catholic Church and some of its most prominent characters in Mexico. In this context, media criticism of the Catholic Church, Catholic leadership, and other powerful conservative or political figures was no longer a taboo in the country.

Although Serrano Limón's general public image never fully recovered, he is still a very respected figure among 'pro-life' groups in Mexico. In his public conference, that I attended during fieldwork in August 2019, he himself explains the scandal, alleging that the accusations were fabricated in order to disgrace him and the *"Comité Nacional Pro-Vida"*.[16] From the atmosphere during and after the conference (at a Catholic university in San Luis Potosí), it was clear that he remains well supported and respected by a large public who identifies as 'pro-life', but also that he is seen as a 'martyr advocate' of sorts, who was publicly attacked specifically because of his activities as a 'pro-life' figurehead.

Interviewed 'pro-life' advocates speak of him as an undoubted leader of earlier and current anti-abortion movements in Mexico.[17] Before Serrano Limón's scandal, the *Comité Nacional Pro-Vida* had been the undisputed 'umbrella' organization leading unified anti-abortion activities throughout the country. Following the scandal, 'pro-life' groups had started to break apart,[18] fragmenting into many other smaller groups. Only recently, from around 2016, has the newer group "National Front for the Family" (*Frente Nacional por la Familia*) emerged as one of the leading organizations advocating against abortion; but the Mexican 'pro-life' groups in general remain somewhat fragmented until today.[19]

... And the Backlash Everywhere Else: When Federalism Came to Life

The Mexico City reforms of 2007 prompted political and social backlash, as well as opposite legislation in other Mexican subnational states, in a way that surprised many of the advocates at the time – those in favour *and* against legalization. After 2007, almost all other Mexican states saw a backlash to the Mexico City reform, in toughening their own anti-abortion norms at the subnational level. The fact that this happened at all, but also the specific way in which it did, merits peculiar commentary about what it represented for federalism in Mexico and for 'pro-life' movements.

The first of these backlash measures began in 2009 with a few subnational states reacting in the opposite direction and the last of such reforms having come to pass in 2018. The changes in the subnational states, however, did not concern reforming the Criminal Codes, as was the case with Mexico City. Instead, reforms were made to the subnational Constitutions, generally by amending the articles concerning "the right to life" by making them include a provision along the lines of *"from the moment of conception"*.[20] To date, 18 Mexican states have so reformed their Constitutions.

Perceptions by the interviewed advocates, concerning these series of subnational reforms, reveal a curious clash in perceptions. Firstly, it should be noted that these reforms in the subnational states mostly concern just the subnational Constitutions – not the subnational Criminal Codes. In the words of one pro-legalization advocate, *"they changed the Constitutions, but they would not dare touch the Criminal Codes"*.[21] In fact, in some subnational states, the penalties for abortion have been lowered, despite it remaining illegal in the same terms – such as in Tlaxcala, where the punishment for abortion is a combination of a monetary fine, combined with a time of mandatory community service. This 'untouching' of the Criminal Codes (or at least the absence of any hardening of penalties for abortion) is explained by pro-life advocates as the idea that "we are not seeking to punish women, only to make abortion a meaningfully unavailable choice".[22]

The legal basis or 'green light' for having passed these subnational reforms was, precisely, the same ruling by the Supreme Court, at the time of the Constitutional Controversy to abortion decriminalization in Mexico City in 2007: declaring that subnational states could each have the autonomy to decide on their own about abortion-related reforms. For many long-time pro-legalization advocates, this was a rather unforeseen development: that subnational states would, for the first time in many decades and in most issue areas, 'dare' to move in the opposite direction as Mexico City, and done so precisely by using a Supreme Court ruling which was interpreted as allowing them (even urging them) to do that very thing.[23] In a way, for some pro-legalization advocates, it felt as "a backfire" of the Supreme Court ruling – an unforeseen negative consequence.[24]

On the other hand, several 'pro-life' advocates not only spoke of these reforms as clearly positive and as a sign of the freedoms granted to subnational states by the federal system. More than one referred to this event as *"federalism coming alive"*,[25] or *"the true spirit of Mexican federalism finally awakening"*.[26] For the first time, subnational states were truly divided and diverse in their rulings and regulations on one specific issue, *"an important step in strengthening true federalism"*.[27] Up until then, it was common legislative practice in Mexico that subnational states would merely copy the laws approved in the capital: abortion was truly the first case where inconformity was signalled through the approval of different and even opposing laws.[28]

It is likely that the legislators who passed the reforms in Mexico City in 2007 expected the rest of subnational states to eventually 'align' and follow suit, as usually happens with most laws in the country. Despite being a federation, Mexico had always had a 'centralist' tradition regarding legislation, where progressive legal reforms concerning all sorts of human rights and liberties (or laws generally considered 'progressive') would first be passed in Mexico City, with the rest of the subnational states eventually copying the exact same reforms for their own local laws, or with generally minor changes or smaller adaptations. Mexico City would normally be 'the trailblazer', while the rest of the states, however begrudgingly or slowly, followed. With abortion the opposite happened, which many 'pro-life' advocates see as a signifier that the 2007 legalization was illegitimate,[29] an overreach, un-representative of *"the true will of the Mexican people"*,[30] or 'wrong' in some other way, given the fact that it elicited such a sharp opposite reaction in the rest of the country.

Another part of the anti-abortion argument, for 'pro-life' advocates, is the fact that all of the subnational Civil Codes in Mexico grant unborn children the right to inherit property, subject upon the condition that they are born and eventually presented alive to the Civil Registry, which *"could not be possible if they were considered mere things"*.[31] For some legal effects, the unborn or *nasciturus* can be considered as a born person (conditional to their live birth), for others it cannot. This is another instance showing that indeed the abortion debate, in legal terms, is hugely complex, if one is to consider that the unborn child gradually gains legal personhood and there is no single 'point' at which full rights realization distinctively occurs. Legal rights and legal protection are rather progressing along a continuum existing between the point of conception and the point of birth. A foetus of, for example, 26 weeks' gestation, can be the subject of care efforts by advocacy organizations defending the well-being of premature infants. That such protection might depend 'merely' on which side of the womb the foetus happens to be on, or on the will of the mother, strikes many 'pro-life' activists as arbitrary and unfair.[32]

Other 'pro-life' legal experts refer to something unexpected, when discussing the legal basis used to pass these local Constitutional reforms protecting life from the moment of conception. They mention the fact that Mexico abolished the death penalty in 2005, by eliminating all mentions of it in the National Constitution. Today, only Article 22 mentions it, by declaring that Congress shall never be permitted to pass any laws sanctioning the death penalty under any circumstance. For some pro-life advocates, the local reforms protecting life "from the moment of conception" hinge also on this abolition: they interpret it as *de facto* meaning that abortion should be banned, too. In the words of some of them, *"they had taken abolition to mean that abortion would be prohibited by default"*,[33] or, more precisely, that life would be protected from conception by default. In their words, this interpretation stems from "reading the reformed constitutional Article 22 *in contrario sensu"*.[34]

In a similar manner, another of their arguments about how "life from the moment of conception" is supposedly protected by default, even if the National Constitution doesn't literally say it, is that Article 29 protects life in the context of naming the rights that cannot be suspended even in cases of grave perturbation of public order, nor in any other exceptional situations. Thus, according to them, *'absolute protection of life'* belongs to a 'hard core' of fundamental human rights,[35] even if not explicitly mentioned so – it can be inferred from the prohibition to sanction the death penalty in legislation, and from 'life' being considered as a right that cannot be taken away even in exceptional circumstances,[36] with the *"basic right to life as a sine qua non condition to the fulfilment of any other right"*.[37] This interpretation might not be accurate, however, seeing as there are legal situations where a life can be taken by the state or by an individual, without punishment: for example in legitimate self-defence, or if a person presents a severe and immediate threat to armed forces.

When questioned about this, pro-legalization advocates state that the Constitution (as well as the Supreme Court's rulings on the matter) can be interpreted as protecting life from the moment of conception *in principle,* but that this does not have to mean criminalizing abortion,[38] nor should it prevail over a woman's rights to her own body. The matter brings us back full circle to fundamental questions about 'the beginnings', not so much of *'life'* itself, but those of *'legal personhood'*. To other pro-legalization advocates, it is nonsensical to mix together the issues of death penalty and abortion, as they are fundamentally different in every aspect that one cares to image: dealing with different subjects, scenarios, agents, and threats to the public order – real or imagined.[39]

Concerning Article No. 4 of the Pact of San José (the Inter-American Declaration on Human Rights), which protects *"life, in general, from the moment of conception",* at the time of the Court dispute that followed abortion legalization in Mexico City in 2007, the words "*in general*" were interpreted by the Supreme Court to mean that each subnational state can legislate the moment at which such explicit protection should begin.[40] Part of the debate on these specificities about the right to life, its legal beginnings, or legal endings stems from the fact that the Mexican Constitution does not specify boundaries to the right to life, neither does it mention the death penalty indeed except for the paragraph prohibiting Congress to pass any laws that sanction it.

Polarization at the constitutional and legislative level ensued, as the Mexican Supreme Court ratified that the Legislative Assembly of Mexico City had the autonomy to redefine abortion. Therefore, in the words of a 'pro-life' advocate, all local congresses 'got the signal' that they, too, had the autonomy to elevate 'protection of life from conception' as a fundamental right, setting it at the constitutional level of their subnational states.[41] Such polarization showed *"the profound rejection with which abortion legalization was met in the rest of the country"*.[42] Many advocates referred to this dispute and to the Supreme Court ruling in a somewhat accusatory tone, as something that the Court used in order to *"polarize the country"*[43] – as if trying to say that the country was previously 'unified' in its anti-abortion stance, until the Supreme Court *'allowed for chaos'* by permitting abortion legalization to stand in Mexico City. 'Pro-life' movements, however, later took advantage of this chance to further their very own anti-abortion norms.

Another concept that would come up time and again when interviewing 'pro-life' advocates, and especially those with legal expertise, is their idea that through these reforms they are 'armouring' the local Constitutions, in the sense that they are 'protecting' their subnational state from passing legislation that permits abortions. The term that they commonly use in Spanish is "*blindaje Constitucional*", or "*blindar la Constitución*".[44] The verb '*blindar*' in this context is not easily translated, but amounts to 'armouring'. In Spanish, the word evokes iron-clad protection: the word and its derivatives can be interpreted as *"to shield, to armour, to armour-plate"*. It is their idea, and their legal interpretation, that if the local Constitution declares that *"life shall be protected from the moment of conception"*, then this reform *de facto* accomplishes what they had believed that abolition of the death penalty was to accomplish: to make it by default impossible to legalize abortion.

They saw these subnational constitutional reforms as a 'padlock' against future, pro-abortion legislation. The subnational constitutions could be considered, within the legal 'micro-cosmos' of Mexican subnational states, as a Type 1 norm: rather abstract laws which do not directly regulate practice, but instead only set general principles. For this reason, some prominent Mexican 'pro-life' advocates (as does also their aforementioned book *Abortion: The Policy of an Abdicating State*, gifted by advocates during fieldwork) refer to these instances of 'constitutional armouring' as a 'padlock' that would supposedly prevent the passing of pro-legal-abortion reforms in the subnational Criminal Codes (which could then in turn be classified as containing T2 or T3 norms). Advocates believed that these *'blindajes'* would prevent the creation of constituting norms allowing abortion practice, procedure, or regulation; and are very much framed by them as a reaction *against* "what happened in Mexico City".[45] Their attempt to 'armour' their local constitution against 'pro-abortion advancements' can thus clearly be identified as a form of *reactive contestation.*

Legal experts on the 'pro-legalization' side of the debate speak of these supposed *'blindajes'* as more cosmetic than legally meaningful, and "quite empty as a legal reform".[46] They suggest (as eventually did the Supreme Court in September 2021) that reforming the local Constitution to "protect life from the moment of conception" does *not* conflict with eliminating penalties for abortion in the Criminal Code. The *'blindajes'* may still pose a problem for *legalizing* abortion in some regions (or for the creation of constituting and regulating norms, on how to provide abortion services), depending on contextual factors and on *what* exactly is done and *how*, but pro-legalization advocates have stated that eliminating penalties for abortion in a Criminal Code is not affected by whether the Constitution says that *"life is protected from the moment of conception"*.

This interpretation is, naturally, disputed and deemed illegitimate by 'pro-life' advocates, who insisted that any step towards decriminalization would run contrary to the 'armouring' reforms and be blocked by the *'blindaje'*.[47] The later section discussing NOM0046 will again touch upon these confronted interpretations of the Constitution, upon what exactly these *'blindajes'* are or are not capable of doing, and generally the complexities posed by the various 'layers' of laws in Mexico, and the opposed visions about which norm is 'most directly' binding towards a medical or legal practitioner.

Throughout these disputed visions about what a 'constitutional armouring' is or is not, and about what constitutional reform means in terms of allowing or blocking other legal changes, federalism itself merits comment on the complexity that it has allowed for in the legal landscape of Mexico, for better and for worse – especially in a country where each subnational state has its own Criminal Code, something uncommon among federal nations. In this case, the federal system has allowed for political fragmentation with considerable effects on legislation: there is an overarching Constitution, Criminal Code, Health Law and other federal regulations; but each subnational state has its own local version of each of those, and additionally there are other, executive-power created[48] norms such as the NOMs (*Norma Oficial Mexicana*).

This means that in Mexico, each state can decide on its own variant of the prohibition-and-exception mix, and regardless of the constitutional 'armourings', most states did not modify the Criminal Codes at all, thus still allowing for exceptions to the abortion bans. All of the subnational states allow for the exception in cases of rape; the rest of the exceptions vary throughout the nation. Two states only, Yucatán and Michoacán, allow for a curious 'economic cause' where a woman is allowed to have an abortion if she has "severe and justified economic reasons"[49] and has at least three other children already. That clause exists in written norm; however, it has apparently never been invoked in any case or legal dispute so far. This shows two relevant things: firstly, the fact that the very women who would be in a position to invoke this economic exception are likely not familiar with the law (nor would they have access to adequate legal representation); and secondly, that it is one thing for a written norm to exist, and a very different thing for actual awareness, access and implementation to meaningfully be in place.

Analyzing interview data, at times it seemed that Mexico's federalism presents a challenge, not only for the research itself, but for advocacy in such a complex and fragmented legal landscape. Many advocates in this debate seem to only reach out towards the international realm whenever it is convenient to the position they are defending at a certain moment. At other times, the international is dismissed as *"irrelevant"* to subnational states' local laws,[50] or even as worthy of opposition within narratives that construe the international as *"foreign interests with financial motivations or perverse goals"*.[51] As a general rule, however, most of the advocates saw the international as relevant, even when they themselves carried their advocacy in a more strictly local way or aiming for subnational reforms.

Only one interviewed advocate (who is a retired legal expert and now an independent citizen advocate) was rather keen to dismiss the international realm as *"irrelevant to national law and national matters within Mexico"*,[52] mentioning often how national sovereignty is much more important than any international treaty or convention, a vision that reflects traditional legal paradigms of past decades. Another advocate seemed not opposed to, but rather unconcerned with the international, feeling that their activities should prioritize attending to women in need within their community.[53] But for most interviewees, the international is relevant especially after the 2011 Constitutional reform (in favour of international treaties as part of the state's obligation to protect human rights). Every interviewee was able to quote at least one international document as being 'on their side', and several of them had been part of Mexican delegations attending international forums of some sort. A substantial part of their activities however, remains confined to the strictly subnational.

It stands to reason that, during the 2013 and 2018 cycles of Mexico's Universal Periodic Reviews at the UN Office of the High Commissioner for Human Rights, other national states made the recommendation that Mexican subnational laws be unified throughout the country – not necessarily saying that all subnational laws have to permit or ban abortion but rather that the existence of such a fragmented and unequal legal landscape may put women across the country in situations of unfair discrimination by virtue of *where* in Mexico they happen to live.

Every victory in either direction has had a 'temporary' feel to it, in an environment where opposed 'sides' of the debate each have created their own norm typology: distinct and incompatible with the other sides. It is an issue of high complexity, where meanings and interpretations, through the active practices of advocacy and contestation (proactive as well as reactive), have shaped legislation and public policy.

Constitutional Assembly of 2016: Mexico City towards a New Constitution

Another scenario of importance happened in 2016 and 2017, in the context of major administrative and political reform in the Mexican capital. The capital city had previously been called *"Distrito Federal"* and was historically an administrative capital with slightly different autonomy rights than the other subnational states. With this reform, the previous "Federal District" officially became "Mexico City" (what it was already often called, for many unofficial purposes). Its previous "Legislative Assembly" became a local Congress like those in the rest of subnational states, and its political autonomy and rights also became equal to those of subnational states. For most intents and purposes, Mexico City already had its own local laws previous to the reform: its own Criminal Code, Health Law, Civil Code, etc., but not its own local Constitution. The reform process included forming a Constitutional Assembly which, for a period of time comprising late 2016 and early 2017, would draft the new text. The Assembly was formed by parliamentarians proportionally representing Mexico City's landscape of political parties, and it was also open to proposals for constitutional articles submitted by NGOs, advocacy organizations and individual citizens.[54]

In this scenario, the legality (and as with any norm, the *legitimacy*) of abortion was once again called into question by advocates and stakeholders, in the various proposals and public debates for drafting the constitutional text. While 'pro-life' advocates saw this new Constitution as their opportunity to roll back the legalization of 2007, by arguing that it had always been 'spurious', 'extra-legal', 'arbitrary', or simply 'illegitimate and unfair',[55] pro-legalization advocates engaged in proactive contestation to defend that which had been achieved in 2007, arguing and explaining why it was necessary that abortion stay legal.

So while the former advocated for a local Constitution which would also "protect life from the moment of conception", the latter pushed for including a subsection on women's reproductive rights that would enshrine access to legal abortion ("legal interruption of pregnancy") as one of such rights. Of the legal experts that I interviewed, two had participated in directly sending proposals to the Constitutional Assembly (the proposals were shared by them, but were also publicly available on the online platform of the debates): a representative from the association *"Constituyentes Feministas"* (a coalition of feminist groups formed with the specific purpose of participating in the Constitutional Assembly)[56] and one independent citizen who sent a proposal on why legal abortion should be 'rolled back'.[57] The latter also shared a similar proposal, by another 'pro-life' citizen advocate. Seeing these different proposals side by side is a stark example of colliding interpretations: one calling legal abortion 'a right', and the other, 'a legal fallacy'.

In the end, the adopted final text of Mexico City's new Constitution includes neither one thing nor the other. While it does not protect "life from the moment of conception", it also doesn't enshrine a "right to abortion" as some advocates wanted. This can again be analyzed in a similar light as to how other local Constitutions, in containing rather 'abstract' or 'fundamental' (at the subnational level) Type 1 norms, don't necessarily go into further details of a regulatory nature, nor do they regulate specific practices that appear in other texts of a 'lower hierarchy'. It is also conceivable that even if an article in the new Constitution of Mexico City *did* enshrine a protection of "life from the moment of conception", legally this could still be interpreted as not conflicting with the Criminal Code stating that abortion can be exempt from penalties until week 12 – although of course many 'pro-life' activists would strongly dispute this.

The absence of any references to abortion is seen by some advocates as a victory (as *"at least it was not rolled back"*),[58] and by others, as a defeat: it was not codified into law as some wanted it to be.[59] The absence of a law can be interpreted as leeway, or as permitting something to exist by omission, or as a failure to regulate for better and for worse. It shows not only the diverse legal interpretations but also the aforementioned *'pendularity'* and the fragile nature of regulations, when it concerns such a disputed case. Although conservative political parties are not dominant in Mexico City, it is not impossible to foresee a situation where, with enough political weight and influence in local Congress, indeed abortion legalization could be 'rolled back' there – unlikely but always possible.

Transnational and Global Engagements: OHCHR Draft Comment No. 36, Argentinian Protests, and Others

Other significant arena for analysis, although one not as clearly defined in time and with blurrier boundaries, is the one generally comprising Mexican advocates' global and transnational engagements. This comprises different modes of 'global engagement'. Some have been the occasions where Mexican advocates for and against legal abortion have established links with their larger 'parent' organizations internationally, or with 'sister' institutions abroad (such the local chapter of "Catholics for the Right to Decide" with "Catholics for Choice International"; or "Pro-Vida" in Mexico and "Pro-Life International").

Two clear instances of transnational advocacy happened while I was researching on the field, with a chance to focus strongly on them: one in 2018 when Argentina was having a similar debate on abortion legalization, and the second one when Mexican advocates participated in the global forum of contestation seen at the United Nations Office of the High Commissioner for Human Rights (OHCHR), where multiple states, NGOs, civil associations, and expert individuals worldwide engaged in discussion through oral and written comments about the "Draft Comment No. 36 on the Right to Life".

Transnational advocacy on this issue is of course not new; it did not start with the Argentinian protests of 2018 or with the debate about Draft Comment No. 36. It has been happening on this issue since at least the 1980s, when *Human Life International* joined forces with the "Pro-Vida" civil association in Mexico, through the *"Organización Vida Humana"* ("Organization on Human Life") which coordinated 140 other organizations in 23 Mexican states.[60] For more focused analytical purposes, I take the two mentioned cases as clear, recent instances of these activities across borders and in global forums and two that left clear traceable footprints which I could personally gather while on the field.

In 2015, the OHCHR began the creation of "Draft General Comment No. 36 on the Right to Life", as a General Comment to the International Covenant on Civil and Political Rights (ICCPR). This Draft General Comment, in its Article 8, encourages states to "adopt measures designed to regulate terminations of pregnancy",[61] with a general view of protecting women's life and health, and to stop the criminalization of certain pregnancies as well as the criminalization of abortion.

Comments by state delegations, civil society, UN organizations, specialized agencies, national human rights institutions (*ombudsmen*), and individual experts were received until late 2017.

More than 180 written statements were sent from around the globe, a substantial amount of them contesting (and often opposing) Article 8, and expressing viewpoints on abortion, both for and against. The OHCHR's own Committee on the Rights of Persons with Disabilities, itself objected to some of the wording in Article 8, challenging the notion of disability as grounds for legal abortion and bringing awareness about the cases where this may amount to discrimination. Through their intervention, the final text of Draft Comment 36 was changed from *"fatal impairments in the unborn"* to *"when the pregnancy is inviable"*,[62] as a justifiable reason for legal abortion. This showcases the lack of a monolithic voice on abortion even within different bodies of the United Nations Human Rights system.

The discussions, negotiation, and drafting of General Comment No. 36 is a very straightforward example of contestation at the global level within a *multilogue* of stakeholders, where advocates who usually work at the domestic level can (and do) address a global organization to express a viewpoint and propose changes to a legal text. Among them, seven comments were received from Mexican advocacy organizations or individuals, some also as coalitions of several organizations.[63] I interviewed two advocates who directly participated in the creation of such comments. The strong response and participation that the drafting of this Comment generated among NGOs and individuals worldwide also shows clashing perceptions of rights – at the fundamental level as well as that of *organizing principles*.

Another crucial moment for transnational advocacy happened when Argentina also had a nation-wide debate about legal abortion in 2018: fieldwork data reveals that there were strong and constant transnational exchanges between advocates in both countries. 'Pro-life' and 'pro-choice' organizations and institutions in Mexico had communications with Argentinian counterparts, sending relevant documents and also with Mexican advocates adopting the symbology of the Argentinian movement: light blue scarves worn at the 'pro-life' protests and green scarves at the 'pro-choice' protests (often with written slogans on each of the coloured scarves or handkerchiefs).

These handkerchiefs and corresponding colours were taken as a signifier throughout the rest of the continent. Until today, bandanas identical to those shown in Argentina are used as a personal flag to signal a 'clear-cut' position within the abortion debate. Argentina was therefore the recent source of new signifiers, adopted transnationally: colours as well as phrases, with 'pro-life' groups adopting the slogan "Let Us Save Both Lives" (*Salvemos Las Dos Vidas*),[64] while the pro-legalization side adopted not one but several phrases, seeming not to find one succinct enough to encompass pro-legalization demands. One of the most important pro-legalization phrases (though somewhat long and convoluted for a protest slogan) was "Education to Decide, Contraceptives to Avoid Abortion, Legal Abortion to Avoid Deaths" (*Educación para Decidir, Anticonceptivos para No Abortar, Aborto para No Morir*). But other green handkerchiefs sported other pro-legalization messages, such as "Legal Abortion Now!" (*¡Aborto Legal Ya!*) or another popular one, "It Will Be Law" (*Será Ley*).

The Argentinian protests also originated new, parallel names for the movements themselves: the 'pro-life' movement became known as the "Light Blue Wave" (*Ola Celeste*, the colour itself appropriated from the similar hue of the Argentinian flag), whereas the pro-legalization movement was named "The Green Tide" (*La Marea Verde*). Both names carry the connotation of an unstoppable natural force: a "wave" and a "tide", each claiming to represent the millions of people 'who are in the moral right'. Thus new names, colours, slogans, and symbols have been brought to the opposed sides of the abortion debate – carrying a certain unified simplicity, for better and for worse.

The popular slogans from both movements, "Let's Save Both Lives" and "Será Ley" represent important narrative shifts of recent years, if we analyze how the anti- and pro-abortion messages have changed throughout time in Spanish-speaking Latin America (acknowledging that advocacy messages in the Anglo or other linguistic worlds may have had different trajectories). Some advocates with long histories of activity on the matter spoke of the evolution of these discourses, including the transnational influences. The advocates that today identify as 'pro-life' (*pro-vida*) very consciously use this positive reframing of their message, as a change from earlier 'anti-abortion' messages of past decades (mainly the 70s and 80s).[65]

The reframing from being *'anti-'* something into *'pro-'* something has been a conscious shift in perspectives that helps to engage more people into a propositional, proactive sounding message rather than a 'reactionary' message.[66] Not only was the effort reframed as a positive rather than an *'anti'*, but they also have, as a movement, appropriated the fundamental notion of 'life': leaving their ideological opponents in a position where they, by default, appear as being *'anti-life'* or *'pro-death'*.[67] This reframing, as a fundamental narrative shift, has undoubtedly been a victory for that side of the debate, where many women, younger people, representatives of indigenous communities, and individuals from all walks of life seem much more ready to embrace a *'pro-life'* rather than an *'anti-abortion'* message.

In a curious example of intersectionality, one small contingent (of about four or five people) attending the 'pro-life' protest of October 20, 2018, in Mexico City carried also rainbow banners and signs declaring them as a 'pro-life LGBTQ+ group'.[68] Of course, there are no rules in place which keep people from LGBTQ+ communities from associating with 'pro-life' groups and embracing their ideas, but it is at least an interesting place to stand ideologically; given that in Mexico and much of Latin America, most of the self-proclaimed 'pro-life' groups also advocate against homosexual marriage and other equal rights for the LGBTQ+ community.

Not only has there been a narrative shift where '*anti*-abortion' became '*pro*-life', but since the Argentinian protests in 2018, the narrative has been again re-reframed into protecting not only one, but two lives. This further increases the appeal of the message: by embracing this movement, one is allegedly not only *not anti-something,* but in favour of protecting *two* lives allegedly at risk ('We Save Both Lives').[69] This facilitates a framing of the 'pro-life' advocacy as being decidedly in the moral right, further increasing their appeal to many.

On the other hand, pro-legalization advocates have also made narrative shifts and re-framings of their messages, some with admittedly more success than others. Since the late seventies, one of the main concepts that started to be attached to the (often harder to 'sell') pro-legal abortion message was the concept of 'consented motherhood'. It gained strength and acceptance among secular, liberal, and progressive sectors of Mexican society, especially in Mexico City. One highly symbolic moment from those earlier movements was when several feminist groups added a plaque reading "Because her Motherhood was Consented" (*'Porque su Maternidad fue Voluntaria'*) below the original plaque of the Monument to the Mother (*Monumento a la Madre*), in Mexico City, in 1998.[70] Both plaques could be seen until recent times at the base of the statue, of a mother with indigenous facial features holding her child. (Following the 2017 earthquake that hit Mexico City, the Monument suffered significant damage and needed rebuilding. Once rebuilt, this latter plaque about "consented motherhood" was not re-added, leaving only the original plaque saying "Monument to The Mother. To Her Who Loved Us Before Meeting Us").

Also in past decades, two important re-framings of the pro-legal abortion movements (in attempts to gain more acceptance) were, on the one hand, the declaration of being 'pro-decriminalization' (*"a favor de la despenalización del aborto"*), and not necessarily pro-abortion as such.[71] And, on the other hand, the reframing of the term 'abortion' into "voluntary interruption of pregnancy"[72]; however, this applies mostly to legal texts. The 2018 Argentinian protest, and the transnational contacts with advocates in other countries, seemingly encouraged more boldness from pro-legalization advocates who now demand that abortion be considered "a right"[73] and that the state should provide free access.

The other, longer phrase sometimes used and written in pro-legalization protests, about the "Education to Decide, Contraceptives to Avoid Abortion, Legal Abortion to Avoid Deaths", seemingly serves the purpose of providing more explanation and nuance – as a way in which advocates 'remove themselves two steps' from abortion when they clarify that the 'first two options' in order to avoid abortions should be education and contraceptives.[74] This helps to increase the acceptance of a concept inherently rejected by substantial parts of the population, perhaps 'softening' the pro-abortion approach.

Another phrase commonly seen throughout the Argentinian protests (not as widely adopted in Mexico) is the short and simple "It Will Be Law" (*Será Ley*). Even if this is decidedly a bold re-framing of the narrative, in the spirit of norm contestation theory,[75] we can point out that *"it will be law"* does not mean the same thing as "*it will be legitimate*". This *"will be law"* reframing can come across (and it is so expressed by some 'pro-life' advocates)[76] as vaguely threatening rather than argumentative, declaring that abortion "will be law" regardless of *who* stands against it, or *why*. A phrase such as "*Será Ley*" risks finding acceptance only among those who already believe that abortion "should be law (legal)": a form of preaching to the choir, or issuing warnings to opposed advocates, rather than being a strong convincing argument by itself. So for pro-legalization advocates, while some of the narrative shifts have consisted of them going for a 'bolder' approach, others have been the opposite: aiming for nuance and for taking a certain 'distance' from the idea of directly embracing abortion.

Instances resembling what Keck and Sikkink deem "the boomerang pattern" in advocacy could be observed in these arenas of transnational contestation – where domestic NGOs may directly seek international allies to try to put pressure on their states 'from the outside'.[77] In 2018–2019, at the peak of these exchanges when both Mexico and Argentina were hosting intense advocacy for and against legal abortion, I encountered ample proof of transnational exchanges between Mexican and Argentinian advocates, among opposed groups: one interviewee from the "Catholics for the Right to Decide" office in Mexico showed proof of communication with their counterpart in Argentina (sharing news of the publication of OHCHR's General Comment No. 36)[78]; a 'pro-life' advocate shared the screenshot of an invitation to a public conference in the state of Sonora, where Argentinian doctor Chinda Brandolino would share viewpoints against abortion and "how the initiative was stopped in the Argentinian Senate".[79] Another 'pro-life' advocate shared a video message where a Congressperson in the state of Oaxaca denounced the alleged presence of Argentinian activists in the Oaxacan local Congress, at the time when it was debating (and eventually decriminalized) abortion in 2019. This Oaxacan congressperson's message appropriates feminism, when declaring that 'pro-life' women are "the real feminists".[80]

About the "boomerang effect", Keck and Sikkink comment that *"justifying external intervention or pressure in domestic affairs is a much trickier business, except where lives are at stake"*.[81] In this case where opposed sides of the debate certainly believe that "lives are at stake"; for this and other reasons (and simply because transnational advocacy is easier today than ever, and we see it happen across many issue areas), they seek and justify connections and alliances with partners abroad. Advocates on opposed sides, however, tend to see their own connections abroad as justifiable, while being more prone to denounce opposed advocates' transnational advocacy efforts as illegitimate acts of 'infringing on national (or subnational) sovereignty'[82]. . . In what I may paraphrase as *"calling it transnational advocacy when I like it; and infringements on national sovereignty when I don't"*.

The book *Abortion: the Policy of an Abdicating State*, gifted during fieldwork by a 'pro-life' advocate and quoted by many others, denounces these transnational exchanges: the alleged "pro-abortion intervention" by international organisms such as the "Inter-American Pro-Human Rights Network" *(Red Iberoamericana Pro Derechos Humanos)* to the IACHR, demanding that subnational states free women who were imprisoned for abortion in much-publicized and mediatized cases. The book accuses of *"transnational links in the pro-abortion camp, including financial support"*.[83] It isn't surprising, perhaps, that such instances of "foreign intervention" or transnational advocacy carry a label of legitimacy when they are perceived to be 'morally correct'. . . and 'morally correct' meaning *'what our group does'*.

The Unplanned Birth of NOM0046

In the structure of Mexican laws and written norms, "NOM" is the acronym for "Official Mexican Norm" (*"Norma Oficial Mexicana"*). NOMs are typically thought of as a 'lower' type of written norm, which is meant to set standards of practice; typically for fields such as manufacturing industries, extractive industries, food regulations for public health, medical practice, or procedural matters in some government instances. NOMs set standards of quality and regulations for how to carry out specific practice. Most of them are ultimately designed to protect human and environmental health or to ensure the quality of manufactured products, through technical and procedural regulation.

Despite the perception of them being 'lower-tier' kinds of laws, they are the type of regulation that most directly apply to practitioners in the fields that use NOMs, setting obligations and regulations and constraining their practices. NOMS are typically created by the executive branch of power, through government ministries or by commissions on varied issue areas, as long as such institutions are recognized as "*dependencias normalizadoras*" ("normalizing dependencies", in this case 'normalizing' means 'a government office with the capacity to create binding written norms').[84] The official Mexican institutions related to public health, especially the Secretariat of Health (*Secretaría de Salud*), have created numerous NOMs related to disease prevention and treatment, as well as general guidelines for the protection of human health.

The story of how one NOM became a crucial piece in the recent abortion debate was recounted by many advocates interviewed in Mexico, and in this case, the officially called NOM0046-SSA2-2005[85] (or 'NOM0046' for a shorter identifier) played an unexpected role.[86]

NOM0046 came to be by means of a reform to a previous one: NOM190, which had existed since the mid-nineties and dealt with procedures on how to give attention and healthcare to victims of domestic violence; its full identifier then being "NOM190-SSA1-1999; Health Services; Criteria for the Attention towards Victims of Domestic Violence". This previous version did not mention abortion or interruption of pregnancy. One reform was made in 2009, changing the name of the ruling into "NOM0046-SSA2-2005; Domestic Violence, Sexual Violence and Violence against Women; Criteria for the Prevention and Attention". The 2009 version also didn't mention abortion, but it did state that emergency contraception must be provided to victims of sexual violence, for up until 120 hours after the assault.

The precedent for this NOM0046 later including abortion services was set in a different law, in 2013, with the creation of the *General Law on Victims of Crime* (*Ley General de Víctimas*), recognizing interruption of pregnancy as an emergency medical service which must be granted to all victims of sexual assault. This General Law rested on two legal bases: firstly, on the fact that abortion in cases of rape was already an admitted exception to prohibition in all subnational states, as well as in the Federal Criminal Code; and secondly, on the legal precedent set by Mexico City, where abortion had been legalized in 2007 and reframed as "Legal Interruption of Pregnancy".[87]

Much more strongly contested was the second reform to NOM0046 which took place in 2016. While the previous text only granted victims of sexual assault access to emergency contraception, after the 2016 reform, it now grants the victims access to abortion (building on what was stated in the "*Ley General de Víctimas*" three years prior). It also eliminates any need to first prove that the crime happened, or to report it to any authorities at all: abortion is to be performed following a written declaration by the victim, stating that the pregnancy is a result of sexual assault. With this reform, underage girls can also access abortion in such cases without parental consent, from the age of 12.

Bartolini and Alarcón recount how, at the dawn of the reform to the NOM0046, women's groups supporting abortion had been setting precedents for this change: they *"concentrated their efforts on two distinct groups of women, according to specific cases: women who are arrested for their possible involvement in the crime of abortion or infanticide, and victims of violence (specifically sexual violence and rape). In this way, they would more easily gather empathy and support, in order to pressure public health institutions into accepting the practice of safe and free abortion, pushing so far as to have abortions performed on the grounds of rape without even denouncing the alleged crime of rape"*.[88]

These two changes to NOM0046 have prompted intense reactions from 'pro-life' expert advocates. Firstly because they see it as a *de facto* legalization of abortion in the whole country (as do some pro-legalization activists also), because even though a woman is only 'supposed' to access abortion if the pregnancy results from sexual abuse, the only 'proof' needed that the abuse took place shall be a good-faith declaration and nothing else, opening the door for "anyone aborting anywhere, acting merely on their word that sexual abuse took place".[89] Secondly, others have intensely reacted against what they see as an override of parental authority, if a girl from the age of 12 can herself choose an interruption of pregnancy, "casting aside the civil and family laws concerning parents and tutors".[90]

Others, regardless of any stance on abortion, see it as deeply troublesome that there is no need to prove that the sexual assault happened, nor any obligation or incentive to report the crime, raising understandable concerns about victims going back to spaces of re-victimization and further abuse once a pregnancy has been "dealt with".[91] NOM0046 has certainly raised interesting questions not only on abortion access but also on the contestation of another principle regarded as a fundamental, Type 1 kind of norm: the need to prove that a crime happened before taking consequent action (rule of law), and whether it is acceptable to disregard it in this case, for the sake of giving a requested intervention to a woman who likely was the victim of a crime.

Interviewed advocates, especially those identifying as 'pro-life', shared their feeling that the latest reform to NOM0046 was a sort of *"attack coming from an unexpected place"*.[92] They would refer to it in appalled tones, sometimes using metaphors related to criminology (*"a forced entry through the back door"*) or to the world of sports: a "score" or "goal" or "offensive move" coming from an unexpected corner of the playing field.[93] For many, it was certainly unexpected that a NOM would become part of this debate at all: most of the Mexican public is largely unaware of them (since they apply to experts in specific fields), and most of the advocates themselves were unaware of them, until these reforms – unless they already were legal experts to begin with.

Given the years of efforts that 'pro-life' advocates had invested into changing subnational Constitutions "to protect life from the moment of conception", the

"NOM0046 move" certainly brought astonishment – as well as much further questioning about the nature and reach of NOMs in general, and NOM0046 in particular. Regarding the norm typologies analyzed before, NOM0046 can be placed as a Type 3 norm, a "technical regulation" of a higher complexity and narrower moral reach, being placed 'in the eye of the storm'.

Debates and ponderings about NOM0046 have focused on some legalistic and technical aspects. 'Pro-life' advocates insist on its illegitimacy, or at least its inoperability in those subnational states that amended their Constitution "to protect life from the moment of conception".[94] At the same time, pro-legalization advocates declare that the subnational Constitutions set abstract norms as basic principles, but that it is the technical regulations (in this case the NOMs) that practicing stakeholders such as doctors and medical personnel are "directly bound by" or must "directly respond to".[95] The issue has become, at times, a discussion on which law 'comes first' or 'is at a higher level', and *who* is bound by *what*, exactly. While the public at large tends not to be too aware of NOMs, experts on medical, legal or scientific fields are very much aware of them, because it is NOMs rather than the Constitution or even the Criminal Codes that directly regulate and constrain their practices. A doctor would allegedly have to *"look at the NOM first, and be mostly unbothered by whatever the local Constitution says"*, because they *"are directly bound by the NOM, even if the Constitution is hierarchically superior"*.[96]

Building on the sayings of many advocates, what is happening in practice with NOM0046 is a "contestation at the implementing stage".[97] Since NOMs are created by dependencies of the Executive branch, what has been occurring on the ground is that the governors of each subnational state 'decide' (through their personnel leading the subnational health dependencies), as part of their executive competencies, if they will or will not "activate the implementation of NOM0046"[98] (i.e. to actually greenlight the protocols for their administrative personnel, in the public health institutions). While it is deeply troubling that the implementation of such a consequential norm should ultimately depend on the political will of the local executive power (and also, remembering *'pendularity'*, that this may be subject to changes depending on the political ideology of the party in power on each subnational state), in reality, this is how several of the advocates recount the "on-the-ground" implementation of the NOM0046[99] – and something not entirely foreign to the way the laws function in Mexico.

To some of them, this resonates with the ever-present "Mexican problem" of having *"great laws, but very bad implementation"*.[100] At the time of carrying out the second cycle of fieldwork in 2019 (with abortion still being illegal at that moment, it should be remembered, in all Mexican subnational states except Mexico City), one pro-legalization advocate stated that, as of September 2019, *"only the governor of Jalisco had agreed to implement NOM0046"*.[101] This acceptance or refusal to implement a norm could be seen as a way to contest *behaviourally* and *reactively*, by subnational executive powers refusing to implement a norm because of disagreement and perceptions of its illegitimacy.[102]

"Law on Conscientious Objection": The Law That Wasn't

After the 'blow' dealt by the reforms to NOM0046, many 'pro-life' advocates concentrated their further activities into not just the aforementioned 'armouring' of subnational Constitutions (the most recent one passed in the state of Sinaloa in 2018) but also a newer effort towards what they call "the Law on Conscientious Objection",[103] in 2018. This ruling supposedly grants doctors or medical personnel the right to abstain from performing abortions, even in situations where another regulation would require them to do so – for example, NOM0046. 'Conscientious Objection' as a concept already existed in other regulations of the medical field, concerning procedures that are contested or controversial for moral and ethical reasons.

For a brief time, it became one of their much-touted 'victories'. This, however, is not really a new law, but rather the addition of a paragraph within the General Law on Health (*Ley General de Salud*), granting medical personnel said right to abstain from controversial procedures, including abortion, but with the obligation to refer the patient to "other available, non-objecting personnel".[104] However, a ruling by the Mexican Supreme Court in September 2021 declared it "unconstitutional" to grant a right to conscientious objection in those cases where women need access to abortion, especially cases of sexual abuse. While individuals do have a right to conscientious objection, hospitals are obligated to have non-objecting personnel.[105]

Latest Events: Decriminalization in Other Subnational States, Supreme Court Rulings in 2021 and 2023

It was only on September 25, 2019, very close to the end of my second cycle of fieldwork, that the state of Oaxaca became the second to decriminalize abortion, the first subnational state to do so after Mexico City in 2007.[106] Abortion was decriminalized until the 12th gestational week, in the same terms as Mexico City did 12 years earlier: through the conceptual redefinition of the practice in the local Criminal Code. Advocates whom I could interview after the day on which this reform was approved, spoke of the reason for decriminalization being the leftist political forces in power in Oaxaca, represented in a local Congress dominated by the Morena party (the party of president Andrés Manuel López Obrador).[107] The states of Hidalgo and Veracruz quickly followed suit in 2020, and Baja California and Colima in 2021, also partially as a consequence of the leftist political forces represented in the local Congresses.[108]

That such rapid change has cascaded in other subnational states, after a decade of what had seemed like progress in the opposite direction (i.e. for the 'pro-life' movements and especially their efforts to amend the subnational Constitutions), is not merely a story of political representation but also one of sociocultural change where the efforts of the '*green tide*' and their pro-legalization demands are slowly gaining more acceptance, at least in some regions of the country. The 'green tide' movements have, in the words of other activists, not focused that much anymore on the 'public health' argument but have rather continued to frame access to abortion as a feminist/progressive demand.[109]

However, the state of Oaxaca has been, as of late 2021, precisely an example of what can happen when 'decriminalization' is not converted into 'legalization' in terms of real on-the-ground policy, nor is it being translated into real access yet: despite the Criminal Code now stating that abortion shall only be considered a crime after the 12th gestational week, no other piece of legislation was amended or implemented, no protocols have been put in place to give meaningful access to abortion, and as of that point, the only change had been the elimination of penalties, without necessarily translating into meaningful access, regulation or institutionalization.[110]

In September 2021, the Supreme Court of Mexico ruled that criminalization of abortion, in general, is unconstitutional and goes against women's rights to freely decide over their own lives. In late 2023, the Supreme Court has gone beyond in declaring that abortion should be decriminalized in the Federal Criminal Code and that federal healthcare institutions should provide the service. While this has been framed in news articles as "abortion having been legalized in Mexico",[111] the Court ruling does not automatically create any new law – but it does set a powerful precedent, one of the strongest that can exist in the Mexican legal and judicial tradition, calling for *decriminalization* of abortion to be an accepted principle. While it should be reiterated that this is not the same as *legalizing* abortion, that the Mexican Supreme Court has now set this precedent at least opens the path now for a more complete acceptance of *decriminalization* as a starting point that many opposed views can agree upon.

Enabling and Contextual Factors of Abortion-Related Contestation and Reforms

Three factors were often brought up by experts, as contextual enablers that can help to explain, on the one hand, the increased contestation of abortion-related norms in Mexico (but especially a contestation where both sides *claim to be defending human rights principles*), and on the other, the possibility that so many legal reforms on the topic of abortion have happened in recent years. These factors also, in and of themselves, make Mexico a particularly interesting case study for contestation of norms related to abortion.

The Constitutional Reform of 2011

An important constitutional reform was carried out in Mexico in 2011, where international Human Rights treaties are granted equal importance as that of national laws. This represented a major paradigm shift in Mexican law, which until that point only recognized (in its first 30 Articles) the existence not of human rights but of "Individual Guarantees" (*Garantías Individuales*), granted *by* the Mexican state *to* the individual Mexican national. The newly adopted text recognizes those articles as "Human Rights and Their Guarantees" (*De Los Derechos Humanos y Sus Garantías*), recognizing that such rights are inherent to the human person, mentioning in its Article 1 that International Treaties signed by Mexico[112] are to be considered as an equally valid source of law as the Constitution, while also upholding the *pro-persona* principle of highest protection of rights (where the source of such protection can be either the Constitution itself or international legal documents signed by Mexico).[113]

Mexico is also a country with a high degree of integration and interaction with what can be called the 'international norms systems' of the United Nations as well as the Organization of American States. It is signatory to numerous Declarations, Conventions and Treaties of the international Human Rights normativity (and a signatory to all of the OHCHR's main Conventions); thus bound by international norms, especially after this Constitutional reform, and it periodically sustains reviews by Human Rights Treaty bodies. As such, there is an interaction between Mexican members of civil society and international institutions of the UN system, Inter-American system, and international NGOs. Several of the advocates that I interviewed deem Mexican laws quite "progressive" and state the fact that much of this progress has happened *because* Mexico is close to the international realm.[114] The discussion on abortion remains perpetually 'unfinished', partially because *"if we consider the central role that human rights and their interpretations now play in the Mexican judicial system after the 2011 constitutional reform"* (in the words of Alarcón *et al*),[115] opposed advocates all find what they see as solid, international legal grounding in their pro- and anti-legal abortion activities.

Legislative Fragmentation and Several "Layers" of Laws

The political and legal nature of Mexico as a federation was also mentioned by opposed advocates as a crucial factor in how advocacy has had varying results at the subnational level. The very complex legal landscape in Mexico, perceived by some advocates as making for a very 'confusing' or 'chaotic' system with overlapping laws, has provided them regardless with a variety of possible "avenues" for contestation.[116] In this context of high complexity, fragmentation, and the existence of so many 'layers' of normativity, some of them have concentrated efforts on changing known federal rulings,[117] others on somewhat 'obscure' regulations such as NOM0046 (also created at the federal level), while others concentrate their efforts on a variety of possible subnational laws.[118]

The overlaps also make for situations of alleged 'conflict' or 'clash' between different laws, often with conflicting perceptions about which law supposedly 'comes first' or 'is higher up' in a hierarchy of laws, or, in the case of NOMs and similar technical regulations, about which law is more 'directly binding' to a specific stakeholder.[119] Mizrahi and Zúñiga recount this conflict in 2013, at the time when the General Law on Victims of Crime (*Ley General de Víctimas*) was created. In its current version, this law states that public health institutions at every level must offer abortion services (now redefined as "Voluntary Interruption of Pregnancy") to any victim of a sexual crime. In their words, the way that this law is written, it seems to *"attempt to override the competence of local state congresses in redefining the crime of abortion, substituting it by "voluntary interruption of pregnancy" which does not have a specific definition, ignoring the fact that abortion is an* *anti-legal or unlawful behaviour (*"conducta antijurídica"*), which may admit some attenuating excuses, but instead presenting it as a right which can be demanded by law. A simple bureaucratic procedure is all that is now required to dispense with the unborn's life".*[120]

Growing Strength of a Diverse Civil Society, Transnational Advocacy Networks

A third contextual factor explaining increased norm contestation on abortion is that, in recent decades, Mexico has seen growing plurality in the realm of civil society, social participation, and political representation. This growing plurality of the Mexican state is reflected in, for example, increased citizen participation in NGOs and civil associations[121]; the existence of newer political parties as well as the growing influence of older, but previously marginalized parties; and the role of civil society and other stakeholders (e.g. religious institutions) in shaping policy and representing citizens' interests. Under the decades-long rule of the PRI party until the year 2000, civil society had not been so active or diverse as it is now. Political change, however, is not the only explanation: newer communications technologies, and the rise in the use of social media, also greatly facilitate exchanges (including transnational exchanges) which would have not been practically possible in previous decades.

Geographical proximity to the United States and the historic ties between both countries also has a repercussion in Mexican social and civil life, advocacy, and NGO 'culture'. Large and transnational advocacy organizations (many of them headquartered in the United States), on various issue areas, have offices or local chapters in Mexico: it is the case for example of Amnesty International, Greenpeace, or relevant for this case, Marie Stopes International, and the International Planned Parenthood Federation. There are links between Mexican advocates and other advocates in 'sister' organizations abroad,[122] very often in the United States. Pérez Hernández mentions 'pro-choice' groups being internationally funded by organizations such as Planned Parenthood International, the Ford and Rockefeller Foundations, and the Population Council.[123]

Civil society advocacy on many issues and greater availability of information online has progressively brought heightened awareness about human rights, for groups that were historically disadvantaged and silenced in practice or in public life: younger people, women, persons with disabilities, indigenous groups, etc. Growing numbers of civil society associations can now represent their interests to the government. Or also, in other instances of conflict, their cases can be brought to the attention of international forums: to institutions such as the Inter-American Court of Human Rights (IACHR) or the Inter-American Commission on Human Rights.

In relation to this and to the anti-abortion backlash measures that ensued in Mexican subnational states after 2007, academic and advocate Marta Lamas points at the cases brought to the attention of the Inter-American Commission as a relatively recent development in the Mexican contestation scene. In various Mexican states, women who *"feel negatively affected by the (anti-abortion) reforms have resorted to national and international judicial instruments . . .; and 860 female citizens from seven Mexican states . . . have sued their state before the Inter-American Commission of Human Rights in Washington, for affectations to their Human Rights"*.[124]

Lamas mentions that these women based their claims on the American Convention on Human Rights (the Pact of San José), which guarantees *"freedom to choose one's life project, life in dignity and personal integrity; the right to private life, freedom of thought and conscience and equal protection before the law with no discrimination"*. She sees such developments as encouraging (despite most of such complaints not progressing before the Inter-American Commission), as they signal new precedents and paradigms where consideration is given to international legal instruments: often as a means to argue against the local laws of one's own national (or subnational) state.

On this last point however, it may well be the case that the Inter-American legal system is less likely than the UN legal system to provide clarity in matters related to abortion because, as mentioned, the American Convention on Human Rights is precisely the one international rights treaty that makes a mention of 'conception' as the beginning of legally protected human life. The endless contestation likely to emerge between the Article that protects life *"in general, from the moment of conception"* and those that protect other rights and principles, such as privacy, freedom of choice for one's life, or non-discrimination, are likely to remain where they are now: firmly entrenched in a legal stalemate. The cases brought to the Inter-American Commission on Human Rights arguing for a 'right to abortion' are, if anything, *less* likely to prosper than if brought forward to similar mechanisms within the UN system.[125] Nevertheless, the combined factors of Mexico's federal fragmentation in laws, as well as this growing and stronger presence of civil society and advocacy organization, has meant an incredibly wide variety of avenues and possibilities for access to contestation.

Another sign of the increased avenues for participation of civil society and citizens in general in Mexican political life is the possibility to create independent citizen initiatives for law reform, such as those proposed to the Constitutional Assembly of Mexico City in 2016. Other legal avenues exist for citizen propositions of legal reform, contingent on having a minimum number of verified signatures as well as other validation processes. These avenues for law reformation and constitution stand as proof of the growing strength of civil society in Mexico, where citizens have more direct access to contestation, both discursive and behavioural.[126] Advocates on legal abortion who have seen these changes in the last few decades mention how the topic's 'internationalization' helped place it within the country's political agenda.[127]

Interviewed activists mentioned many instances in which not only the growth of civil society, but also the growth of transnational advocacy networks has influenced contestation and outcomes in national and subnational events.[128] Mizrahi and Zúñiga also refer to recommendations by international organizations as "mechanisms for public pressure"[129] and recount how, when in 2014 in the Mexican state of Nuevo León various pro-life advocates wanted to pass the local Constitutional reform for the protection of life from conception, international organizations *"made their presence felt, through private lobbying meetings and by sending letters"*.[130] Again, and perhaps naturally, interviewed advocates speak more positively of such instances when the "mechanism for public pressure" features a narrative aligned to their own, and rather negatively when it is the 'opposing side' engaging in transnational advocacy.[131]

Multidimensional Discourses: The Many Contested Dimensions of the Abortion Debates

In such a multidimensional issue, there are numerous norms and concepts that can be found within the Mexican case alone. This relates to the earlier concept of *framing* in relation to norm contestation: functioning as a constant 'negotiation of meanings' in the abortion debate. During the extended interviews, I engaged with the advocates not only on their personal advocacy journey but also on their ideas and interpretations of various different concepts, as well as on what exactly do international norms and documents establish in relation to abortion, and in consequence what 'should' Mexican national and subnational laws establish in turn. I probed them on their own views of the legitimacy gap, on what do they perceive as a 'workable compromise in policy', and how they explain links (or the perceived lack thereof) between the Mexican norms and the efforts by advocates, as well as links with advocates in other countries, or in the international organizations and institutions such as those at the UN Human Rights System or Inter-American Rights System.

Subject to contestation by opposed advocates are many different concepts: even such basic and foundational ones like *life, health, reproductive health*, who is a *victim* or a *transgressor*, who may forfeit certain rights and why, or what constitutes an acceptable and unacceptable *family planning* practice. They were interviewed about their ideas and interpretations of diverse practices and social experiences, as well as meanings and relationships between concepts, such as the link between abortion and women's health, or many diverse and socially constructed concepts. Some can refer, for example, to motherhood and the cultural constructions around it, gender roles and transgressions to said roles, who is 'a rights holder', or who is entitled to a specific right in a specific society – and who has 'given up' or 'lost' rights because of transgressions to social norms.

Some advocates tackle also what they perceive as larger issues that influence women's decisions to have legal or illegal abortions: also subject to contestation in this debate are, for example, overarching concepts such as *patriarchal systems of oppression*, which, in the eyes of pro-legalization advocates, create such gendered inequalities that many poor and disempowered women risk their lives in unsafe abortions because they have lacked sexual education as well as access to contraceptives. On the other hand, for the socially conservative 'pro-life' side, the *global liberal order* is worthy of contestation and overt rejection: in their understanding, this '*global liberal order*' overly privileges values of individualism and hedonism and underprivileges *family values* or a certain sense of *a collective* where women and men play traditional gender roles that are strongly related to that sense of collectivism and tradition.[132]

Analyzing contestation as carried out by the advocates also provides a deeper understanding of other fundamental clashes, not only those already mentioned but also others such as religious and scientific principles, a clash sometimes between 'public health' and 'human rights' (specifically the right to life), the 'moral' versus the 'pragmatic', as well as discussions on 'the agent' with regard to 'the structure'. Universal paradigms versus global organizing principles – that is, Type 1 and Type 2 global norms – are also shown as part of the perceived dichotomies within the debate. Particularly interesting is also the mutual constituency of structure and agency in norm creation and change, as well as the constitution of normative meaning.

When analyzing the issue of agency versus structure in this debate, it is worth noticing that the two directly affected individuals (the woman having or wanting an abortion, and the unborn) tend not to have a voice: not at all, in the case of the unborn but also a greatly reduced one in the case of women, and especially if we are looking at the debate from the pro-legalization side. This should be further explained because it seems counterintuitive and I have previously hinted at the opposite: that women are indeed prominent voices in the Mexican abortion debate, on 'both sides', and roughly half of the experts interviewed for this book were women, evenly split between the opposed 'sides' of the debate as well. But it becomes an issue of rather 'indirect' representation: voices that are 'one step removed'.

Throughout Latin America, there are still strong elements of taboo around the subject of abortion, particularly being in favour of its legalization. And it is quite rare for a woman to admit that she's had, or even desired, an abortion, and those women (the ones who maybe lacked access and would want to advocate for it) overwhelmingly tend *not* to become advocates themselves. To be clear, women are very present in advocacy throughout all the spectrum of the abortion debate (and in leadership positions as well), but because of the social taboo still attached to it, they tend to purport to speak *'for other women'*[133]: most often speaking in a position of allegedly being 'removed' from the issue.

This can be attributed to a principle of personal privacy, but what is notable is that 'pro-life' advocates do tend to be more personal: one can more easily find, for example, testimonies by women who claim that they 'were going to have an abortion but decided against it' and carried their pregnancies to term. Also present, though less common, are the testimonies by women who claim to have had abortions and deeply regret them, deciding later to become 'pro-life' advocates.

So in a curious way, in this case it seems as if everybody else speaks for the actual stakeholders; the agent (woman) is often not fully an agent, or not properly represented, but it is rather the others who speak on her behalf (even if that means 'other women'). We can find here, therefore, a clash of rights of two differently recognized individuals, but both without a voice that is directly, publicly heard. Sometimes there is a third type of stakeholder whose voice is 'louder', too: the doctors providing (or refusing) abortion services, who in their position of expertise often have a higher degree of agency than the woman herself (in Mexico, many doctors are involved in advocacy either for or against legalizing abortion).[134]

With these considerations about the affected stakeholders, and *other* agents claiming to represent them, it stands to reason that the dichotomies of *agency* and *structure* are rather complex in this case. Opposing sides of various debates on the legality of abortion have curiously differing ways of approaching the dimensions of individual agency versus social (and other kinds of) structures, which largely shape their discursive conceptualizations. Pro-legalization advocates tend to mention structural problems, obstacles, or injustices such as religious institutions, patriarchal systems, poverty, public health systems and their failures, as well as the rigidness of gender norms. 'Pro-life' advocates rather have the tendency to emphasize individual agency and responsibilities (and particularly the negative aspects thereof) in a way that portrays individuals, especially women and particularly women who have aborted or who would opt for an abortion, as the willing or coerced agents of a transgression,[135] in a legal as well as moral sense.

Their framing of such individual women is complex, as the individual responsibility and individual agency for an act of abortion tends to be framed by 'pro-life' advocates in a morally isolated way, in almost total abstraction from societal structures. The agency of such women can be portrayed as either morally questionable ("*Women should not be able to make that decision*"),[136] as divided among two beings and not only one ("*It is not only 'your' body!*"),[137] or as questionable in terms of the woman's capacity to make such a choice ("*All women who abort will regret it later*",[138] "*It is their partners who pressure them into it*"[139]). 'Pro-life' advocates rarely mention institutions or social structures, whereas 'pro-legalization' advocates tend to delve deeper into structural issues.[140] In Mexico, as in other Latin American countries where abortion has become a politicized debate, distinct political factions construct and frame a human rights-related discourse very differently. Their constructed realities mean that, when it comes to dimensions of structure and agency, they tend to see the world very differently and shape their advocacy accordingly.

Advocates themselves can be analyzed, in how their own positionality in *their* field affects what norms and avenues of contestation they have access to. In this manner, part of the questions during interviews (especially when probing the advocates to tell about their own 'advocacy stories') focused on several points: the advocate as a *contester* of the local and international norms and principles (if and when they establish a link with the global, or links across borders); the advocate as an *interpreter and translator* of local and international norms and principles; and the advocate as *an agent* (and often a *transnational* agent) in shaping new norms through the ongoing process of contestation and meaning-making. In this way, the focus can be placed on both the advocates and the discursive frames that they use; tracing the discursive patterns through which they interpret international norms, laws, and treaties, while taking into consideration how the validity or legitimacy of norms is always filtered through the lens of the individual and their particular interpretations and perceptions, their respective 'baggage' and experiences.

Looking at the highly multidimensional discourses used by the advocates helped to 'unpack' the enormous complexity of the debate itself, as well as the complexity of the advocates' worldviews: despite how often the debate, and their very own discourses, appear as 'simplified' into a few, supposedly 'black and white' notions. What I found in the field, instead of any such simple notions, is two complex sets of meanings-in-use, two entire *ontologies* (in the sense of having many different dimensions contained within), framed as opposed views within one issue. The way in which the discourses have developed over time also helps to understand where they are today. These sets of complex meanings (or 'competing ontologies') include their understandings of international relations and international norms, what their role should be in relation to the Mexican context, and potential ideas on the (global) organizing principles that can be applicable to abortion-related policies on the ground.

Opposing, Polarized, and Competing Discourses

The analysis of advocates' discourses reveals three main characteristics in regard to how the 'sets' of meanings stand in relation to each other: *opposed*, *polarized*, and *competing*. These three characteristics respond to the way in which advocates have constructed the discourses, as well as how they are framed in relation to one another. I briefly explain them along with some examples, as a preamble to the analysis that will follow on all the main points of contention where advocates have interpreted concepts and meanings in fundamentally different ways.

The discourses are opposed (or 'opposing'), in the sense that they 'look in opposite directions', and also reject each other. They have different views on rights, on the appropriate role of the state, as well as discourses that remain strong within different large segments of society and backed up by legal principles, national and international. One simple example of the ways in which advocates see and frame their discourses as 'opposed' is (going back to the fundamentals of the debate), that while many of the interviewed 'pro-life' advocates see abortion as "a murder",[141] many in the opposing side of the debate see it as "a right for women"[142] – clearly not just a difference in nuance, degree, or other marginal distinction, but one of frontally clashing interpretations of the same practice or concept.

Calling the discourses 'opposed' is relatively straightforward and easy to understand, intuitive even, for those familiar with almost any abortion debate. The second characteristic, 'polarized', merits more nuance as this polarization also is embedded within a larger context of *general* sociopolitical polarization in our current days. In this context, '*polarized*' refers to the fact that not only are these groups in the abortion debate presenting fundamentally different interpretations, effectively clashing with each other in their propositions, but the term is meant to bring attention to the fact, confirmed on the ground, that the individual advocates in this debate have exceptionally little contact to opposing advocates, or to people outside what could be called their ideological network or 'echo chamber'.

Looking at online debates and exchanges for example on social media platforms, one could have the illusion of a lively debate where opposed sides are indeed discussing in-person, on similar forums or by being present on the same platforms. But it is known (and intuitive also in this day and age) that 'online debates' on social media platforms are not reflective of how the true in-person exchanges play out (if they are happening at all) and that online exchanges rarely are fruitful for policy creation (even in the cases where they can still be called 'rational debates'). At least in the Mexican case, during the cycles of fieldwork for research, it was surprisingly difficult to see advocates on the 'opposing sides' ever being present in the same times and places for any kind of in-person exchange. Even the opposing marches or public protests happened on different days, presumably attended by entirely different crowds.

One simple but illustrative example of this polarization is that at no point during fieldwork was it possible to obtain a photograph of the blue and green 'handkerchiefs' (the physical 'pro' and 'anti-abortion' signifiers born in the Argentinian protests) being worn at the same time, in the same place: it was always a 'tide' of one or the other colour exclusively. Searching online, too, it is quite difficult to find any photograph, from any recent public protest on abortion *anywhere*, showing both symbols together in one frame: we find either a photo with the 'wave' of blue or one with the 'tide' of green. Rather than foster meaningful dialogue across the 'sides', advocacy (and especially the more modern advocacy carried out through social media) seems to have *solidified* both positions, where they move further and further apart.

Only very exceptionally were the interviewed experts capable of offering contact details of someone from an 'opposite side' of the debate,[143] suggesting an almost complete lack of communication between opposed groups in the wider debate. Advocates also tend towards discursive extremes; representing their opponents at their most radical and caricaturized (using numerous 'strawman fallacies'), and effectively distanced in a way which makes compromise difficult. They often organize conferences, public events (of which I personally attended three with varying audience sizes: the two public protests and the public conference by Jorge Serrano Limón), and use diffusion channels which all tend to be given attention mostly by people who already identify strongly with that similar discourse.

From analyzing similar instances of polarization in countries like Argentina, or in regional organizations such as the Inter-American institutions, it can be observed that in this multilogue (nationally, regionally and internationally), opposing advocates are often not sitting at the same table, nor are they often talking to each other in any way conducive to policy creation. 'Pro-life' and 'pro-choice' groups in Mexico have put forward discourses where they present this binary vision, each group claiming to be 'constantly antagonized' or victimized by the opposing, 'more powerful' group.[144]

Another curious aspect of this polarization is that advocates often ascribe unrelated ideological points to the opposing groups, making assumptions on, for example, economic right- or left-wing sympathies, religious affiliation or lack thereof, stance on and relations to LGBTQ+ movements (especially 'pro-life' advocates tend to see a larger narrative where abortion and LGBTQ+ issues are allegedly part of a larger movement of "anti-family globalist efforts"[145]), or other unrelated political points of contention. Although some of those generalizing connections can sometimes be accurate, they clearly represent problematic, automatic assumptions on the part of advocates, who often simplify the debate not only about their own propositions but also by ascribing an entire, often distorted worldview to their opponents and their ideas – further stripped of nuance and further estranging themselves from dialogue.

Thirdly, on them being *'competing'* discourses, this bears some similarities to what I mean by calling them *'opposed'*, but with a heavier emphasis on how their proposed legal and normative solutions are mutually exclusive in policy enactment: as the debate has unfolded in Mexico, it remains a case where opposed groups of advocates propose competing policies, legal reforms and solutions where they perceive a situation of '*our* laws versus *theirs*'.[146] They do not create 'common', but rather 'competing' policy, in a case of continued "lawfare".[147] As the opposed discourses remain strong and backed by pieces of national and international law, they aim for mutually exclusive legal solutions, the ideas frontally opposed.

We could perhaps say that 'every case of competing laws is a case of contestation, but not every case of contestation is a case of competing laws'. In this debate, the normative changes seen by advocates as 'progress' in either direction tend to rely not on dialogue or compromise about a 'middle ground' but rather on temporary majorities in parliaments or constituencies, or on having larger numbers of supporters than 'the opposing side' has in a particular context or event or instance, in order to push forward a normative proposition.

And every proposition will soon be challenged by opposing advocates, typically in *their* respective 'echo chamber', or by concentrating on furthering opposed norms in another scenario (for example another Mexican state) where they do have a legislative or political majority. While advocates often react directly to the propositions furthered by their ideological opponents (as was seen when reforms were challenged at the Mexican Supreme Court, and when advocates reactively contest a reform), when the direct reaction does not yield the expected result, the strategy then turns to looking at the places, scenarios, and documents where 'success' is more likely. For example, an interviewed expert from the state of Aguascalientes spoke of travelling to another Mexican state, to speak in favour of reforming that other state's subnational Constitution.[148] Another expert from Mexico City also mentioned frequent travels to different subnational states to meet with similarly minded advocates and organize events, conferences, book presentations, etc. and push for policy changes where they seem the most likely to find success.[149]

Advocates on all positions within the debate are very certain in their own advancements, quite enthusiastic about their respective recent 'victories' in local legislation; many of them seemed sure of great progress and 'near victory' (meaning, their belief that the time is approaching for their biggest desired reforms to successfully pass), precisely *because* they concentrate on the places, moments, crowds, and pieces of legislation where they see fertile ground for their proposals and where success is most likely. Opposed advocates all remain enthusiastic that the social and political environment will become ever more receptive of their discourses, ideas, and norm proposals and certain that future generations will fully embrace their message.

Notes

1 Comisión Nacional de los Derechos Humanos, 2016.
2 Wiener, 2014.
3 Fieldwork interview: Expert No. 3.
4 Fieldwork interview: Expert No. 24.
5 Fieldwork interview: Expert No. 1.
6 Fieldwork interview: Expert No. 2.
7 Mexican Government. Criminal Code of Mexico City (Distrito Federal), 2002. Last amended February 2021.
8 Pérez Hernández, 2017, p. 25.
9 Fieldwork interview: Expert No. 6.
10 Fieldwork interview: Expert No. 11.
11 Olivares *et al.*, 2007.
12 No regulation exists that limits the service exclusively to residents of Mexico City; so in practice women from other subnational states travel to Mexico City to use abortion services, public and private.
13 Fieldwork interview: Expert No. 17.
14 Fieldwork interview: Expert No. 25.
15 Fieldwork interview: Expert No. 7.
16 Fieldwork material: Recording of Public Conference by Jorge Serrano Limón, 2019.
17 Fieldwork interview: Experts No. 6, 7 and 26.
18 Pérez Hernández, 2017, p. 25.
19 Fieldwork interview: Expert No. 7.
20 In some states, the reformed articles say that "life should be protected from the moment of *fertilization*". The technicalities concerning distinctions between 'conception' and 'fertilization' are sometimes relevant in other issue areas of medicine and bioethics, for example concerning *in vitro* fertilization, where there might be a meaningful difference. However, the medical minutia distinguishing the two concepts has practically no effect on the abortion debate, nor does it really affect the spirit of the changes desired by 'pro-life' groups.
21 Interviewed expert No. 17.
22 Fieldwork interview: Expert No. 6.
23 Fieldwork interview: Expert No. 11.
24 Fieldwork interview: Expert No. 17.
25 Fieldwork interview: Expert No. 6.
26 Fieldwork interview: Expert No. 10.
27 Fieldwork interview: Expert No. 10.
28 Bartolini Esparza and Alarcón Loayza, 2017, p. 46.
29 Fieldwork interview: Expert No. 11.
30 Fieldwork interview: Expert No. 24.
31 Bartolini Esparza and Alarcón Loayza, 2017, p. 44.
32 Fieldwork interview: Expert No. 7.
33 Fieldwork interview: Expert No. 24.
34 Fieldwork interview: Expert No. 6.
35 Fieldwork interview: Expert No. 11.
36 Bartolini Esparza and Alarcón Loayza, 2017, pp. 49–50.
37 Mizrahi Nedvedovich and Zúñiga Tapia, 2017, p. 59.
38 Fieldwork interview: Expert No. 14.
39 Fieldwork interview: Expert No. 1.

40 Bartolini Esparza and Alarcón Loayza, 2017, pp. 42–43.
41 Fieldwork interview: Expert No. 24.
42 Bartolini Esparza and Alarcón Loayza, 2017, p. 44.
43 Fieldwork interview: Expert No. 6.
44 Fieldwork interview: Expert No. 6.
45 Pérez Hernández, 2017, p. 25.
46 Fieldwork interview: Expert No. 1.
47 Fieldwork interview: Expert No. 6.
48 In this context, "Executive-Power-created" means that these norms are created by the corresponding Secretariats or Ministries. It does not have to do with the President, who has the power to propose legislation his- or herself, but not to create their own NOMs.
49 Criminal Code of the State of Yucatán. 2017, Article 393, IV.
50 Fieldwork interview: Expert No. 11.
51 Fieldwork interview: Expert No. 7.
52 Fieldwork interview: Expert No. 11.
53 Fieldwork interview: Expert No. 26.
54 Santana Ángeles *et al.*, 2017.
55 Fieldwork interview: Expert No. 11.
56 Fieldwork interview: Expert No. 5.
57 Fieldwork interview: Expert No. 11.
58 Fieldwork interview: Expert No. 8.
59 Fieldwork interview: Expert No. 11.
60 Pérez Hernández, 2017, p. 23.
61 UN Office of the High Commissioner for Human Rights. General Comment No. 36 to the ICCPR, 2018.
62 Communications by Committee on the Rights of Persons with Disabilities (CPD) to OHCHR process of drafting General Comment No. 36 to the ICCPR on the Right to Life, 2017.
63 OHCHR Draft General Comment No. 36 on the Right to Life. Communications.
64 All phrases taken from: Fieldwork material, secondary data: photographic documentation gathered at protests.
65 Fieldwork interview: Expert No. 6.
66 Fieldwork interview: Expert No. 9.
67 Fieldwork interview: Expert No. 8.
68 Fieldwork material, secondary data: photographic documentation gathered at protests. Mexico City, October 2018.
69 Fieldwork interview: Expert No. 6.
70 Fieldwork material, secondary data: photographic documentation gathered at protests.
71 Fieldwork interview: Expert No. 14.
72 Fieldwork interview: Expert No. 20.
73 Fieldwork interview: Expert No. 12.
74 Fieldwork interview: Expert No. 22.
75 See Wiener, 2014.
76 Fieldwork interview: Expert No. 6.
77 Keck and Sikkink, 1999, p. 93.
78 Fieldwork material: Documentation piece No. 17.
79 Fieldwork material: Documentation piece No. 27.
80 Fieldwork material: Documentation piece No. 16.
81 Keck and Sikkink, 1999, p. 94.
82 Oaxacan congressperson from: Fieldwork material, Secondary Documentation piece No. 16.
83 Pérez Hernández, 2017, p. 26.
84 Mexican Government, Secretariat of Health, 2015.

85 Comisión Nacional de Derechos Humanos (CNDH), Marco Normativo, 2016.
86 Fieldwork interview: Expert No. 6.
87 Fieldwork interview: Expert No. 4.
88 Bartolini Esparza and Alarcón Loayza, 2017, p. 46.
89 Fieldwork interview: Expert No. 9.
90 Bartolini Esparza and Alarcón Loayza, 2017, pp. 48–49.
91 Fieldwork Materials: Documentation Piece No. 15.
92 Fieldwork interview: Expert No. 24.
93 Fieldwork interview: Expert No. 6.
94 Fieldwork interview: Expert No. 26.
95 Fieldwork interview: Expert No. 1.
96 Fieldwork interview: Expert No. 2.
97 See Wiener, 2014.
98 Fieldwork interview: Expert No. 21.
99 Fieldwork interview: Expert No. 22.
100 Fieldwork interview: Expert No. 17.
101 Fieldwork interview: Expert No. 21.
102 It's possible, however, that in some subnational states, implementation of NOM0046 is yet to happen not because of disagreement or a purposeful contestation through failure to comply, but simply because it has not been a political priority of local executive powers.
103 Fieldwork interview: Expert No. 11.
104 Mexican Government, General Law on Health, 1984. Last amended November 2020.
105 Aristegui Noticias, 2021.
106 Expansión Política, 2019.
107 Fieldwork interview: Expert No. 20.
108 Center for Reproductive Rights, World Map of Abortion Laws, 2021.
109 Fieldwork interview: Expert No. 13.
110 García, 2021.
111 La Vanguardia, 2021.
112 Mizrahi Nedvedovich and Zúñiga Tapia 2017, p. 54.
113 Bartolini Esparza and Alarcón Loayza, 2017, p. 49.
114 Fieldwork interview: Expert No. 6.
115 Alarcón Loayza *et al.*, 2017, p. 15.
116 Fieldwork interview: Expert No. 9.
117 Fieldwork interview: Expert No. 20.
118 Fieldwork interview: Expert No. 21.
119 Fieldwork interview: Expert No. 1.
120 Mizrahi Nedvedovich and Zúñiga Tapia, 2017, p. 57.
121 Fieldwork interview: Expert No. 16.
122 Such is the case for the interviewed advocate from 'Católicas por el Derecho a Decidir'.
123 Pérez Hernández, 2017, p. 21.
124 Lamas, 2014, p. 93 and 116.
125 Fieldwork interview: Expert No. 6.
126 In the likes of the citizen initiatives for articles in the new Constitution of Mexico City, sent by interviewed experts No. 5 and No. 11.
127 Pérez Hernández, 2017, p. 27.
128 Fieldwork interview: Expert No. 16.
129 Mizrahi Nedvedovich and Zúñiga Tapia, 2017, p. 53.
130 Mizrahi Nedvedovich and Zúñiga Tapia, 2017, p. 64.
131 Fieldwork interview: Expert No. 12.
132 National Pro-Life Committee, Mexico, 2003.
133 Fieldwork interview: Expert No. 3.

134 Fieldwork interview: Expert No. 2.
135 Fieldwork interview: Expert No. 7.
136 Fieldwork interview: Expert No. 6.
137 Fieldwork interview: Expert No. 7.
138 Fieldwork interview: Expert No. 23.
139 Fieldwork interview: Expert No. 26.
140 Fieldwork interview: Expert No. 4.
141 Fieldwork interview: Expert No. 7.
142 Fieldwork interview: Expert No. 18.
143 The only instance of this happening during fieldwork was interviewed expert No. 23 (identified as a 'pro-life' advocate) providing the contact details of expert No. 21 (identified as a 'pro-choice' advocate).
144 Pérez Hernández, 2017, p. 19.
145 Fieldwork interview: Expert No. 9.
146 Fieldwork interview: Expert No. 24.
147 See Sieder *et al.*, 2014.
148 Fieldwork interview: Expert No. 6.
149 Fieldwork interview: Expert No. 10.

References

Alarcón Loayza, N., Bartolini Esparza, M., Contreras Díaz, A.J., Mizrahi Nedvedovich, C., Ortiz Trujillo, D., Pérez Hernández, C., and Zúñiga Tapia, F.R. (2017). *Aborto: La Política de un Estado Claudicante*. Todas y Todos Valemos en México. Mexico City: Consejo Editorial de la Cámara de Diputados, LXIII Legislatura.

Aristegui Noticias. (2021). "SCJN no anuló la objeción de conciencia del personal médico en casos de aborto: Arturo Zaldívar." https://aristeguinoticias.com/0710/mexico/scjn-no-anulo-la-objecion-de-conciencia-de-los-medicos-en-casos-de-aborto-arutro-zaldivar/

Bartolini Esparza, M., and Alarcón Loayza, N. (2017). "Análisis de las Normas y Sentencias Relacionadas con el Aborto en México Durante los Últimos 25 Años." In *Aborto: La Política de un Estado Claudicante*. Todas y Todos Valemos en México, 31–51. Mexico City: Consejo Editorial de la Cámara de Diputados, LXIII Legislatura.

Center for Reproductive Rights. (2021). "The World's Abortion Laws: Map." http://worldabortionlaws.com/map/. Accessed November 2021.

Comisión Nacional de los Derechos Humanos (CNDH). (2016). *NOM-046-SSA2-2005. Violencia Familiar, Sexual Y Contra Las Mujeres. Criterios Para La Prevención Y Atención*. Marco Normativo CNDH.

Expansión Política. (2019). "El Congreso de Oaxaca aprueba la despenalización del aborto." September 25. https://politica.expansion.mx/estados/2019/09/25/la-ley-en-favor-del-aborto-en-oaxaca-avanza-es-aprobada-en-lo-general

García, A.K. (2021). *A dos años del aborto legal en Oaxaca: ni tan universal, ni tan gratuito, ni tan seguro*. El Economista. https://www.eleconomista.com.mx/arteseideas/A-dos-anos-del-aborto-legal-en-Oaxaca-ni-tan-universal-ni-tan-gratuito-ni-tan-seguro-20211120-0011.html

Keck, M.E., and Sikkink, K. (1999). "Transnational Advocacy Networks in International and Regional Politics." *International Social Science Journal*, 51(159), 89–101.

Lamas, M. (2014). *Cuerpo, Sexo y Política*. Series Debate Feminista. Mexico City: Editorial Océano.

La Vanguardia. (2021). "El Supremo de México legaliza el aborto en una decisión histórica." September 7. https://www.lavanguardia.com/internacional/20210907/7706049/supremo-mexico-legaliza-aborto-embarazo.html

Mexican Government. (1984). "Ley General de Salud." https://www.diputados.gob.mx/LeyesBiblio/pdf_mov/Ley_General_de_Salud.pdf. Accessed November 2020.

Mexican Government. (2002). "Código Penal para el Distrito Federal" (Criminal Code of Mexico City). https://paot.org.mx/centro/codigos/df/pdf/2021/COD_PENAL_DF_26_02_2021.pdf. Accessed February 2021.

Mexican Government, Secretariat of Health. (2015). "Normas Oficiales Mexicanas." https://www.gob.mx/salud/en/documentos/normas-oficiales-mexicanas-9705

Mizrahi Nedvedovich, C., and Zúñiga Tapia, F.R. (2017). "Las recomendaciones de los organismos internacionales como mecanismos de presión política." In *Aborto: La Política de un Estado Claudicante*. Todas y Todos Valemos en México, 53–67. Mexico City: Consejo Editorial de la Cámara de Diputados, LXIII Legislatura.

National Pro-Life Committee, Mexico (Comité Nacional Pro-Vida). (2003). "Perspectiva de Género: Sus Peligros y Alcances." http://www.comiteprovida.org/articulos-informacion/sexualidad-humana/perspectiva-de-genero/. Accessed May 2017.

Olivares, E., Muñoz, A., and Sevin, M. (2007). "Rechaza Carpizo impugnación de CNDH a la reforma sobre aborto" (Carpizo Rejects court challenge by CNDH to abortion reform). *La Jornada*, May 28. https://www.jornada.com.mx/2007/05/28/index.php?section=capital&article=038n1cap

Pérez Hernández, C. (2017). "Antecedentes del Aborto en México." In *Aborto: La Política de un Estado Claudicante*, edited by Pérez Hernández, *et al*. Mexico City: Consejo Editorial de la Cámara de Diputados, LXIII Legislatura.

Santana Ángeles, F., Vega Millán, I., Méndez Méndez, M.J., and Galván Madrigal, J.A. (2017). "La experiencia de archivo abierto en la Asamblea Constituyente." *Revista de la Biblioteca y Archivo Histórico de la Asamblea Legislativa Plurinacional*, (11), 52.

Sieder, R., Gianella, C., Gloppen, S., Gargarella, R., Bergallo, P., Gonzales, A.C., Peñas, A., de Assis Machado, M. R. R., and Ely Yamin, A. (2014–2017). "Abortion Rights Lawfare in Latin America." Research Project at CMI Chr. Michelsen Institute, Norway. Norwegian Research Council. https://www.cmi.no/projects/1841-abortion-rights-lawfare-in-latin-america. Accessed August 26, 2020.

United Nations Office of the High Commissioner for Human Rights, Human Rights Committee. (2018). "General Comment no. 36, Article 6 (Right to Life)." CCPR/C/GC/35, 3 September 2019. https://www.refworld.org/docid/5e5e75e04.html

Wiener, A. (2014). *A Theory of Contestation*. Springer.

5 Advocates in Times of Lawfare

This chapter engages in a detailed exercise of placing the discourses for and against legal abortion in Mexico 'side by side' in their most important points and the most relevant contested dimensions. This will allow for a true 'parallel' analysis of their strategies, concepts that they propose and those that they react against, what they perceive as recent victories, international texts of most relevance, etc. The analytical focus is placed on how advocates *contest*, *interpret*, *propose*, and *refute* a variety of *concepts, norms*, *meanings*, *principles*, as well as *each other*, through two discourses that remain strong within large sectors of society. They do so by engaging in modes of contestation that can be *discursive* or *behavioural*, *reactive* or *proactive*. Figure 5.1 presents this as a scheme.

Not Talking to Each Other: Separate Ontologies of Two Parallel Discourses

In this in-depth analysis of the discourses side by side, it is helpful to remember that it showcases an example of norm contestation through two opposing, polarized, and competing discourses, with usually colliding interpretations of rights and principles. In this context, 'contestation' (of one same norm) is not the same as 'collision' (of two or more norms). This case displays both events happening, through the advocates' discourses, advocacy, and practice. Opposed groups of advocates ascribe differing meanings to many concepts (*contesting* practically every single one), leading into two entire sets of *colliding* ontologies. Different norms collide when, for instance, various rights are understood to clash with each other, mainly the unborn's 'right to life' colliding with a woman's 'right to choose' over her own body – which might include choosing to interrupt a pregnancy.

Analyzing the discourses as opposed in this manner, the detailed mapping follows the main concepts observed, the notions proposed and refuted, the main recent advocacy achievements, and other noteworthy observations for the case study. In some specific cases, where a possible normative type can already be identified as clearly associated with that observation, it is marked as "T1", "T2", or "T3".

DOI:10.4324/9781032642338-5

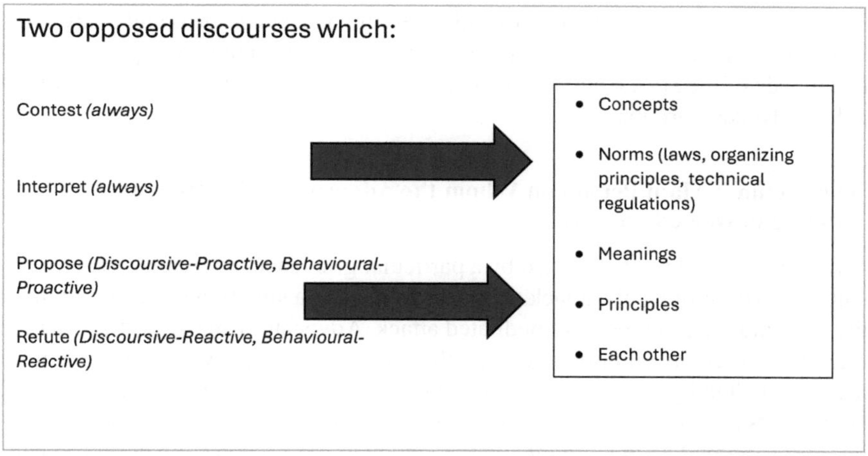

Figure 5.1 Parallel discourses in norm contestation.
Source: Figure by author, based on Wiener, 2018.

The Points in Common

In the intention to ultimately find 'pathways to dialogue', this parallel comparison begins with looking at common points, found within opposed advocates in the abortion debate, to later proceed into the many concepts in which they ideologically 'part ways' and confront each other, in their opposed discourses – to later hopefully point at ideas that may 'reunite' them again in a measure of common ground. It can be observed that the opposed groups:

- Remain strong, vocal; have their own discourse which is often circulated and followed off- and online; claim many recent legislative and advocacy victories (laws reformed, policies put in place, newer NGO's advocating).
- Contest and challenge: existing laws, human rights documents national and international, interpretations, meanings, each other.
- Appeal (with solid legal grounds) to internationally recognized human rights, in Covenants, Pacts, and Declarations.
- Are very active in recent political and public demonstration, having ongoing conversation with their followers.
- Are the case that "brought federalism alive" in Mexico[1]: pushing the diverse subnational states to each create their own specific and differentiated laws for the first time, instead of just roughly copying Mexico City's laws.
- Engage transnationally with allies abroad and are active in the global political community: with 'sister' organizations in other countries, sending communications during debates in United Nations Human Rights forums, often organizing events with international attendance.

The following sections will take several different concepts or ideas and analyze the opposed interpretations given or contested by advocates on the pro-legalization (to the left side of the tables) and the self-identified as 'pro-life' (to the right side of the tables) advocacy groups.

"The Victim": Main Person on Whom the Advocacy Is Centred, or Claiming to Defend and Protect

Victims are those directly affected by a particular grievance, be it a disease, an accident, a violation of rights, a lack of access to justice, a situation of profound inequity, a natural disaster, or a premeditated attack. Advocates usually portray victims in a way that elicits emotion and empathy, in order to amplify the voice of those directly affected by a problem. While 'pro-legalization' advocates claim to defend the interests of women, 'pro-life' groups have centred on the unborn as a clear victim: easily framed as *the ultimate victim*, one who has no voice, no access to contestation or representation, and is clearly incapable of any form of self-defence or agency. Advocates in the field are familiar with the concept of 'victim' and 'victimhood' as a mobilization point for advocacy; often they themselves pose and answer the question: *Who is the victim of abortion?* (where 'pro-life' advocates clearly see the unborn as the victim most in need of protection, although recently they have engaged in a narrative shift by way of painting the woman as 'a second victim').

Meanwhile, pro-legalization advocates rather tend to hinge the 'victimhood question' on a premise of a woman having lacked access to *legal* abortion, asking rather: '*Who is the victim of a potentially unsafe abortion, if it is illegal?*'[2] The woman seeking control over her own body, who cannot have it if abortion is inaccessible and/or unsafe, is framed as a victim. She also usually lacks direct self-representation and access to contestation, most strongly *in this specific case*, due to social stigma.

The portrayal of victimhood in the case of abortion is interesting to analyze: 'pro-life' activists give preponderance to *the unborn child* as the most relevant victim, as opposed to groups who advocate for the liberalization of abortion laws, who tend to see *the pregnant women who desire to end their pregnancies* (especially the poorest and most marginalized) as victims in dire need of healthcare and rights fulfilment, whose injury or death can be prevented by accessing safe and legal abortion. But 'pro-life' advocates contest and reject this notion,[3] for in the words of many of them, the fact that illegal abortions are risky to women is not a good enough reason to legalize them. To most of them, the issue is a clear-cut moral choice where the woman, to protect her own life and health, *"simply should not choose to have an illegal abortion"*,[4] and they often draw comparisons to the

Table 5.1 "The Victim" as an Object of Advocacy

Pro-legalization	*'Pro-life'*
Woman seeking control over her own body	The unborn

choice to commit other crimes for 'selfish reasons' and ending up harmed in the process. For them, the victim is clearly the unborn child, portrayed as the ultimately innocent and defenceless being, for whom it is easy to stir up emotion.

For some in the 'pro-life' movements, the mother becomes a *transgressor* and a guilt-bearer (assuming her abortion was consented) *for even wanting or attempting to abort*, although in recent years, this vision has been changing in favour of the 'pro-life' narrative shift of reframing the woman as 'a second victim' who is also harmed by abortion and "often regrets it, suffering lifelong emotional pain"[5] or who was "deceived into thinking that abortion was a solution".[6] In their view, what a woman needs (if she is to be seen in this case as a holder of unfulfilled rights) is access to "*real* healthcare, not abortion",[7] "government assistance",[8] or "possibilities to give the child up for adoption".[9] But it will still be the case in many traditional societies that women who abort (or attempt to) rarely ever speak about it, for they risk being met with great hostility and vitriol, regardless of if it was legal or illegal, safe or unsafe.

This issue of 'characterization' and 'victim portrayal' also speaks about the characterization of women as 'good' or 'bad' mothers. Across Latin American societies, the archetypical 'good mother' is portrayed as a self-neglecting caregiver, sacrificing individual needs to put others' needs first, always bearing pure intention towards their children. In the context of this debate, for very traditional or religious groups, women can sometimes be portrayed as *victims* whose legal rights were violated in cases of maternal death or injury due to medical negligence, but not often in any other situations, and especially not in situations of voluntary abortion. A recent narrative shift from 'pro-life' groups has been embracing the idea of seeing the woman as 'a second victim of abortion', a more modern approach that attempts to paint 'pro-life' movements as "also feminist, because women are victims and also because half of the aborted foetuses are female".[10] But the more traditional 'pro-life' views would still tend to portray aborting women as "the ultimate *bad mother* or 'irresponsible woman' who does not want to be a mother" – often ignoring the fact that a significant amount of women who abort in Mexico already have other children.[11]

Human Rights: When Opposed Groups All Claim to Defend Them

While opposed groups of advocates claim to protect, defend, and uphold human rights (stemming from the fact that there are two potential rights holders in this case), naturally they do not advocate from the same angle. Advocates all mention 'rights' in the abstract, but the longer discourses that follow tend to sound

Table 5.2 The Angle of Human Rights Defence

Pro-legalization	*'Pro-life'*
Defending human rights from an angle of: Gender equality; feminism; secularism of the state	**Defending human rights from an angle of:** "Tradition", religious and moral principle (family, traditional gender roles)

quite different. The pro-legalization side tends to mention notions of gender equality, feminism (in its many waves and currents), as well as the official secularity of the Mexican state much more often, as well as the "separation of Church and state"[12] – something not mentioned by any interviewed 'pro-life' advocates. The latter are prone to speak of traditional gender roles, the 'traditional' or 'natural' family,[13] as well as religious and moral principle. Many 'pro-life' advocates however are aware that religious discourse does not resonate with everyone when debating public policy and that it is better kept for advocacy on a more 'private' or like-minded sphere.

The messages and symbols observed in the 'pro-life' protest of October 2018 had a strong presence of religiosity, especially Christian and Catholic (and in light of the motherhood-related topic, with much imagery alluding to the Virgin Mary), but in longer interviews with 'pro-life' advocates who are experts in law or policymaking, religion was not often mentioned. They rather frame their advocacy in secular terms such as, the right to life being 'absolute', and its nature as "the fundamental pre-requisite for the protection of any other human right to make sense".[14]

The upcoming section on narrative shifts details this better, but it was also observed that, in recent years, 'pro-life' advocates have also had important narrative shifts in this area: as opposed to the more traditional or religious discourses of the past, many of them now claim to embrace 'true feminism' (e.g. through the idea that they "also protect the unborn girls"),[15] or "true gender equality"[16] (by elevating motherhood to a certain 'sacred' status in policy and social practice, obligating the state to support and protect it) but also "the true protection of human rights for all, from the moment of conception".[17]

Fundamental Principles Proposed through Advocacy

One of the most frontal, fundamental clashes happen at the level of the *principles* that advocates attempt to enshrine (i.e. codify into law), and the way in which they clash with the visions by opposed advocates. Firstly, *abortion* itself, as a practice and as an act, is framed by the pro-legalization advocates as 'a right' (if at least in *some* contexts), whereas 'pro-life' advocates see it as a 'murder' to which few or no permissible exceptions should exist. That one same act is seen as either 'a right' or 'a murder' not only shows a stark confrontation, beyond a mere 'difference in degree', but this clash, in and of itself, is also used by 'pro-life' advocates as alleged proof that the legalization of abortion cannot possibly be 'a right'. One 'pro-life' interviewee was quoted as saying that *"a thing cannot be 'a right' if the very same concept, in other circumstances, is 'a crime', somewhere else within the same legal system or even the same legal document"*.[18]

In Mexico City and the subnational states that have decriminalized it, abortion is still codified as 'a crime', on the condition that more than 12 weeks' gestation have passed – a boundary that 'pro-life' advocates see as entirely arbitrary. In other legal texts of Mexico City and those subnational states, such as their local Health Laws, abortions done before the 12th week are redefined as "Voluntary Interruption of Pregnancy", which is then codified so as to give access in terms of 'a woman's

Table 5.3 Fundamental Principles Proposed through Advocacy

Pro-legalization	*'Pro-life'*
Abortion as "a right", at least in some cases	Abortion as "murder"; life as an absolute human right with no exceptions (T1)
Consented Motherhood and the "right to choose"	The unborn is another separate person with full rights (concept of *personhood*); not all personal choices are morally acceptable
Legal personhood starting from birth (T2); or at some point later than "conception"	Legal personhood from conception (T1/T2)
Abortion as a public health issue	Abortion as a moral/criminal issue
Privacy over one's own body	The life of the unborn overrides the mother's privacy rights
The state as a transgressor: not granting women their rights	The state as a transgressor: not granting the unborn's right to life, but sometimes women and doctors are transgressors as well, if "abortion is murder"

right'. Naturally, the difference between "Voluntary Interruption" and 'abortion' is entirely non-existent in the eyes of 'pro-life' advocates. While it is not within the scope of this book to resolve whether it is true that "something cannot be a right and a crime in the same legal system, depending on factors such as temporality",[19] it is a point that does merit reflection, considering context as well as the intention of the norm itself.

Another concept strongly and often proposed by pro-legalization advocates in Mexico is that of 'consented motherhood', on which 'pro-life' advocates tend to agree only insofar as consent is exercised *before* a conception happens. Once a conception has happened, for the 'pro-life', the unborn is a separate person, deserving legal protection from that moment, overriding any notion of 'consented motherhood' or a 'right to choose'. In their view, not every choice is morally acceptable (a notion that everyone living under the rule of law and human rights principles can accept), and no 'right to choose' can trump the absolute 'right to life' (a Type 1 fundamental principle).

The matters of 'legal personhood' are very clear for 'pro-life' advocates, who in general agree that it exists from the moment of conception. Some of them agree that, in *a few* exceptional circumstances such as the life of the mother being at risk (and only in such a dire case as that of the mother's life being directly at odds with the unborn's), then the legal personhood of the mother may override that of the unborn. On this point, it is telling that in the book "*Abortion: the Policy of an Abdicating State*", Pérez Hernández refers to the exceptions to abortion prohibition, somewhat dismissively, as a *"catalogue of excuses"*.[20]

These situations where the mother's life might be at risk if the pregnancy is continued are constantly pointed out by 'pro-life' advocates as being exceptional and a tiny minority of abortion cases. And while most of them do admit an exception to abortion bans in such a case, the admission is often followed by philosophical ponderings about 'intentionality' (sometimes based on solid philosophical principles, but at times resting on theology disguised as 'bioethics'), regarding how exactly a doctor should proceed in such a case.

"If the continuation of a pregnancy really does put the mother's life at risk, a doctor must not 'abort' in the sense of intentionally causing the unborn's death; rather he or she should treat the mother's condition, knowing that the foetus might die. Or they can induce birth or perform a Caesarean section if possible, causing the child to be born pre-term. If the foetus still dies, it was a natural consequence, but not an intentional killing".[21]

In other words, their vision of protecting the unborn's life at all costs still stands as predominant, even in cases where it is directly at odds with the mother's survival.

For pro-legalization advocates, the matters about the legal beginning of personhood are trickier. The vast majority of them do *not* suggest that abortion should be legal at *'any'* gestational point. Such a view belongs only to a fringe minority (and no advocate interviewed for this book showed support for that idea). The matter of *when* exactly the legal protection of personhood should begin has blurrier boundaries, which can respond to different criteria (viability outside the womb, medical discussions about the existence of sentience, capacity to feel pain, or merely the mother's own will and desire), some of them admittedly arbitrary – and it also depends entirely on the intents and purposes for which the definition is needed. For example, it is obvious that for the purposes of creating a birth certificate with a name and a nationality, 'birth' is the point that matters, but for other legal matters, an existence of personhood before birth can be considered.

Where to draw a line for the beginning of 'personhood' is a matter that clearly depends on what issue one is discussing, and in what context: in Mexico, there are different considerations if one is discussing civil family law (such as inheritances), or a miscarriage caused through violence, or a voluntary abortion because a pregnancy was a result of sexual abuse. 'Beginning of legally protected personhood', then, seems to be a much more context-sensitive matter in the pro-legalization discourses, one existing within the "legitimacy gaps" of different discussions with several possibilities for "Type 2" organizing principles. One of such organizing principles perhaps being the 'gradually increasing protection of personhood' before birth, as has been stated in cases such as *Artavia Murillo vs. Costa Rica* (where the Inter-American Commission on Human Rights determined that, for the matters related to *in vitro* fertilization, embryos do not have personhood).

Then follow the reflections about abortion being either 'a matter of public health' or falling within the 'right to privacy' – both notions rejected by 'pro-life' advocates on the grounds that the absolute 'right to life' trumps any such considerations. They also contest and react against the notion of abortion being 'part of reproductive health', denouncing instead the ideological influences that have placed "newer concepts such as consented motherhood"[22] on the table of social movements. As had been mentioned, publications such as *Abortion: The Policy of an Abdicating State* challenge the idea that abortion legalization in Mexico City actually reduced maternal mortality or improved women's health in any way – something that by nature is not easy to prove, as the true impact of unsafe and illegal abortions is hard to measure due to its illegality.

Numerous advocates identifying as 'pro-life' challenge and contest the consideration of abortion as a health-related issue,[23] placing it rather as a moral issue: one where allowing for exceptions to the abortion ban will eventually lead (through a supposed 'slippery slope') to complete liberalization and to the use of abortion as "a common contraceptive method".[24] In so doing, 'pro-life' advocates attempt to appropriate claims of "true protection of women's health". In their webpages and communications, many pro-life advocacy groups claim (often citing no sources, or sources of dubious quality) that legalizing abortion actively damages women's health by increasing their risk of numerous diseases (including breast cancer),[25] or by failing completely to prevent maternal deaths,[26] or by leading to mental illness (all of which is disproven by medical associations and other institutions such as the World Health Organization).

Similar claims about the supposed risks and damages of abortion, "even when fully legalized", appear in the pamphlet called "Love Life for Me" (*Ama La Vida Por Mí*) that was widely distributed during the 'pro-life' protest that I attended on October 2018 in Mexico City. Photos and copies of the same pamphlet (which is lacking any credible scientific sources, apart from a couple references to studies and magazines from the 1960s) can be found online, as it is apparently a common piece of publicity used in 'pro-life' protests across Spanish-speaking countries in Latin America, from Mexico to Argentina.

One can also analyze the notion of who is a transgressor in cases of abortion, where both sides often agree on *'the state as a transgressor'*, but for different reasons. "Duty bearers" become transgressors when they fail to protect, respect, and fulfil a right, or to deliver justice. It is usually governments that fall under this category, since, according to Keck and Sikkink, they are the primary guarantors of rights, but also usually the main violators.[27] In this particular case, it is governments who are pressured to either legalize or criminalize abortion. Also worth mentioning is the fact that, for anti-abortion advocates, a woman who aborts (or even desires to) is sometimes portrayed as a transgressor who violates the rights of her unborn child. Even if a woman were to die because of consented unsafe abortion (as it indeed happens often, wherever abortion is illegal), it seems unlikely that her image and testimony would garner widespread compassion in many traditional societies, and it's likely that in the eyes of many 'pro-life' advocates, she would still be seen as a transgressor, even if she dies. In Mexico, this has been starting to change only recently, through the reframing of women who abort as 'a second victim'.

This issue patently shows the fluidity of concepts related to human rights, as well as their construction through struggle and through *meaning negotiation* and *meaning making*. In various human rights debates (especially those related to gender roles and roles within the traditional family) oftentimes, rights can be framed as obligations, obligations can be framed as rights, oppression can be framed as a privilege, and a privilege as oppression. As such, many advocates who oppose abortion and declare that it should remain illegal claim to not be affecting women but rather protecting them from a decision that is "evil", "unhealthy", "emotionally scarring", "potentially fatal", and "always regrettable"[28] – similar claims to those found in the aforementioned 'pro-life' publicity piece *Love Life for Me*. In their view, usually, motherhood is always preferable to the "immoral" and "scarring" decision of abortion, no matter the conditions in which it is lived.

Several Mexican 'pro-life' academics, in their book *Abortion: The Policy of an Abdicating State* denounce that the topic of abortion in Mexico has, in the past decade, been "*de-valued from the essential; now becoming a platform for ideological postulates and particular agendas, in contrast to what it would mean to effectively engage in human rights protection such as protection of the unborn and of pregnant women's health and well-being*".[29]

Suggested Legal Model and Other Legal Concepts

Notwithstanding that many 'pro-life' advocates still see the *'causales'* or exceptions to abortion bans as "excuses"[30] to be only admitted in exceptional cases, or as

Table 5.4 Suggested Legal Model and Other Legal Concepts

Pro-legalization	*'Pro-life'*
A model of gestational limits (T2): the Mexico City 2007 reform re-defined the legal figure of abortion itself, as "the interruption of a pregnancy after the 12th week". Therefore, abortion is in reality still penalized, but only considered as such once the 12th week of pregnancy has passed	A model of exceptions (T2): abortion is defined as the deliberate interruption of pregnancy at any point, and penalized according to the subnational state's particular laws, but with some non-punishable exceptions (rape, risk to the mother's life, fatal abnormalities, etc.)
Also, an alternative model of "despenalización" (*de-criminalization*), is by simply eliminating penalties in the Criminal Code, which is however not equal to "legalizing". This being, perhaps, the most workable Type 2 agreement. Or alternatively, to call the first 12 weeks of pregnancy a "Cause for the Exclusion of Responsibility" ("Excluyente de Responsabilidad")	A punitive model, to varying degrees, depending on each state
Progressiveness of rights (understood as women's rights having precedence over the unborn's), in a general context of women having more rights than they did historically. This *progressiveness* can also be interpreted as the unborn progressively gaining rights as time passes, but the woman's 'right to choose' trumps them during the first 12 weeks	Resting on the *widening inclusivity* of Human Rights: to include also the unborn child (a notion of *'foetal rights'*)
National normative unity, for the sake of equal access to abortion for women in the whole country. Can be framed as a principle of non-discrimination (T1)	Federalism as leverage for the creation of anti-abortion legislation: convenient in this case (a potential T2 principle)

dangerous doors towards a 'slippery slope' of more and more exceptions eventually leading to unrestricted legalization, most of them still advocate for a model where indeed abortion is banned with some admitted exceptions. Advocates on pro-legalization groups obviously defend the need to legalize abortion, although the specific demands may vary: from 'decriminalization' to 'legalization', via different types of legislative reforms, along a spectrum of permissiveness. Concerning federalism itself, in this case many 'pro-life' advocates strongly defend it[31] as a factor that has allowed them to pass the local anti-abortion subnational reforms, whereas some pro-legalizers argue for national legal homogeneity, for the sake of giving women equal access throughout the entire country.[32]

Major Narrative Shifts: Recent Discursive Re-Framings for Advocacy

Despite the fact that pro-legalization advocacy has seen steady progress in Mexico in recent years, culminating with the Supreme Court's rulings on September 2021 and September 2023 that it is unconstitutional to criminalize abortion; it can be said that the narrative shifts undertaken by 'pro-life' groups have been equally, if not more successful than the re-framings of pro-legalization groups, despite the latter gaining greater success in laws and in achieving 'legislative victories'.

Table 5.5 Major Narrative Shifts

Pro-legalization	*'Pro-life'*
A narrative shift: from the use of the word "abortion", into the use of "Voluntary Interruption of Pregnancy" in newer laws such as the General Law for Crime Victims (*Ley General de Víctimas),* passed in 2013	***A major narrative shift:*** from mere opposition and being "anti-", to a more positive framing and message: "*pro-vida*", "*Salvemos Las Dos Vidas*" ("We Save Both Lives", a slogan born in the context of the 2018 Argentinian debate); framing themselves as "pro-women too"
Another important shift; although one that is buried deep within *legal technicalities*: the change in some local Criminal Codes, from the term "exceptions to punishability" (*causales de no punibilidad*) into "causes for the exclusion of responsibility" (*excluyentes de responsabilidad*) This redefines whether a crime has been committed: in the former, a crime exists but is not punishable; in the latter, the criminal act does not get configured at all. Major paradigm shift, but only talked about by few legal experts. *Can however be a crucial key to decriminalization as a compromise, a Type 2 kind of agreement*	

The Mexican 'pro-life' movements have undergone a true 'rebranding' especially after 2016,[33] renovating their image in a way that appeals to numerous young people, women, and the public in general, no less among conservative sectors who already for decades embraced the older face of the 'anti-abortion' movements. If the pro-legalization advocates have had solid victories grounded in law and in normative technicality, and despite the 'pro-legal-abortion' message gaining more acceptance over the years than it had before, it is undeniable that 'pro-life' movements have had successful narrative shifts, greatly boosting the appeal of their message: appropriating feminism, identifying the aborting woman as 'another victim', and in the simplicity of appropriating *'life'* itself as the defended principle.

Concerning the technical change mentioned in Table 5.5 about the "Exceptions to Punishability" being made into "Causes for the Exclusion of Responsibility" in the Criminal Codes, most advocates who are not legal experts or legal practitioners are rather unbothered with these sorts of "Type 3" technicalities (if we engage with the theory of norm contestation), appealing instead to broader "Type 1" moral principles such as 'protecting life from conception', or 'a right to bodily autonomy'. Despite its legal relevance, it remains a rather obscure change, rarely mentioned in the arenas of public, broadly appealing protest.

"Calling the Pro-Legalizers Out": The Concepts That the Opposing Side Most Frequently and Strongly Challenges, Denies, or Opposes

Some of the most curious and interesting things to observe while researching were the instances where advocates on either side of the debate directly denied the validity of the concepts touted by their opponents, at times accusing them of lying. This

Table 5.6 "Calling the Pro-Legalizers Out": Arguments Challenged by 'Pro-Life' Advocates

Pro-legalization advocates state that:	*'Pro-life' advocates respond:*
Abortion is a Public Health issue.	Abortion has, in reality, very little to do with maternal health and mortality. Some countries ban or criminalize abortion and have still greatly diminished maternal deaths (such as Chile, Ireland). In Mexico City, where abortion is legal, indicators of maternal health and mortality are still worse than in some Mexican states where abortion remains illegal.
Abortion helps women.	Abortion is risky even when legal; it hurts women physically and psychologically.
Thousands of women in Mexico are unfairly jailed for having had an abortion.	The *actual* numbers of people imprisoned in Mexico for the crime of abortion are quite low, and include many more men than women. News and media sources often conflate *accusations* with *incarcerations*.

(*Continued*)

Table 5.6 (Continued)

Pro-legalization advocates state that:	*'Pro-life' advocates respond:*
Abortion should be a woman's right: part of Sexual and Reproductive Health and Rights (SRHR), under the umbrella of rights mentioned by UN institutions.	Refutes abortion as a right, and even the entire concept of "sexual rights". There are no "sexual rights"; only "a right to reproductive health", which does *not* include abortion.
Very few women have died in Mexico City since abortion was legalized in 2007.	Challenges the official Mexico City numbers and statistics: the government cannot even know the true numbers, because official data about abortions happening in private clinics is not collected. Or alternatively, "government hides the true numbers".
Women should have an unlimited "right to choose" over their bodies, and "abortion rights" should be unlimited.	Abortion is murder and should never be a choice; besides, no choice is 'unlimited' in our lives as social beings. Infanticide could become legal on similar grounds.
Bodily autonomy is a fundamental principle for all.	The embryo is another, separate body: when a woman is pregnant, her body is no longer "only her own".

could be observed for the opposed sides of the debate. Some of the most obvious instances have been mentioned, such as abortion being framed as 'a right' versus 'a murder'. Others are less frequently heard, but opposed nonetheless. This section, and the next, will first detail which of the pro-legalizing 'talking points' are opposed by 'pro-life' advocates, as well as what they respond with. In the next section, *vice versa,* some common 'pro-life' talking points are presented, along with what pro-legalizing advocates refute with.

"Calling the Pro-Lifers Out": The Concepts That the Opposing Side Most Frequently and Strongly Challenges, Denies, or Opposes

In a similar exercise, but inverting the order of the columns, we can analyze the ideas espoused by 'pro-life' advocates, and refuted by those in favour of legalization:

Table 5.7 "Calling the Pro-Lifers Out": Arguments Challenged by Pro-Legalization Advocates

'Pro-life' advocates state that. . .	*Pro-legalization advocates respond:*
Abortion should be prohibited because it is a moral problem, a morally unacceptable act, and making it illegal prevents it from happening, at least to some degree.	Illegalizing does not keep abortions from happening; it only makes them more dangerous, and it disproportionately affects poorer women.
Abortion is a sin and should be prohibited (appealing to immutable religious truth).	Mexico is a country with official separation of church and State, principles of laicity should be upheld, religion should not decide public policy.

(*Continued*)

Table 5.7 (Continued)

'Pro-life' advocates state that...	*Pro-legalization advocates respond:*
Abortion is murder, completely on par with any homicide.	Abortion is a right at least in some cases; the unborn's rights are not yet equal to the woman's. Not even the most restrictive countries treat abortion as "equal to homicide".
Personhood begins at conception/fertilization, and thus so do human/civil/legal rights.	Attempting to protect life "from the moment of conception/fertilization" in any meaningful legal sense is fallacious, and the laws made in this sense only aim to criminalize women. Fertilization cannot even be detected until weeks after it has occurred, and *only if* embryo implantation occurred too: these medical concepts are not helpful for policymaking on abortion and serve only to restrict women's liberties.
Abortion hurts women; "pro-life" advocates really are both "pro-women" and "pro-child".	Advocating against abortion only has the aim of controlling and criminalizing women's sexual behaviour.
Abortion increases the risk of infertility, breast/ovarian/uterine cancer, psychological problems, suicide, etc.	The veracity of such claims is questioned.
Abortion is a multi-billion-dollar business. Its supporters have financial motives; it is a "global conspiracy".	The veracity of such claims is questioned.
Abortion is a highly violent act, gruesome and bloody, is done using sharp objects or through saline injections to the foetus' head.	Almost the entirety of legal abortions today are carried out with drugs (*Misoprostol* and *Mifepristone*), or through manual intra-uterine aspiration (AMEU). Images depicting gruesome "abortions" are in reality stillbirths or exceptional cases, presented in a misleading manner to provoke an outraged, emotional response.
Abortion is a new moral problem, emblematic of current moral decay.	Abortion has always existed and is only now being given greater visibility as a social problem.

Counterproductive Strategies

An interesting aspect to observe was how opposed advocates often engaged in counterproductive strategies, fallacious arguments based on inaccurate data, ideas whose legitimacy is called into question, poorly constructed claims, or discursive re-framings that have at times backfired, been ineffective, or that were used in the past and were abandoned for being ineffective.

Strongest Supporting International Document, Quoted for Advocacy

Advocates on opposing groups are lacking any binding international legal document which firmly sustains their position, each relying instead – for whenever

Table 5.8 Counterproductive Strategies

Pro-legalization	*'Pro-life'*
Inaccurate statements showing ignorance of biology or embryological science such as "*the foetus is only a bunch of cells*", or "*it is part of the mother's body, like a tumour*". *These notions are frequently and easily discredited by opposed activists with more accurate knowledge of week-by-week foetal development and its complexities.*	Inaccurate information about how most medical abortions are performed nowadays, as well as the use of highly gruesome and often misleading imagery: describing the procedure as highly violent, bloody; using incendiary terms such as "*dismembering*", "*burning*", "*ripping apart*"; often using gory images of very late term abortions, or photos pertaining to miscarriages and stillbirths rather than abortions. *This strategy elicits a clear emotional response, invites outrage, and appeals to morality. Many 'pro-life' advocates disagree with the use of such "triggering imagery",*[34] *considering it "in poor taste" or "counterproductive".*
In the same vein, some advocates also resort to calling the foetus "the product of conception": a term that may come from the medical field, but which can provoke moral outrage in some 'pro-life' advocates. The use of the word *"product"* to refer to an embryo or 'potential human', rings undeniably utilitarian and material-like.	Calling for the imprisonment of women who abort; stigmatization. *Calling for the criminalization of women, or for harsher measures against them, is becoming an increasingly unpopular message, even among pro-lifers themselves. Most of them advocate for "the State giving women support and other options, never abortion", and/or "penalties other than jail: monetary fines, community service, etc".*[35]
Advocating for an un-limited right to abortion at any stage of pregnancy. *No choice can truly be "unlimited"; the wide majority of the public disagrees, even among "pro-choicers" themselves. There has to be a "cut-off" line", at some point before the third trimester begins, point at which abortion is no longer permitted, except in extraordinary circumstances.*	

they do reach out to international texts to back up their claims – on a particular non-binding or semi-binding document: pro-legalization advocates rely on the Montevideo Consensus (which recommends that states should legalize abortion at least on *some* specific cases), while the anti-legalization side relies on the Inter-American Human Rights Convention, or "Pact of San José" (which normally would be counted as a binding document, yet Mexico presented a reservation on the issue of "*protecting life, in general, from the moment of conception*", clarifying that each subnational state can decide).

Table 5.9 Strongest Supporting International Document

Pro-legalization	*'Pro-life'*
Pact of Montevideo, which urges states to legalize abortion at least in some of the cases, and to consider women's health and bodily autonomy rights. It is however a non-binding document (in traditional International Law terms)	Pact of San José (Inter-American Convention on Human Rights), with its article No. 4 protecting life *"in general, from the moment of conception"* (although Mexico placed a reservation on precisely that article. Also, the words "in general" allow some room for interpretation)
International Convention on Population and Development (ICPD Cairo 1994), and Post-2014 Cairo Framework; however, they are non-binding in the traditional sense	Declaration of the Rights of the Child, which however does not specifically mention abortion, only vaguely sets a protection of life "*before as well as after birth*"

As was observed through the interviews as well as literature, opposed advocates in the debate claim to have solid international legal grounds for their advocacy, defending the solidness and binding-ness of the documents which appear to give them the best support and the most favourable interpretation. Argentinian legislators advocating against abortion legalization also made mentions of the Pact of San José and its protection of life "from the moment of conception", throughout their advocacy. So did Mexican legislators in 2016, when debates were being held for the creation of the new local Constitution in Mexico City.[36] It was observed however (and perhaps is to be expected) that advocates reach into international documents if and when it is convenient, otherwise preferring to ignore or dismiss them as 'irrelevant to subnational policy' or 'contrary to national sovereignty', in instances of what I previously deemed as *"binding recommendation when I like it, and mere soft law when I don't"*. Quoting Andrew Clapham: "the vocabulary of human rights helps to formulate demands" and can also "reveal competing interests at stake",[37] but it does not in itself resolve fundamental questions about whose interests should prevail in a given situation, or why.

As an additional note, there is also a parallel tendency among 'pro-life' advocates to often reject the international realm in general, with arguments that resemble conspiracy theories: the United Nations or international NGOs as part of an alleged "*big abortion*"[38] lobby, abortion as a part of efforts to reduce population in less developed countries, 'anti-family' policy, its relation to "global LGBTQ agendas",[39] etc. Such a tendency of rejection towards 'the global' in general was not observed in pro-legalization advocates in Mexico.

Most Recent Legislative Victories

The opposing sides, through their advocacy efforts, have each had some recent 'legislative victories'. Pro-legalization advocates influenced the creation of the regulation called NOM-0046, which grants access to legal abortion for any woman who has been a victim of sexual assault, without any requirement of proof of the

Table 5.10 Most Recent Legislative Victories

Pro-legalization	*'Pro-life'*
NOM0046, especially after its 2016 reform, which grants women the access to abortion in cases of sexual assault, *with no need to prove in any formal way that the assault took place* (contesting the need for proof of a crime, before granting a service meant for crime victims). A written statement by the woman, under oath of truth, suffices as proof. This has been "the unexpected battleground", as NOMs are rarely ever so contested or even known. Clearly a Type 3 kind of norm, among the least contested discursively (but most contested behaviourally), according to theories of contestation.	***Law of Conscientious Objection,*** through the addition of an article to the *Ley General de Salud*: granting doctors the right to refuse to carry out any medical procedures, as long as their objection is not immediately life-threatening to the patient (contesting doctors' obligation to provide a legal public service).
The precedent set by the *Supreme Court rulings of September 2021 and 2023*, which have declared the unconstitutionality of criminalizing abortion. Though this is likely to still be contested by "pro-life" advocates, the Court has set a powerful precedent for eventual decriminalization throughout the country, one which advocates will most likely use in the future as a discursive tool in their advocacy.	Several reforms to subnational constitutions across various Mexican states (asserting "right to life from the moment of conception"); this however is a more abstract change with barely any legal "teeth": a cosmetic change, rather than legally meaningful. Many 'pro-life' activists call these reforms "*blindar la Constitución*", taken to mean "shielding, armouring" of the subnational Constitution in order to "prevent" abortion legalization as happened in Mexico City in 2007. *However, with the recent ruling by the Supreme Court on the unconstitutionality of criminalizing abortion, it is likely that the subnational Criminal Codes can be amended, regardless of what the local Constitution says.*

assault (nor requiring any previous existence of a report about the crime). 'Pro-life' activists, through advocacy and alliances with conservative legislators, recently achieved the creation of a "Law of Conscientious Objection": the addition of an article to the General Health Law, allowing doctors to refuse to carry out any procedures that they disagree with. During the interviews, advocates frequently referred to these texts: defending the norm accomplished by their side and attacking the opposing norm.

Both texts have become that respective group's most recent 'legislative weapon'. They contest and reject the 'opposed' text, questioning the principles that it aims to protect or uphold, and calling for its withdrawal. Analysis of these and other similar texts, and of the construction of their meanings, presents a fascinating and detailed map of diverse laws, national and international, and how they have been created, constructed, and contested as either Type 2 or Type 3 norms (contingent upon their complexity and moral reach), as well as how the proactive and reactive contestation of both has shaped the debate.

In September of 2021, the Supreme Court set a powerful precedent (one of the strongest that can exist in the Mexican legal landscape) for abortion legalization or at least de-criminalization: through its resolution that criminalizing abortion is unconstitutional and directly violates women's rights, especially in the cases resulting from sexual abuse. The Court has ruled that decriminalizing abortion is not unconstitutional and does not conflict with protecting life, even if the subnational Constitutions specifically protect life "from the moment of conception". Although 'pro-life' advocates are likely to keep challenging this notion, the Court has now ruled what many pro-decriminalization advocates have long said: that decriminalizing is not the same as 'legalizing', and it doesn't have to come in conflict with protection of life.

A Norm-Typological Analysis: Two Sets of Meanings-In-Use on the Abortion Debate

Recalling the notions introduced in Chapter 3 about norm typologies, the findings during fieldwork can further be combined with a norm-typological analysis of what the advocates on the ground have contested, proposed, and reacted against, in terms of types of norms as well as modes of contestation. In the abortion debate in general, but also concerning legal typologies in particular, it is of course important to remember that the aforementioned Types 1, 2, and 3 are not distinct and separate categories. This is especially true in the debate about abortion: I rather refer to '*a continuum of law*' in this case especially, a case which blurs many boundaries of anything resembling a clean-cut categorization. The "types" are to be taken as

Table 5.11 Types of Norms as a Continuum of Law

Three types of norms as a "Continuum of Law"	
Type 1	Abstract principles, a meta-social discourse on generally upheld principles of justice (i.e. democracy, human rights, rule of law). Wide moral reach.
Type 2	**Organizing Principles** as axes along which to adjoin and balance, in practice, differing and competing interests, various potentially colliding rights, opposed visions of the world. *The Legitimacy Gap*
Type 3	Technical regulations, more precise rules with narrower moral reach. *This Type 3 seems relatively less debated, in general, in the abortion debate in Mexico, with the notable exception of NOM0046. Advocates are rarely contesting technicalities or procedures, focusing rather on larger ideas and more general principles.* This also depends on whether we refer to reactive or proactive contestation, as NOM0046 has been a clear example of a highly contested (behaviourally and reactively) T3 norm.

Source: Based on Wiener, 2014.

distinct, yet fluid (not strictly separated) norms, using the typology for analytical reasons and not for strict categorization.

Within a similar analytical point of view, Table 5.12 shows how the competing principles and texts furthered by opposed sides of the abortion debate might be typologically organized, looking at the national and international norms, documents, laws, and principles that they each have focused their advocacy on, or spoken in favour of.

Table 5.12 Norms Proposed by Advocates along a "Continuum of Law"

Norms proposed by the advocates along "Continuum of Law".

	Pro-legal abortion	*Anti-legal abortion*
Type 1 – Fundamental Norms	"Right to Choose" "Women's Rights" – abortion as part of women's reproductive rights International Declarations: ICPD Cairo '94, CEDAW "Consented Motherhood": personal choice as a deciding factor over a pregnancy	"Right to Life", absolute and unbounded National Constitution in Mexico: through its abolition of the death penalty, "indirectly giving absolute protection to life" Inter-American Convention on Human Rights or "Pact of San José", protecting life "in general" from the moment of conception
Type 2 – Intermediary-level laws, as well as potential *Organizing Principles*	*Decriminalization* as a potential Organizing Principle, within subnational Criminal Codes – through clauses of "exclusion of responsibility" Gestational Limits as a criterion for access to legal abortion Rulings by the Mexican Supreme Court (2021 and 2023), in favour of decriminalizing abortion The Montevideo Convention (in its non-binding nature), urging states to consider decriminalizing abortion and considering it part of reproductive rights General Comment No. 36 on the Right to Life (soft law), to the ICCPR "Progressive protection" of rights for the unborn	Subnational Constitutions, and the reforms made to them, protecting life 'from the moment of conception' Federalism itself as allowing autonomous subnational decision-making
Type 3 – Technical Regulations	Regulatory laws: NOM0046	Regulatory Laws: Law (Article) on Conscientious Objection

Source: Table by author, based on Wiener, 2014.

As with the similar tables and visual schemes used for this analysis, the interest of engaging in this exercise is not to create strict categorization but rather to help visualize norms, principles, and documents as they relate to each other. Seeing norms and laws displayed in this way helps to gather new analytical insights into how the advocates are doing what they do: if some are focusing more on a certain 'type' of norms or another, going towards either the fundamental or the technical, within what should always be taken as a 'continuum of law' rather than strict categorizations. Norm implementation reveals the meanings-in-use that the advocates on the ground are instrumentalizing in their advocacy efforts.

Contestation Modes and "Levels" in Advocacy on Abortion in Mexico

Analysis of field data allows also for a more detailed mapping of 'contestation types', while incorporating the notions of *discursive*, *behavioural*, *proactive*, and *reactive* contestation into my observations of the way in which advocates carried out contestation, as well as how 'highly' contested each type of norm is in the Mexican debate on abortion (bearing in mind, of course, that to call a norm 'highly contested' or 'not so highly contested' is rather subjective, in this case the notion has been informed by how often advocates or media referenced said norm). Table 5.13 helps to 'organize' and visualize the contestation modes in which opposed sides of the debate engage and to analyze several dimensions: how high or low the contestation has been, which texts or principles have been contested and in which manner, etc.

Table 5.13 serves as a general approximation of how highly contested the Types have been, across the different "modes", in this debate. It is further useful to draw a similar table, seeing the "modes" of contestation for the opposed advocates within the debate, considering which norms and principles they have most often contested discursively and behaviourally, as well as reactively and proactively.

In their study of the UN System's "Women, Peace and Security Agenda" (WPS), True and Wiener present their selected case as an example revealing "constellations of contestation", mapping out the diverse contestation modes within one case[40] in what is deemed the "dynamics of dissent". It shows the constellation and interplay between discursive and behavioural contestation, where distinctions can be made between *"a reactive practice of contestation, or a proactive practice of critical engagement"*.[41] *"Proactive contestation denotes an agent's capability to engage with norms on a macro-scale; reactive contestation, by contrast, indicates an agent's capability to merely object to a norm on the micro-scale"*.[42] Engaging in a similar exercise in the case of abortion can serve as one analytical approach.

The tables serve as approximations of how and where to place concepts and modes of contestation, as has been suggested by analysis of the gathered data, remembering that every boundary represented by every one of these lines is blurry to some extent. Furthermore, it isn't always easy to define with precision a difference between contesting something "proactively" versus "reactively", or "discursively" versus "behaviourally". Contestation, almost by definition, requires some

Table 5.13 Contestation 'Modes' and 'Levels' in the Abortion Debate in Mexico

Contestation in the abortion debate in Mexico				
Mode:	*Discursive (Heavier focus on "principle")*		*Behavioural (Heavier focus on "written law")*	
Mode:	*Proactive*	*Reactive*	*Proactive*	*Reactive*
How is the contestation carried out?	Suggesting new Meanings/ Interpretations	Contesting established Meanings/Interpretations	Law changes/Emerges (legal reforms)	Protest/Disobedience of laws/ Failing to comply
Main engaged stakeholders:	Activists, mainly	Activists, mainly	Activists and Policy Makers/Legislators	Activists and Women/Doctors/ Institutions
Type 1 (more focused on "fundamental principle")	LOW	HIGH	MEDIUM	LOW
Type 2 (Intermediary Laws, as well as the middle ground between principle and practice)	MEDIUM	HIGH	**VERY HIGH**	**VERY HIGH**
Type 3 (more focused on "standards in practice")	LOW	MEDIUM	**VERY HIGH**	**VERY HIGH**

individual agency and could be classified as "a behaviour", even if such behaviour consists mostly of uttering or writing a certain discourse. The issue of abortion in Mexico is also a decades-long history of advocates 'reacting' to someone else's previous act, or speech, or to a perceived injustice, making it difficult to make a claim of "proactiveness" that *doesn't* also come as a response to something else. That being said, this serves as an analytical tool to reflect deeply about concrete cases (e.g. one instance of a particular law reform being proposed in Congress), to look at such instance and ponder on questions such as: *Who is doing this? How are they doing it? Are they doing what they do, or saying what they say, as an immediate reaction to something else, or is this a new idea?. . .*

Main Concepts and Laws Contested by 'Pro-Life' Advocates in the Mexican Abortion Debate (in Bold, What They Oppose)

Table 5.14 Main Concepts and Laws Contested by 'Pro-Life' Advocates

Mode:	*Discursive (Heavier focus on "principle")*		*Behavioural (Heavier focus on "written law")*	
Mode:	*Proactive*	*Reactive*	*Proactive*	*Reactive*
How is the contestation carried out?	Suggesting new meanings/ interpretations	Contesting established meanings/ interpretations	Law changes/ emerges (legal reforms)	Protest/ disobedience of laws/failing to comply
Main engaged stakeholders:	Activists, mainly	Activists, mainly	Activists and policy makers/legislators	Activists and women/ doctors/ institutions
Type 1 (more focused on "fundamental principle")	Absolute "right to life" Convention on the Rights of the Child			
Type 2 (Intermediary Laws, as well as the middle ground between principle and practice)	Pact of San José, Article 4: "protecting life, in general, from the moment of conception"	**Recommendations by the Universal Periodic Review at the OHCHR, on legalizing or decriminalizing abortion (reacting against)** **Reforms to the local Criminal Codes, decriminalizing abortion – as Mexico City did in 2007 (reacting against).**	Reforms to subnational Constitutions Law on Conscientious Objection **General Comment No. 36 on the "Right to Life" (contestation at the process of negotiation, and reacting against its final provisions on abortion)**	
Type 3 (more focused on "standards in practice")				**NOM0046 (reacting against)**

Source: Author's own creation.

Main Concepts and Laws Contested by 'Pro-Legalization' Advocates in the Mexican Abortion Debate (in Bold, What They Oppose)

Table 5.15 Main Concepts and Laws Contested by 'Pro-Legalization' Advocates

Mode:	*Discursive (Heavier focus on "principle")*		*Behavioural (Heavier focus on "written law")*	
Mode:	*Proactive*	*Reactive*	*Proactive*	*Reactive*
How is the contestation carried out?	Suggesting new meanings/ interpretations	Contesting established meanings/ interpretations	Law changes/emerges (legal reforms)	Protest/ disobedience of laws/ failing to comply
Main engaged stakeholders:	Activists, mainly	Activists, mainly	Activists and policy makers/legislators	Activists and women/ doctors/ institutions
Type 1 (more focused on "fundamental principle")	Women's "right to choose" Consented Motherhood			
Type 2 (Intermediary Laws, as well as the middle ground between principle and practice)	Convention of Montevideo. General Comment No. 36 to the ICCPR, on the "Right to Life", including some instances where abortion should be permitted. Decriminalization as a potential organizing principle	**Pact of San José – reacting against its established meaning on "protecting life from the moment of conception", clarifying that this is only a general principle**	Reforms to subnational criminal codes, decriminalizing abortion	
Type 3 (more focused on "standards in practice")			NOM0046	

Source: Author's own creation.

Mapping Laws and Texts across the Norm Typology

Figure 5.2 (similarly to Figure 3.1 in Chapter 3) lays out various texts containing laws, written norms, or principles, which advocates in the abortion debate in Mexico most use, propose, contest, or attempt to reform in the context of their advocacy. Recalling the analysis of norm typology according to Wiener's theory of contestation,[43] it was established that two relevant dimensions to differentiate between Types 1, 2, and 3 are "*Moral Reach*" and "*Complexity*". A norm can be understood to have a wide or narrow moral reach, according to how much it aims at universality, the number of different policy fields upon which it touches, and the potential number of stakeholders involved in its design and implementation.

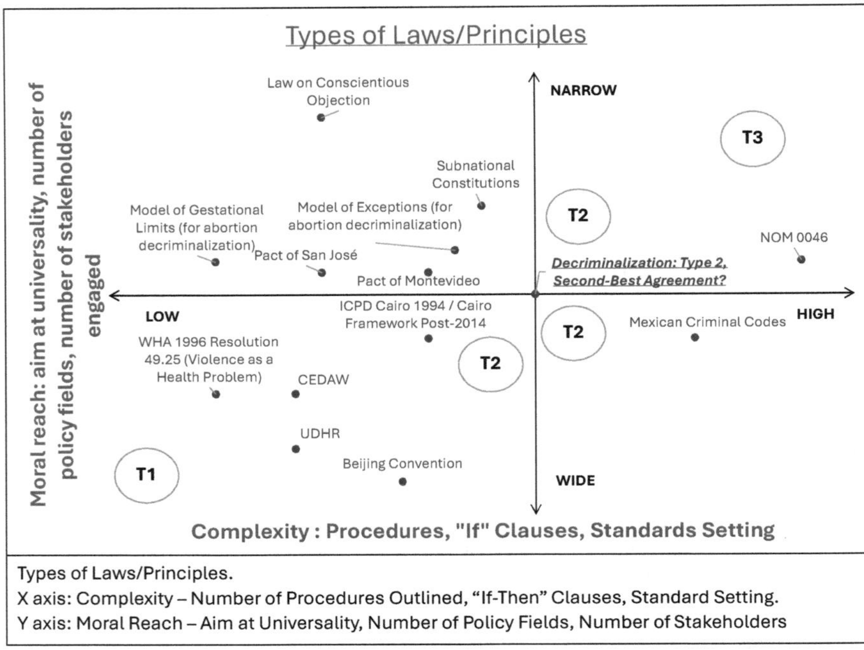

Figure 5.2 Mapping the contested laws in the abortion debate, along dimensions of Complexity and Moral Reach.

Source: Author's own figure, based on theory by Wiener, 2014.

Complexity, in turn, refers to the number of procedures or legal mechanisms that it details, the *"if"* clauses it may contain, or the extent to which it sets specific standards.

Building on these conceptualizations, Figure 5.2 maps the different and most prominent texts, laws, or general principles that activists on opposing sides of the abortion debate in Mexico use in the context of their advocacy, and how they fall across this legal spectrum. Such an effort of 'classifying' or 'quantifying' laws in dimensions, which can admittedly be vague, is not meant as an exercise in precision, but rather to provide general ideas of how these norms relate and compare *to one another*. A strict and exact classification of norms and texts in this way is not only impossible but also as the present research is constructivist in nature, this should exclude attempts at precise categorization or classification. It can, however, be useful to better understand a detailed mapping of the types of norms that these advocates most often use, propose, and attempt to reform throughout their advocacy.

As a tool for visual and comparative analysis, it is useful to create 'overlap' between the laws (or legal concepts) that advocates on opposed sides have used, contested and reacted against in their advocacy. As such, it is not meant for theory creation nor drawing final conclusions, but as a useful visualization of a fluid continuum of law, with the "Type 2" norms clustering around the middle, and to further visualize the many 'shades of grey' existing in this topic.

The Convoluted 'Ways to Get There': A Normative Analysis of Strategies Used by Pro-Legalization Activists

'Pro-life' activists in Mexico are, for the most part, looking to either maintain or solidify what is effectively the *statu quo* (or in their own words regarding the local Constitutions, "*blindar*": "to armour" or "shield" the *statu quo*). In this case, abortion 'starts out' as default illegal, since every local Criminal Code, as well as the Federal Criminal Code, all define abortion as a crime. Yet through intense advocacy and lawmaking efforts, it is sometimes legalized or de-criminalized in some places, in some instances, in some circumstances, and even when legalization is not achieved, certain sectors of civil society continue to press for its legalization. As a response to these changes (or to the pressures to change), 'pro-life' movements intensify efforts to reverse any pro-legalization gains, to thwart any reform attempts, or to solidify the outlawing of abortion. In this section I analyze how enacting change has been possible for those facing the 'uphill battle': pro-legalization activists.

Analyzing interviewees' answers, as well as the actual reforms proposed (those which have passed and those which haven't), we can identify several different ways of attaining, in practice, a de-criminalization of abortion:

- *Claiming abortion to be "a right"*. This entails redefining a controverted practice, framing it as a right that a group of people needs access to, and demanding that the state give such right. This rather "Type 1" endeavour aims to redefine principles and, in practice, will be very hard to attain: abortion is likely to remain unacceptable to a significant part of the Mexican population. Such a T1 shift is likely to have a high level of discursive-reactive contestation. A major, much more *'meta'* cultural shift would be needed (and indeed such shift might never arrive) for a majority of the population in Mexico to think of abortion as 'a right'. Also in a strictly legal sense, as one of the interviewed 'pro-life' experts remarked, in their view it is rather difficult (not to mention arbitrary) to frame a certain practice as 'a right' when the same practice is considered 'a crime' under different circumstances, just by virtue of having crossed a temporal line (of gestational weeks),[44] one which also seems arbitrary to many opposers.
- *Legally redefining abortion itself.* This is what lawmakers in Mexico City did in 2007, redefining it as an interruption of pregnancy after the 12th week. This other type of T1 (principle- or concept-focused) reform, which some of the 'pro-life' interviewees called "a true legal somersault"[45] or which they described as arbitrary, ungrounded, and unreasonable, was able to gain traction in Mexico City thanks to a local congress dominated by progressive political parties and has been able to stay in place thanks to Mexico City's more liberal society (which includes strong feminist advocacy groups) and the Supreme Court's rulings on its constitutional validity. As per a norm contestation analysis, this

redefinition provoked a high level of *discursive-reactive* contestation. This contestation might also be a sign that this reform is perceived by many as a push for a cultural shift that 'pro-life' advocates would never find acceptable, as it is often the case that one of their conceptual cornerstones is on *conception* as the beginning of legally protected life; therefore, an abortion will be any voluntary interruption of pregnancy happening after that precise point.

- *By means of technical laws, the 'devil in the details'*. With the unprecedented passing of NOM0046, and especially after its subsequent 2016 reform, activists on opposed sides of the debate were met with an unforeseen new battleground for activism: the very technical realm of the NOMs (*Norma Oficial Mexicana*), which are often highly technical regulations, typically only known to experts in specific fields such as doctors or industrial engineers. NOMs are rarely ever controversial or even subject to public attention. In our norm typology, they would comfortably be classified as Type 3 norms, with a high degree of complexity and a narrow moral reach, normally touching upon few policy fields.

  NOM0046 is being held in the spotlight, as many anti-abortion advocates feel that "the attack came from an unexpected place",[46] as if pro-legalizers had used a sort of 'back-door' to usher in a new social and legal reality, which they ('pro-lifers') resist and resent. Being a Type 3 norm, it comes both as a result of, and with the accompaniment of, rather low discursive contestation yet intense behavioural contestation, both proactive and reactive: for example, with doctors and policy makers refusing to comply with it or to implement it in their fields, or expert advocates taking it to the Supreme Court, more than once, to challenge the constitutional legitimacy of NOM0046 (as did the local executive governments of Aguascalientes and Baja California in late 2018).
- Another similar, very 'technical' kind of change is the rewriting, in the Criminal Codes, of the exceptions to abortion prohibition (the *'causales'*) from being 'causes of extinction of the penalty' into 'causes for exclusion of responsibility'. This change did not immediately bring changes to abortion policy, but it set a precedent to non-criminalization, and at the time (early 2000s) it was barely noticed by anyone other than legal experts.
- *Back to the origins: 'despenalización'* (decriminalization) *as the current workable compromise?. . .* The very first pro-legalization activists in Mexico, decades ago, were not referring to abortion as 'a right' that should be crystallized in law. They rather referred to '*despenalización*' as a way to ensure that women would not be criminalized for their reproductive choices, pushing this idea especially through a framework of public health. *Despenalización* is still one of the fundamental concepts in the abortion debate, even though in recent years, many pro-legalization activists aim for wider acceptance of the practice, rather than 'merely' decriminalizing it. As shown throughout this book, advocacy on opposed sides has only further solidified the clashing positions, strengthened opposed discourses, polarized and estranged different groups, and widened the legitimacy gap between the 'sets' of meanings-in-use.

  Can this *'despenalización'* become the main organizing principle, the compromise, or 'middle ground', on which opposed sides of the debate might (at least for now) meet halfway?. . . And how to achieve this in existing laws?. . . In the Mexican legal system, a cornerstone of criminal law is the "*principio de taxatividad*", or *nulle crimen sine lege stricta*[47]*:* in short, the principle that every punishable crime shall be strictly specified by the law, not allowing for sentencing by extrapolation or similarity. Therefore, if abortion is to be criminalized, it is to be detailed in a law referring to it specifically. It is highly telling that, when trying to fight against legal abortion, 'pro-life' activists have proposed reforms only to the local Constitutions and, in the words of one pro-legalization activist, "they have not dared touch the Criminal Codes",[48] as that's where the anti-abortion penalties take on real legal meaning. No 'pro-life' group in Mexico has successfully advocated for stricter punishments to abortion (stricter than those currently existing), as it remains a highly unpopular proposal.

A way in which pro-legalization activists have tried to achieve decriminalization is by proposing to either eliminate the references to penalties for abortion, or by listing exceptions to the penalties (such exceptions could be cases of rape, incest, risks to the mother's life, or the low number of gestational weeks). Looking at the typologies table, a proposal of this nature could be considered a Type 2 kind of proactive contestation, as it sits squarely at the legitimacy gap – not just between the clashing discourses, giving a bit of agreement to both but also with *'despenalización'* as an organizing principle for this exceptional case (and arguably a kind of rule with a low level of complexity, and within a narrow moral reach).

However, 'mere' decriminalization is nowadays not enough progress in the eyes of many pro-legal abortion advocates, as they rightfully argue that eliminating penalties for an act is nowhere near the same as providing access, creating constituting norms, or regulating a practice in a way that it can be meaningfully acceptable in a society.

The Successful Rebranding: A Normative Analysis of Strategies Used by 'Pro-Life' Advocates

Although they have not faced 'the uphill battle' and rather defend the *statu quo* staying as is, 'pro-life' advocates have also embraced new strategies and narrative shifts which brought them successes in some regards, especially in the realm of the public and transnational advocacy itself. Even if they have been less successful so far on the "lawfare"[49] (with strong opposing blows having recently come from the Supreme Court itself, in 2021 and 2023), their renewed 'marketing' strategies have given way to a powerful revitalization of pro-life movements in Mexico. In what Pérez Hernández calls *"new faces of civil society in pro-life activism"*,[50] it was observed on the field that these revitalized 'pro-life' movements, especially the post-2018 movements of the 'blue wave' (*Ola Celeste*) in connection to the Argentinian movements, have attracted a great number of women, young people, and young families. There is no longer truth to the notion that the pro-life movements comprise 'only conservative men' or 'only conservative people of an older age cohort'.

Probably the narrative shift which is simplest, but most crucial in importance and perceptions, was the one that happened already in the late eighties: when the reactive 'anti-abortion' movements renamed themselves as a proactive 'pro-life', softening the messages and reframing them as positive. In 2018, in the context of the transnational exchanges with Argentinian advocates, came the second successful 'spin': when 'pro-life' groups adopted the slogan "We Save Both Lives". This "Saving Both Lives" comes as a message of massive appeal, reframed as positive, human rights-defending, and taking into consideration "the woman as well".

From *'the transgressor bad mother'* into *'Abortion has two victims!'*, the rebranding into a much more appealing framework is one that many younger people have embraced, as a manner of supporting 'pro-life' ideas while still 'being pro-woman'. The protest that I attended in Mexico City in 2018 clearly showed, in shared messages and phrases (all coming from the organizers as well), that these modern 'pro-life' movements have appropriated to themselves many progressive concepts: a concept of 'true feminism', embracing feminism if at least cosmetically ("we protect the woman too, as well as the unborn girl child"[51]), a concept of 'life' (where opposing them would give the impression, by inference, that one is 'against life' or 'pro-death'), 'family' (where they see a larger narrative connecting abortion, marriage, the 'traditional family' and LGBTQ+ agendas), 'true gender equality' (by enshrining and protecting motherhood, and the interest of upholding it as a social good) as well as 'fundamental liberties'.

This point about 'fundamental liberties' has more convoluted explanations, and their perceived connection between banning abortion and 'liberties' is harder to see: intuitively one would perceive that they oppose the 'fundamental liberty' of a right to choose over one's own body. They tend to explain it in rather vague notions about their fundamental liberties to 'raise their children in a morally correct way' or to give them 'the religious education of their choosing', more often circling back to 'life' as the fundamental cornerstone of any liberty. They also perceive the connection to abortion in a larger sense of respecting parental authority, parental rights and their discretion regarding sex education (teaching their children that many forms of contraception are unacceptable and so is abortion), and generally pushing 'pro-family policy'.

However, regarding their law proposals, the most successful of their efforts and their most touted recent victories have been the reforms to the subnational Constitutions, as well as the creation of the article about "the right to Conscientious Objection" within the General Health Law. Their proposed and accepted law reforms have mostly moved in an 'abstract realm', or in the words of an opposing pro-legalization advocate, *"the 'pro-lifers' have moved in a much greyer area, where the laws that they have managed to reform have little impact on reality"*.[52] In terms of norm contestation theories, it translates into victories that are closer to Type 1 and Type 2 norms: advancing the acceptance of some fundamental principles, in the former case, and reforming intermediary laws of a rather abstract nature, in the latter.

Another observed fact was that several 'pro-life' advocates were involved in proposing law reforms which often touch upon other tangential topics and not abortion itself: they advocate on issues like facilitating adoption procedures, government support for working mothers and single mothers, expanded access to childcare, etc., all of which, in their eyes, "constitutes pro-family policy and therefore discourages abortion",[53] which is admittedly an unproven claim. It gives the impression that 'pro-life' advocates are losing legal battles when it comes to 'the laws with real teeth', concentrating instead on the abstract laws (such as the subnational Constitutions, which do not oblige or directly bind medical doctors and health authorities in the way that NOM0046 clearly does), or on advancing laws that don't directly concern abortion but 'family policy' (something that, in principle, any pro-legalization advocate could support as well).

'Pro-life' advocates seem to respond to the pro-legalization advances by 'firing in all directions', preferring to propose initiatives that either concern more general laws, or to concentrate on other family-related aspects. As another pro-legalization advocate commented, however, "too many solutions are none",[54] meant in the sense that so many diverse 'pro-family' proposals seem to signal a dilution of their efforts into many other directions, rather than directly addressing abortion as such.

While pro-legalization advocates have recently achieved legal reforms of much more concrete significance, the 'pro-life' side has managed a successful 'rebranding' through many crucial discursive shifts, carrying out intense national and transnational advocacy with a large following – even if their successful law reform proposals have been more abstract, more tangential to the abortion issue, and with less 'legal teeth'.

Operating in Different Realms: Normative Types, Legal 'Teeth', and Concrete Victories

I conclude this chapter by reflecting on the fact that opposed groups of advocates seem to operate on different normative realms. At first sight it may seem that the opposed groups are on equal footing when it comes to recent normative and legislative victories; upon close inspection, we can see a strong difference in the types of 'victories'.

'Pro-life' advocacy has, thus far, managed to gain good terrain within segments of conservative Mexicans, especially related to Catholic and other Christian churches. They have created a strong discourse in favour of the rights of the unborn, stemming mostly from grassroots civil society and religious groups, with a message of both proactive and reactive contestation against legal abortion. However, most of their advancements and steps forward remain within an abstract realm of values, principles, and mostly Type 1 and Type 2 kinds of texts.

Their biggest (and by far most touted) recent victories, the various '*blindajes*' of the local state constitutions, still lack legal 'teeth' except for their temporary capacity to rebuke any intentions to chance the local Criminal Codes – and this has been recently declared all but invalid by the Supreme Court, who ruled that criminalization of abortion is unconstitutional and that the de-criminalization does *not* contradict protection of 'life from conception' in the subnational Constitutions. Even before the Court ruling, it still was a 'meta' sort of victory, one that in the end failed to show its supposed legal 'teeth': by reforming local constitutions, 'pro-life' advocates had allegedly instituted a Type 1 kind of "padlock" whereby other reforms and other constitutive rulings would supposedly be blocked.

Another example of 'pro-life' advocacy indeed operating in a much greyer legal area is the aforementioned statement by a few interviewed advocates that "the abolition of the death penalty means that abortion is by default forbidden, or that life is protected from the moment of conception". We could call abolition of the death penalty (in any country), to be a very Type 1 kind of reform: one of extremely low complexity, extremely wide moral reach. That the 'pro-life' advocates would draw such a conclusion (that abolition also means prohibiting abortion) seems to indicate that their 'lawfare moves' are staying confined to a much more abstract normative realm.

The legal advancements achieved by pro-legalization groups have had more concrete legal 'teeth'; however, they bear two disadvantages. One is that despite their advancements in "lawfare", their message remains unaccepted by a strong segment of conservative people and associations. The second is that, by sometimes operating in the realm of obscure technicality, such as the changes concerning NOM0046 or the legal reforms changing "causes of the extinction of penalties" into "causes for the exclusion of responsibility" (details unknown by the non-expert public at large), they risk always carrying a certain feel of 'illegitimacy' in their achieved changes – or a sense of temporary-ness, where opposed ideological tides could one day reverse the advancements.

Notes

1 Fieldwork interview: Expert No. 6.
2 Fieldwork interview: Expert No. 5.
3 Fieldwork interview: Expert No. 10.
4 Fieldwork interview: Expert No. 11.
5 Fieldwork interview: Expert No. 26.
6 Fieldwork interview: Expert No. 11.
7 Fieldwork interview: Expert No. 15.
8 Fieldwork interview: Expert No. 23.
9 Fieldwork interview: Expert No. 15.
10 Fieldwork interview: Expert No. 23.
11 Fieldwork interview: Expert No. 1.
12 Fieldwork interview: Expert No. 5.
13 Fieldwork interview: Expert No. 7.
14 Fieldwork interview: Expert No. 11.
15 Fieldwork interview: Expert No. 26.
16 Fieldwork interview: Expert No. 15.
17 Fieldwork interview: Expert No. 11.
18 Fieldwork interview: Expert No. 10.
19 One could point at marriage, for example, being 'a right' but becoming 'a crime' if one intends to marry a minor, also on the grounds of *temporality*: the act becomes legal if more time passes and the person becomes an adult. It is not entirely clear that the argument stands, whether 'something cannot be both a right and a crime, depending on timing'.
20 Pérez Hernández, 2017, p. 28.

21 Fieldwork interview: Expert No. 10.
22 Fieldwork interview: Expert No. 7.
23 Balbontín, 2016.
24 Balbontín. 2015.
25 DeSíde Organization, 2017.
26 National Pro-Life Committee, Mexico, 2005.
27 Keck and Sikkink, 1999, p. 93.
28 Fieldwork interview: Expert No. 26.
29 Alarcón Loayza *et al.,* 2017, p. 15.
30 Pérez Hernández, 2017, p. 28.
31 Fieldwork interview: Expert No. 6.
32 Fieldwork interview: Expert No. 20.
33 Fieldwork interview: Expert No. 6.
34 Fieldwork interview: Expert No. 6.
35 Interviewed Expert No. 11.
36 Interviewed Expert No. 11.
37 Clapham, 2007, p. 160.
38 Interviewed Expert No. 7.
39 Interviewed Expert No. 23.
40 True and Wiener, 2019.
41 True and Wiener, 2019.
42 True and Wiener, 2019.
43 Wiener, 2014.
44 Interviewed Expert No 24.
45 Interviewed Expert No 10.
46 Interviewed Expert No 24.
47 Interviewed Expert No 19.
48 Interviewed Expert No. 17.
49 See Sieder *et al.*, 2014–2017.
50 Pérez Hernández, 2017, p. 27.
51 Fieldwork materials: photographs gathered in public protest in Mexico City, October 2018.
52 Interviewed Expert No. 1.
53 Interviewed Expert No. 15.
54 Interviewed Expert No. 21.

References

Alarcón Loayza, N., Bartolini Esparza, M., Contreras Díaz, A.J., Mizrahi Nedvedovich, C., Ortiz Trujillo, D., Pérez Hernández, C., and Zúñiga Tapia, F.R. (2017). *Aborto: La Política de un Estado Claudicante*. Todas y Todos Valemos en México. Mexico City: Consejo Editorial de la Cámara de Diputados, LXIII Legislatura.

Balbontín, A. (2015). *The Government Does Not Solve Any Social Problem by Decriminalizing Abortion.* Chile: El Demócrata. https://www.eldemocrata.cl/opinion/el-gobierno-no-resuelve-un-problema-social-al-despenalizar-el-aborto/

Balbontín, A. (2016). *Minister of Health Provides Key: Abortion is Not a Public Health Issue*. Chile: El Demócrata. https://www.eldemocrata.cl/opinion/minsal-da-la-clave-aborto-no-es-tema-de-salud-publica/

Clapham, A. (2007). *Human Rights: A Very Short Introduction.* Oxford University Press.

DeSíde Organization. (2017). "Abortion Doubles Risk of Breast Cancer." http://www.embarazoinesperado.com/cancerdemama.htm.

Keck, M.E., and Sikkink, K. (1999). "Transnational Advocacy Networks in International and Regional Politics." *International Social Science Journal*, 51(159), 89–101.

National Pro-Life Committee, Mexico (*Comité Nacional Pro-Vida*). (2005). "Legalizing Abortion Does Not Reduce Maternal Mortality." http://www.comiteprovida.org/aborto/mortalidad-materna.htm#.
Pérez Hernández, C. (2017). "Antecedentes del Aborto en México." In *Aborto: La Política de un Estado Claudicante*, edited by Pérez Hernández, *et al*. Mexico City: Consejo Editorial de la Cámara de Diputados, LXIII Legislatura.
Sieder, R., Gianella, C., Gloppen, S., Gargarella, R., Bergallo, P., Gonzales, A.C., Peñas, A., de Assis Machado, M. R. R., and Ely Yamin, A. (2014–2017). "Abortion Rights Lawfare in Latin America." Research Project at CMI Chr. Michelsen Institute, Norway. Norwegian Research Council. https://www.cmi.no/projects/1841-abortion-rights-lawfare-in-latin-america. Accessed August 26, 2020.
True, J., and Wiener, A. (2019). "Everyone Wants (a) Peace: The Dynamics of Rhetoric and Practice on 'Women, Peace and Security'." *International Affairs*, 95(3), 553–574.
Wiener, A. (2014). *A Theory of Contestation*. Springer.
Wiener, A. (2018). *Contestation and Constitution of Norms in Global International Relations*. Cambridge: Cambridge University Press.

6 Abortion in International Laws, Institutions, and Global Debates

This chapter, where I undertake a 'zooming out' into the overarching realm of global and international norms, has a dual purpose: on one hand, to understand and explore the current status of the global abortion debate across international organizations and agencies; and on the other, to draw the connections between Mexico and the transnational and global context. In previous chapters, I have analyzed ways in which Mexican advocates and policy makers on the abortion issue engage globally and transnationally, so it is relevant to understand this global context in more detail.

The participation of Mexican advocates 'beyond borders'[1] has taken the form of attending and organizing regional forums; building transnational alliances with like-minded advocates, experts, and organizations; engaging in global debates; communicating with representatives from 'sister' or 'parent' organizations abroad; and generally accessing diverse forms of contestation in the "*multilogue*" facilitated by international institutions. Such connections are found in the transnational advocacy across nation-state boundaries and in the ways in which Mexican advocates and institutions have participated in global forums and in the drafting and adoption of international legal texts, through their own various interpretations of norms and principles of justice.

Another important point to keep in mind is the degree to which human rights norms and principles are subject to interpretation, mostly at the implementing stages.[2] The more abstract and 'universalist' they may be, the more they are in practice subject to widely varying interpretations according to cultural norms, practices, and traditions. When it comes to *practice* as a point of study, the issue of 'access' also becomes unavoidable,[3] not only in the sense of *'which actors have access to which specific kinds of practices?'* but also for contestation itself in a more *'meta'* kind of sense: *Who has access in the first place to contest certain norms, principles or written laws, and how do they do it?. . .*

Abortion is embedded within a global normative environment of major historical shifts in ideas and concepts regarding human rights. As explored earlier, the history of human rights as a philosophical and legal concept has been a history of an ever-enlarging concept of rights, having come a long way since its inception as a narrow set of mostly political liberties for a few kinds of (exclusively male) individuals. Since then, the path of human rights has been one of progressive

DOI:10.4324/9781032642338-6

inclusion (through the drafting of new international legal documents as well as reforms to the existing ones) of groups such as women, children, many kinds of minorities, and disadvantaged groups as well as 'newer' rights such as the rights to food, housing, clean water, and a healthy environment, among many others. The future is likely to bring us newer conceptions and 'generations' of human rights, in accordance to newly appearing global concerns, or by presenting new solutions to older problems.

In the international human rights systems, no right is taken to be absolute or unbounded (with the exception of the absolute torture prohibition); and it is accepted that nation-states can sign international legal documents with reservations to certain articles, with comments and interpretive observations – a process which allows states enough room to interpret articles to fit their specific cultural and local context.[4] Even as basic and fundamental a right as the *'right to life'* is not taken to be 'unlimited' and sees contestation with issues at both of its '*ends*', concerning, on one end, when can abortion be legally permitted, and on the other, discussions such as the legality of euthanasia, assisted suicide, the death penalty for serious crimes, or instances where state actors are allowed to confront individuals using lethal force.

Abortion presents a case where not only are the rights of two distinct subjects at odds with one another but also the human rights norms *themselves* are subject to varying interpretations and where, in this context of the ever-more encompassing concept of 'human rights', any talk of *'protecting human rights'* risks losing any meaning – as we have seen in the Mexican debate where opposed advocacy groups claim to be defending internationally recognized human rights.[5] Compromises have been rather attained when the 'rights' framework is complemented by other notions, such as *public health* (in an attempt to prevent deaths of women from unsafe abortions) and through the construction of a carefully nuanced discourse where the woman's rights are proven to trump those of the unborn, at least during the earlier stages of a pregnancy.

Re-visiting the notion of the 'ever-expanding' human rights, this is precisely the argument put forward by some advocates on the 'pro-life' side. They argue that the rights of the unborn ought to be included, too, in this ever-widening recognition of human rights for specific individuals or, argued differently, for groups with particular vulnerabilities. They invoke a notion of "foetal rights"[6] or "foetal protections",[7] arguing that human life is a continuum that begins at the moment of conception and contesting the notion that any 'threshold' other than conception can be reasonably established as a beginning of personhood – that is, of *legally protected* human life. As explored further in this chapter, there is no consensus in international legal documents to fully support this notion, but some experts consider that it also cannot be outright rejected, as several international legal documents do lay out some protections – vague as though they may be – to life before birth.

This lack of consensus on what the precise boundaries of 'the right to life' ought to be in this case also means a lack of a monolithic position about what kind of policy should states adopt in regard to abortion: what are, or what should be, the boundaries of the constituted norms to protect life or to protect women's reproductive choices. Especially at the international legal stage, abortion is the prime example of a case where: *"in the absence of social recognition, where nothing seems intuitively appropriate, individuals will turn to their individually held normative baggage for reference"*.[8] Ample room is provided for interpretation by the states – and by extension, allowing also varied interpretation by different cultural or ideological groups.

One of the oldest debates within human rights normative frameworks is, for instance, the one about where exactly should the boundaries lie between 'the public' and 'the private' spheres of life: when should governments intervene in individuals' private matters, for the sake of protecting others or protecting the common good. Within the topic of abortion, this makes for some unusual contradictions within, sometimes, even individuals themselves: people who usually have strong stances against government intervention in economics, family life, healthcare, etc., advocate in favour of government intervening to impede, block, and prosecute abortion. These 'conservative libertarians' (just as much as the modern liberals who are *'pro big government'*) showcase the increasingly complex – sometimes internally contradicting – panorama of modern debates when framed solely in 'human rights' terms and discourses.

Since the times of drafting the first modern rights documents, already the feminist movements of those years brought attention to how this broad human rights framework failed to *"address the structural inequality between the sexes, issues of private violence against women, and the need for greater inclusion of women in decision making"*.[9] The inadequacy of just arguing 'on human rights terms' in a general sense has shown itself in the abortion debate, where opposed advocacy groups all claim to defend internationally protected *fundamental* rights.

In light of these clashes and collisions of principles, it might be difficult to turn either a prohibition or an endorsement of legal abortion into a "Type 1" fundamental or universal norm. '*Right to life*' and '*Freedom of individual choice*' are both taken to be fundamental, T1 principles; yet neither is an unbounded or unlimited principle, nor is there full clarity on which interpretation should prevail when the two of them collide. Thus, it is only at the level of "Type 2" norms, or organizing principles, that the real 'on-the-ground' compromises can be made at the national level.

However, the clash in viewpoints will occur at this level too, the space for a potential compromise situated between the two extremes of the 'total ban on abortion with no recognized legal exceptions', on the one hand, and the 'total freedom of abortion on-demand and with no constraints as to gestational period', on the other. It is important to point out that the majority of advocates, either for or against abortion, advocate for *something in the middle*. It is only the rare, fringe minorities on both sides which defend either of those two extremes – in the Mexican advocacy as well as in other contexts.

Most expert advocates interviewed in Mexico are aware of the relevant international human rights documents, integrating them as part of their advocacy discourses in order to engage in *"lawfare"* which can be expected to continue across the region. The aforementioned lack of consensus does not undermine the legitimacy of abortion-related norms – following on the theory of contestation; it rather strengthens the case for a dialogue that looks carefully into opposing sides and their respective claims.

Abortion Laws as a Global Matter

Abortion could seem to be a strictly national issue, and even within the nation-state, some perspectives would prefer to treat it as a private matter, rather than one where the state or the law need be concerned beyond some medical regulations. Why examine it through this global lens? In our modern interconnected world, hardly any social movement, or any social justice cause that the public might consider pressing enough, remains strictly local. A growing network of transnational advocates, as identified by Keck and Sikkink,[10] increasingly seeks alliances abroad – constantly cross-pollinating their expertise with that of academics and experts from other (geographical as well as issue) areas.

In analyzing of the history of global public health, Kickbusch and Ivanova[11] explain major changes which, since the late 19th century, started to shape "international public health" into "global health" as one ramification of modern IR.[12] Recognition of the AIDS epidemic (around the late eighties), coinciding with major political shifts at the end of the Cold War, brought 'cosmopolitan momentum' to international health diplomacy, as well as a new need for collective (i.e. *global*) action in the realm of health. In this modern normative dimension of global responsibility, defending national interests will necessarily be balanced with the realization that modern health challenges can only be resolved jointly across national borders. Public health becomes the same as '*global* public health', as the interconnectedness of people, transport means and systems, resources, and knowledge all increase. A part of this shift has also been the appearance of other stakeholders than states, towards the inclusion of voices from civil society, advocates on a variety of issues, industries, and private corporations. Health is now a global public good, and as such it needs to be negotiated multilaterally.

The recent COVID-19 pandemic came as proof that major public health issues can quickly become *global* public health issues, not only because communicable diseases can cross borders much more quickly than experts can detect them but also because populations across the world also now share a multiplicity of the causes for *non*communicable disease (i.e. shared food habits and sources, similar cultural habits of sedentary lifestyle). Cultural chances such as delaying marriage and childbearing, having smaller families, and the demand for contraceptives have happened across most of today's societies – however unequally and variedly across regions and subnational contexts. In the same way that the World Health Organization (WHO) deals with global public health issues more generally, the United Nations Population Fund (UNFPA) is one of several UN agencies that treat abortion and its legal complexities as an international issue.

It is a relevant issue within women's health because unsafe abortions (legal or illegal) can cause maternal mortality, morbidity, or problems with future fertility. Illegality rarely keeps abortions from happening. In countries where the practice is illegal, many abortions are still carried out, but they are often unsafe and carry the aforementioned risks.[13] In almost all countries where abortion is banned, complications from unsafe abortion are a leading cause of maternal mortality.[14] The burden is unjustly high on economically disadvantaged women, who do not have access to a discrete procedure in a safe private clinic, as women in a better economic position can often access.

In international law, mentions of abortion are embedded within norms and declarations related to the human rights of women, particularly the right to sexual and reproductive health and autonomy. This has become relevant for advocacy itself: as mentioned earlier, the debates at the national level tend to stall when framed exclusively as 'rights' issues, yet the discursive framework of public health has, at times, allowed for compromise and organizing principles pivoting on women's health.

International law can give actors ideas for advocacy and standards on potential compromises. General propositions are not necessarily decisive in concrete cases, which is why 'interpretation matters', yet the endeavours during fieldwork and data analysis showed that the current national debates are being influenced by the global ones.[15] Advocates 'on the ground' are listening to what United Nations agencies do and say, and UN agencies are opening spaces for advocates and NGOs to inform them, in turn. The ongoing contestation and negotiation of meanings in treaties and declarations, and the contestation of actions and practices as well, prove that such global debates matter (and they matter because advocates, stakeholders and individuals decide that they do) and that the international legal texts are generally accorded legitimacy.

These 'opposing voices' present in the abortion debate throughout many different regions are opposed on a debate that the advocates themselves present as polarized and binary. Hence looking first at *why* abortion is a complex and polarizing problem and, at the 'bigger picture' of the international arena, where a 'global *multilogue*' of stakeholders seeks cultural validation and shows great ideological diversity. It is not the aim of this book to declare whether there 'should' be a universal IR norm in relation to abortion. In that sense, it will not be the job of IR theorists to 'solve' the issue, not even to declare that it's necessarily a problem in need of a 'universal' solution. Dialogue will still vary across different contexts.

Abortion 'Goes Global': Cairo 1994 and Beyond

In 1994 during the International Conference on Population and Development, in Cairo, Egypt (ICPD Cairo '94), abortion was first addressed by international institutions as an issue of public health – rather than 'human rights' or an individual 'right to choose', or merely gender equality for women. It was recognized by states as "*a major public health concern*".[16] It has a dimension of psychological health, as some experts argue that being in control of her own reproductive choices improves a woman's chances in life and therefore her emotional health; others consider that forcing a woman to carry a foetus which is the product of sexual abuse, or one that will eventually die from severe malformations, is "*a form of cruel, inhuman and degrading treatment*".[17] Also there are cases of women who, during pregnancy, develop conditions which endanger their life and who need an abortion – though such instances are exceedingly rare, as many so-called pro-life advocates often emphasize.

Data from the WHO and UNFPA shows that in most countries where abortion is illegal – and therefore more women risk unsafe procedures – maternal deaths resulting from abortions are significantly higher than in those countries where it is legal.[18] Medical institutions as well as women and girls' rights organizations state that unsafe abortion remains one of the leading causes of maternal mortality and morbidity, and legal prohibitions often have little to no effect on the number of abortions carried out in a given setting.[19,20] Using this argument along with other 'pro-choice' discursive framings, advocates and organizations have, in recent decades, fought for the legal recognition of a 'right to access' abortion as a medical service. The United Nations Commission for Latin America and the Caribbean (CEPAL), in its follow-up examination document after 15 years of the Fourth World Conference on Women (Beijing Conference), notes that some Latin American countries have seen progress in expanding the cases where abortion should be legally permitted, following global concerns about the dangers that unsafe abortion presents for women.[21]

The most recent report following up to the Framework of Action of the International Conference of Population and Development (called *ICPD Post-2014* or *Cairo Beyond-14*) presents study cases such as that of Uruguay, where abortion was legalized as a part of comprehensive measures for reproductive health. It is a model that treats abortion "*as a public health issue rather than a legal or criminal matter*".[22] As a result, Uruguay made important progress in reducing maternal deaths from unsafe abortion (with the numbers reaching zero in 2011), as well as very low maternal mortality and better scores in reproductive health overall. The issue remains, however, a major challenge in Latin America, and such framings and discourses are opposed by conservative political factions as well as by practically all major religious institutions, which often reject the very notion that discussions on abortion should be related to public health at all.

The Irreconcilable Viewpoints: Human Rights Grounds on Opposing Discourses

At times when international legal documents have been adopted, especially those touching upon issues of women's sexual and reproductive health and rights such as the Beijing Declaration and Platform for Action of the Fourth World Conference on Women of 1995, or the final text adopted at the International Conference on Population and Development (ICPD) in Cairo 1994, or the Convention on the Elimination of all forms of Discrimination Against Women (CEDAW), the written records of the negotiation processes by which these documents came to be is telling evidence of the contested nature of such issues in the international arena.

The informative documents on such Declarations contain detailed descriptions of the negotiations themselves, recording not only each country's signature and ratification date but also each of their observations, remarks, interpretive statements, and reservations to the documents. Oftentimes, the sections on interpretive statements and reservations are as lengthy as the declarations themselves, with numerous countries presenting objections to different aspects of sexual rights, gender equality provisions, and reproductive rights in general – with a particular focus on abortion.

International legal documents are often made vague on purpose, in order to get many states to agree with them and adapt to their cultural context. Nations can then have much leeway to interpret according to contexts, cultures, and circumstances. *"Given this emphasis on general agreement, the subsequent contested interpretation of the details of the agreement (whether of legal quality or not), at the implementing stage in specific local contexts is to be expected".*[23]

The upcoming section takes a brief look at the international legal documents and human rights documents which are relevant to the abortion debate, providing an overview of why they are. Some of them because of recommendations in relation to abortion laws, or for providing statements about life before birth and its judicial recognition, ideas on the recognition of personhood before birth, or because of how certain reservations and interpretive statements by specific nations have made them relevant. They are relevant especially if advocates for and against legal abortion tend to mention them in their messages. This shall provide an overview of the current 'international legal panorama' on abortion and related norms.

Specificities about Mexico are provided when relevant: either because it is a document pertaining to Mexico exclusively (results of the Universal Periodic Review cycles for Mexico) or because Mexico presented reservations or interpretive comments. It is intended as an analysis of what the most relevant and notable international documents state about abortion, situating this practice (and the related concepts and ideas) within the global normative environment of human rights, public health and gender equality. These are the main documents that advocates referred to in their defence of their specific positions and on which it was of interest to engage them in their interpretations and perceptions.

ICPD Cairo 1994

The text of the Cairo Declaration on Population and Development, following the International Conference on Population and Development (ICPD '94), is one of the most relevant documents topic-wise – though not necessarily the one providing the most legal clarity, or the one that advocates in Mexico use a lot. It was however the first international document of its nature to mention abortion explicitly; thus, I begin this section with it. Contrary to beliefs by some advocates, it does *not* state that abortion must be legalized but it does draw connections between unsafe abortion and health risks for women, urging states to avoid a criminalization of (or the withholding of medical treatment for) women who have abortions. It argues against using abortion as a method of family planning, in favour of strengthening commitments to women's health by improving access to other methods and prioritizing the prevention of unwanted pregnancies, to "eliminate the need for abortion".[24] The text emphasizes that "any measures or changes related to abortion within the health system can only be determined at the national or local level according to the national legislative process" and that wherever abortion is lawful, it should be safe.

The Records of Proceedings written at the time of the adoption of the Programme of Action subsequent to this Declaration (*"Programme of Action of the International Conference on Population and Development (ICPD) of 1994 in Cairo, Egypt"*) contain numerous written statements and reservations that nations presented as the negotiations took place.[25] There is strong representation of African, Middle Eastern, and Latin American countries among those states who presented reservations to specific articles and paragraphs. Most objections refer to sexual and reproductive health and rights, with an emphasis on abortion, with various countries' delegations reaffirming their official stance that life is to be legally protected from the moment of conception and that they shall not recognize abortion as a part of legitimate reproductive choices.

A remarkable number of countries object to the word '*individual*' when it is part of a statement about reproductive health and fertility, emphasizing the more collective nature of such decisions (meaning, belonging to a couple or family unit), often stressing that only a married couple of one man and one woman can, jointly, claim a right to make reproductive decisions (but never after conception has occurred). The Vatican, as well, submitted lengthy comments and reservations, rejecting any notion that abortion should ever constitute a legitimate choice, as well as challenging any *"individualistic understanding"* of sexuality and reproductive rights.

ICPD Cairo Post-2014 (Framework of Actions)

The 2014 "Framework of Actions for the Follow-Up to the Programme of Action, of the International Conference of Population and Development" (known as the Cairo Conference of 2014 or Cairo Post-2014) makes a more pressing case for the advantages of legalizing abortion, than the Cairo Declaration of 1994. It does not openly say that states 'should' legalize or liberalize access to abortion, but it is taken by some advocates to be one of the international documents that comes the closest to affirming a supposed *'right to access abortion'*. As a "Framework of Actions", however, it is not considered to be a binding legal document.

It emphasizes the *"relationship between restrictive abortion laws, maternal mortality and unsafe abortion"*[26] condemns absolute bans and urges states to *"eliminate punitive measures against women and girls who undergo abortions and providers who deliver abortion services. . . . At a minimum, States should decriminalize abortion and ensure access to abortion when the pregnancy poses a risk to a woman's health or life, where there is severe foetal abnormality, and where the pregnancy is the result of rape or incest"*. It notes that these exceptions however might be insufficient to ensure women's rights.

Like its predecessor document, it stresses that abortions should be carried out safely *in contexts where it is already legalized.* A similar message is stated in informative documents of the United Nations' Office of the High Commissioner for Human Rights, showing that even when the issue of abortion is tackled by international Human Rights institutions and by the international legal system of

Human Rights, the focus has had to be placed on *health* rather than private individual choice[27]: a framework of only individual human rights has not been helpful to the negotiations for more liberal abortion laws.

Universal Declaration of Human Rights (UDHR)

The cornerstone and foundational document of the international system of Human Rights, the UDHR is also the most intentionally vague legal text – so as to encourage universal signing and later adaptation within domestic contexts. It does not mark specificities about the precise point at which life, personhood, or the judicial protection of either should begin. No topic pertaining mostly to women is mentioned, nor to any other disadvantaged group, for that matter. Article 1 states: *"All human beings are born free and equal in dignity and rights"*[28]; and Article 3 on the right to life is 11 words long: *"Everyone has the right to life, liberty and security of person"*. The UDHR does not mention the word 'conception', mentions 'birth' and 'born' only in the context of non-discrimination and equality, and does not make any attempt to define a precise point where life or rights begin. Though not very used in advocacy, some 'pro-life' activists might mention it as protecting life in the most general terms, which in their view means *absolute* terms.

Convention on the Rights of the Child (CRC)

The UN Convention on the Rights of the Child (1989) mentions in its preamble – quoting the earlier Declaration on the Rights of the Child of 1959 – that a child *"by reason of his physical and mental immaturity, needs special safeguards and care, including appropriate legal protection, before as well as after birth"*.[29] The sentence is still interpreted by many to be rather vague (for intents and purposes of the abortion debate), not specifying a point at which legal obligation to protect life begins. Some anti-abortion advocates construe this as opposition to abortion, even if the word 'conception' (which they take as such starting point of protection) does not appear.

OHCHR Covenants: ICCPR and ICESCR

The two international Human Rights Covenants, the International Covenant on Civil and Political Rights (ICCPR), and the International Covenant on Economic, Social and Cultural Rights (ICESCR), also contain no specificities on abortion or the boundaries of the right to life. The ICCPR's article on the right to life is almost as vague as that of the UDHR, mentions 'birth' and 'born' only in the context of non-discrimination and equality, and also does define a precise point where life, personhood, or rights begin.[30] The ICESCR, in turn, does not contain an article on the right to life, nor does it attempt to define its beginning. It makes only one reference to protections towards the period before childbirth, but these are for the expecting mother: *"Special protection should be accorded to mothers during a reasonable period before and after childbirth"*.[31]

ICCPR General Comment No. 36 on the Right to Life

The two covenants themselves only provide these points and therefore are not commonly used by advocates in either pro- or anti-abortion advocacy. However, much more relevant is the aforementioned *"General Comment No. 36, on article 6 of the International Covenant on Civil and Political Rights, on the Right to Life"*,[32] which contains specific references to abortion and whose process of negotiating and drafting was in itself a fascinating instance of norm contestation at the global level. For the purposes of this section, the General Comment reiterates and reemphasizes the points laid out by Cairo Post-2014 that states are strongly encouraged to reconsider the links between unsafe illegal abortions and risks to women's health, to guarantee access to abortion in the cases where it is legal, to strive for the prevention of abortions, and to avoid stigmatizing women who undergo them. It does not call abortion 'a right', except (closely so) in cases where the woman's life would be at risk, or when she was a victim of sexual assault.

Universal Periodic Reviews (UPR), Recommendations to Mexico: Cycles of 2013 and 2018

As an instrument of soft law, the Universal Periodic Review (UPR) is one of the UN Human Rights System's strongest accountability mechanisms. Each time that a state undergoes examination (in five-year cycles), other states provide specific legal recommendations, which the examined states can accept or reject. Other stakeholders such as representatives of domestic NGOs also have opportunities to inform on the status of domestic affairs. The concluding documents of the UPR do not constitute a binding, signed Treaty, but they are nevertheless a strong instrument for accountability and standards-setting – one that advocates use domestically to pressure their governments into compliance with these commitments and accepted recommendations, publicly made in a global forum.

In Mexico's second cycle in 2013,[33] comments by the Netherlands concerned abortion laws: recommending harmonization of state-level legislation on abortion to grant equal access country-wide (Recommendation 148.153, publicly accepted by Mexico). A recommendation in the opposite direction came from the Holy See of the Vatican: *"Respect and defend life from conception to natural death, based on amendments of state constitutions, promoting a similar protection at federal and local levels"* (Recommendation 148.8). To the latter, Mexico gave the following non-accepting comment: "*The Supreme Court has confirmed the power of the federal entities to legislate in this area . . . It is therefore not possible to implement recommendation 148.48 since uniformity in the various legislations cannot be ensured under the current Federal Pact*". The responses show that while Mexico (or at least, *the delegation representing the country's government then*) accepts a stance towards abortion decriminalization (to match the legalized status of Mexico City), it still mostly resorts to federalism in granting each subnational state the power to decide internally.

By the time of the third cycle of examinations in 2018,[34] two things were remarkable. The first is that many more countries made suggestions concerning abortion, most of them towards more liberal laws. The second is that this time, however, explanatory statements were not given, instead the Mexican delegation simply decided to take recommendations as either "supported" (no longer called "accepted") or, when in disagreement, as "noted". Mexico responded with "supported" to all recommendations suggesting harmonizing laws giving access to abortion across the country (from Denmark, France, Slovenia, Georgia, Azerbaijan, Albania and New Zealand). The only recommendation not supported but only "noted" was again the same recommendation coming from the Holy See of the Vatican, about protecting life "from conception, based on the amendments to state constitutions".

It is notable that most countries' position, when they touch upon the subject of abortion at all, lean in the direction of pressing towards legalization. Mexico's responses also seem more receptive to the idea of legalization; however, they tend to give more weight to federalism as a system where each subnational state decides on its policies.

OHCHR: Committee on the Rights of Persons with Disabilities (CRPD)

In past Country Reviews and Country Reports by the Committee on the Rights of Persons with Disabilities (not Mexico's however, but other countries', such as Austria in 2013), the OHCHR's Committee itself has criticized laws in some states allowing abortion until very late stages of pregnancy, when it is detected that the foetus has a disability. The Committee has urged to *"abolish any distinction in the period within which a pregnancy can be terminated based solely on disability"*.[35] Overly permissive abortion laws for reasons of disability are not the case in Mexico; the interest of mentioning it is to touch upon the many aforementioned dimensions of the debate and to showcase the various angles from which the issue is breached also within the UN system.

Disability rights and their potential clash with abortion-related norms had been mentioned as one aspect of the 'contestedness' and controversies inherent to this debate. Indeed it is not just a simplified clash between a religious dogma on the 'right to life' versus an absolute and unquestioned 'right to choose'. It has many more nuances where other, perhaps non-obvious rights, can be at stake and where the reasons *'why'* someone might choose an abortion carry a certain weight in the discussion. Other dimensions of the debate are to be considered, even if advocating for legalization and for rights over one's own body and reproductive choices. This also challenges the notion held by many 'pro-life' advocates, that the UN is *'a pro-abortion organization that pushes states to legalize abortion everywhere, at any time and for any reason'*[36] or the paradigm that there is a single, monolithic vision on abortion within the UN.

CEDAW: Comments and Reservations

Similar to ICPD Cairo '94 and its Follow-Up Frameworks, for the Convention on the Elimination of all Forms of Discrimination Against Women (CEDAW), lengthy comments and reservations were presented by many signatory countries.[37] CEDAW is however less focused on reproductive rights than the Cairo documents; it elaborates less on such rights and does not mention 'abortion'. Only two countries (remarkably, two European ones: Malta and Monaco) specifically objected, in their reservations to CEDAW, to some articles which they interpret as a potential imposition to legalize abortion. Most reservations to CEDAW are about defending or maintaining domestic laws that discriminate against women, and most of such objections came from countries with predominantly Muslim populations. Still, the existence of so numerous and long reservations and interpretive statements presented to documents like CEDAW shows that the issues related to women's equality are still highly contested in many traditional cultures and in their derived legal practice.

Beijing Declaration: Comments and Reservations

The 1995 Beijing Declaration and Platform for Action of the Fourth World Conference on Women mentions abortion in a similar manner to ICPD Cairo '94 but not in an explicit push towards legalization. It calls attention to the dangers of illegal abortions that tend to be unsafe, urging states to do everything they can to reduce the need for abortions through education and contraceptives, as well as to give adequate post-abortion care to women regardless of the legality status of the practice. The Declaration quotes and refers to Cairo '94 in most of its mentions about abortion.

At the time of adoption, 64 countries (from a total of 190 attending) presented observations, reservations, and interpretive statements to various articles.[38] Fourteen of them were Latin American countries, the rest mostly African, Southeast Asian, and Middle Eastern states. Most interpretive statements express challenges to notions about which actions and practices are 'acceptable' as individual choices in reproductive rights. Out of the 14 Latin American countries that presented reservations, 5 of them referred to the articles that mention abortion, rejecting the idea that it should be legally permissible, and reaffirming their interpretation that life shall be legally protected from the moment of conception.

Also noteworthy for its religious and cultural influence in Latin America is the lengthy written statement presented by the Vatican State, in representation of the Catholic Church. It reaffirms the official doctrine rejecting not only abortion without exceptions but also "*contraception or the use of condoms, either as a family planning measure or in HIV/AIDS prevention programmes*".[39] Other remarkable words, showing the Vatican's interpretation of human rights is: "*My delegation regrets to note in the text an exaggerated individualism, in which key, relevant, provisions of the Universal Declaration of Human Rights are slighted – for example, the obligation to provide "special care and assistance" to motherhood. This selectivity thus marks another step in the colonization of the broad and rich discourse of universal rights by an impoverished, libertarian rights dialect. Surely this international gathering could have done more for women and girls than to leave them alone with their rights!*"

The Pact of San José (Inter-American Convention on Human Rights)

The legal existence of a 'right to life before birth' is a contested concept in national legal systems, as well as international ones. In the Inter-American human rights system, the regional American Convention on Human Rights does mention a specific right to life before birth – the UN's Universal Declaration does not, nor does any other UN rights treaty, in such a specific manner. The American Convention on Human Rights of 1969, also known as the "Pact of San José", states in its Article 4: "*Right to Life: 4.1 Every person has the right to have his life respected. This right shall be protected by law and, in general, from the moment of conception*".[40]

Such a defined statement on the protection of life *"from the moment of conception"* is, for better and for worse, an anomaly in the international panorama of human rights conventions, declarations, and treaties. Other documents in international human rights regimes do not lay out such a clear mandate to protect life starting at one specific moment, whatever it may be. The few that allude to life before birth only do so as assumed to be encompassed within the special care that must be given to motherhood and childhood in general. The *Pact of San José*, unlike equivalent UN documents, is the only international legal document containing such a provision.

Debates which invoke Article 4 of the Pact tend to focus on the exact meaning of the words "in general".[41] The vagueness of those words (and the diverse interpretations about what kinds of exceptions they might allow for) gives room to interpretations that could fit a strict anti-abortion agenda, or a 'general anti-abortion, with some exceptions' agenda, or even a more permissive decriminalization scheme. This is context-sensitive and depends on what meanings and constructions are attached to the "in general", particularly constructions not mentioned at all by the Pact such as *'who decides?'* or, *'who has access to define and elaborate on those meanings in the first place?'*. . .

This specific recognition of a right to life from conception is deemed by some as a notion of *"foetal rights"*.[42] It highlights the controversial nature of abortion in the Americas, especially in many Latin American countries. Rather than such countries' opposition to abortion stemming from a document like the Pact of San José, it is likely the opposite: the fact that such wording was included in the Pact at all, is something that showcases the efforts of the strong anti-abortion advocacy that has been in place for several decades, and it reflects the contested meaning of 'life' with regard to its legally protected beginning across Latin America. It's likely not the case that a lot of the Americas have a rather conservative stance on abortion because of the Pact of San José but instead that Article 4 came to be *because* the region has strong conservative trends, a consequence rather than a cause.

At the time of ratification of the Pact, two interpretive declarations and one reservation were presented by the Mexican delegation. The first reads as follows: "*With respect to Article 4, paragraph 1, the Government of Mexico considers that the expression "in general" does not constitute an obligation to adopt, or keep in force, legislation to protect life "from the moment of conception," since this matter falls within the domain reserved to the* (subnational) *states*".[43]

Taken at face value, this does not reflect opposition to the protection of life before birth, but rather a note on the federal nature of Mexico's highly fragmented legal system – where matters of protection of life before birth fall within the realms of subnational laws.

Many experts interviewed for this book mentioned the Pact of San José, either as 'pro-life' advocates remarking on this international legal protection before birth and the transnational advocacy that put those words into the text or as pro-legalization advocates commenting on the process of coming up with this interpretive declaration and on the flexibilities granted by the words *"in general"*. Their statements and comments on this article showcase human rights-focused advocacy working in both directions: from the global into domestic policies, and vice versa. Local and regional advocacy made its mark in the drafting of the Inter-American Convention, and meanwhile 'the global' has influenced (and continues to influence) the local, when advocates especially in 'pro-life' groups quote this document in their efforts.

Jurisprudence by the Inter-American Court of Human Rights, and the Inter-American Commission on Human Rights (IACHR)

Relevant cases having to do with abortion (or legal personhood before birth) presented to the Inter-American Court of Human Rights, or to the Inter-American Commission on Human Rights (IACHR), are relatively scarce. Among the ones existing, most concern the countries with the strictest bans such as El Salvador and Nicaragua, and even then, they normally concern only 'extreme cases' such as the jailing of women who abort, or pregnancies resulting from sexual assault towards very young underage girls – not cases demanding access in general. Relevant to Mexico are two in particular: one because it directly concerned the Mexican state, and another because it marks the closest that the Inter-American Court has come to presenting a stance about legal personhood before birth.

The first was the "Caso Paulina" in the very early 2000s, where Mexican advocacy institutions (GIRE and the Alaíde Foppa group of Baja California) representing an underage girl who was denied abortion by the local Baja California authorities after sexual assault denounced the Mexican state to court, demanding reparations of the damage done to "Paulina".[44] After local authorities failed to adequately respond in the case, GIRE and the Alaíde Foppa group denounced to the Inter-American Commission on Human Rights. The case culminated six years later with an 'amicable solution settlement' between the Federal Government of Mexico and the victim, signed before the IACHR in Washington.

It is recognized as a major stepping stone towards eventual legalization of abortion in Mexico City in 2007.[45] Similar cases have been presented to the IACHR, where individuals attempt to bring their respective governments into accountability for failing to respect a particular woman's right to abortion. However, such cases do not focus on abortion as 'a right for all women': those that 'make it' to the IACHR in the first place (and are followed up on by the Commission) tend to be exceptional, for example, concerning high-risk pregnancies where a woman is being denied necessary abortion to save her life or health, or pregnancies resulting from the assault of very young underage girls. Such cases are not representative of claims to a more 'general' liberalization of abortion, and the Court's jurisprudence highlights the absence of an international consensus on abortion rights.

The second relevant ruling is *"Artavia Murillo vs. Costa Rica"* of 2012, which came as a result of debates in Costa Rica on whether in vitro fertilization (IVF) should be permitted or not, because of embryos' potential personhood.[46] Though initially not concerning abortion, the controversy and the subsequent ruling are mentioned often by pro-legalization advocates and by scholars who write on the topic,[47] as the case concludes that embryos do not have legal personhood, only progressively attaining rights.

Artavia Murillo is a remarkable instance of an idea previously mentioned: that newer advancements in medical technology are bound to change our views and considerations on what 'life' means, medically and legally. Some of its ponderings stress on the fact that 'conception' can mean different things clinically, remarking the distinction between 'fertilization' (of an egg) and 'implantation' (of a fertilized egg into the womb) – relevant to mention only because, in medical terms, a pregnancy is considered to begin only when *implantation* successfully occurs, essential for the woman to even notice that the *fertilization* took place. In the amendments to Mexican subnational Constitutions to protect life before birth, some of them mention *'conception'*, but a few mention *'fertilization'* instead. None of them protect life *'from the moment of implantation'*. These distinctions could seem like a form of 'hair splitting' on medical technicalities. But because of the fact that both abortion and IVF can become the subject of legal controversy about allowed or prohibited reproductive practices, it is important to discuss on clear medical terminology – something not always given proper mind by advocates or policy makers.

With *Artavia* and the ponderings about IVF, debates ensued on whether an embryo that comes into existence through 'fertilization' without 'implantation' could be considered 'a person' and whether the relevant criteria to be considered 'a human person' in early stages of life is to be born, or merely to possess human DNA, or to be an embryo that successfully implanted into a womb. Proving, therefore, that even some meanings that could appear simple or timeless such as 'human life', 'conception', 'person' or 'pregnancy' can be subject to interpretations depending on *how* they are defined, and *by whom*. The Court declared that foetuses do not possess personhood in a form equal to the woman but that protections to the life of a foetus are *"gradual and incremental"*.[48]

It is curious, then, that opposed groups in the abortion debate refer in their advocacy to two different documents, both under the larger umbrella of the Organization of American States: while so-called pro-life advocates use the Pact of San José's Article 4 as part of their advocacy efforts, some pro-legalization activists refer to the Inter-American Court's ruling on *Artavia Murillo vs. Costa Rica* as a supposed indicator that the IACHR does not support the protection of life from the moment of conception. The Supreme Court in Mexico stated in 2015 that *"sentences published by the Inter-American Court of Human Rights are binding to national justices, independently if Mexico was part of the litigation . . ., as these criteria determine the content of the rights established in the (Inter-American)*

Convention (on Human Rights)".[49] The idea stands that consensus is lacking and that even within one institutional umbrella, different documents can be used to support opposed positions.

Other Human Rights Systems: The European Court of Human Rights

While the European Court of Human Rights obviously does not concern the Mexican state, it serves as a reference of another regional rights system and another 'lack of consensus' on the issue. The European Court has declined to adopt a general position on abortion, as there is no regional agreement on a recommended legal status.[50] Clapham quotes the European Union's Court of Human Rights Law's statement that *"in the absence of any European consensus on the scientific and legal definition of the beginning of life, the issue of when the right to life begins comes within the margin of appreciation which the Court generally considers that States should enjoy in this sphere".*[51]

Other Human Rights Systems: The African Charter's Maputo Protocol

Quite remarkably, the Maputo Protocol to the African Charter on Human and Peoples' Rights on the Rights of Women in Africa is the first legal document on human rights of a binding nature, recognizing some cases where abortion is 'a right', mentioning that states shall take appropriate measures to "*protect the reproductive rights of women by authorising medical abortion in cases of sexual assault, rape, incest, and where the continued pregnancy endangers the mental and physical health of the mother*".[52] Mexico is naturally not a signatory to the Maputo Protocol either, but this text sets a globally relevant precedent – in a continent also hosting many developing and middle-income countries, some with a similar level of socio-economic development as that of Mexico and where many women also struggle for their equal rights in contexts of conflict, violence, and patriarchal tradition.

Montevideo Consensus on Population and Development (2013)

The 2013 *Montevideo Consensus on Population and Development*, adopted at the first session of the Regional Conference on Population and Development in Latin America and the Caribbean, is a non-binding legal document that adopts recommendations similar to ICPR Post-2014, urging states to reconsider the criminalization of abortion as problematic and to allow for at least some exceptions. Thus, it declares that *"penalization of abortion leads to higher rates of maternal mortality and morbidity and does not reduce the number of abortions"*, urging states *"to consider amending their laws, regulations, strategies and public policies relating to the voluntary termination of pregnancy in order to protect the lives and health of women and adolescent girls, to improve their quality of life and to reduce the number of abortions".*[53]

As the years have passed since Cairo '94, the international documents dealing with abortion and related issues have adopted a progressively bolder stance in denouncing the criminalization of abortion: if they do not explicitly call it 'a right', nor advocate for its unrestricted liberalization, they have become clearer in their message that criminalization is an undesirable legal status that leaves many women in situations of vulnerability and potential rights violations. This was, therefore, a document frequently mentioned by pro-legalization advocates in their messages.

Geneva Consensus Declaration of 2020 (at the Margins of the World Health Assembly 2020)

On the margins of the 2020 World Health Assembly in Geneva, Switzerland, representatives of the United States government (under the Republican leadership of then-President Donald Trump) spearheaded the creation of a brief document called the "Geneva Consensus", a non-binding declaration on "Promoting Women's Health and Strengthening the Family".[54] This document, however, is not related to any of the Geneva-based international organizations and was done rather as an independent project of sorts, of the US Republican administration at the time (especially at the initiative of Secretary of State Mike Pompeo). It was supported and co-signed by another 33 countries, most of them African and Latin American (not including Mexico).

In its short text, the anti-abortion stance seems to be a rather central point. Thus, it is perhaps the first international Declaration against abortion. It affirms that states should "*improve and secure access to health and development gains for women, including sexual and reproductive health . . . without including abortion*", and it reaffirms "*that there is no international right to abortion, nor any international obligation on the part of States to finance or facilitate abortion*".

Despite the *"consensus"* in the name, this short text rather consists of a declaration made by 34 states, through a letter to the United Nations Secretary General, and independently of any international organizations or international legal bodies. It was made separately from any of the conventional negotiation, ratification, and signature procedures normally complied with, when creating internationally accepted legal texts. In a strong display of the political *'pendularity'* of abortion-related policies (and in a manner so short-spanned as to come across as strangely bipolar), US Democratic President Joe Biden removed the United States from the declaration on January 28, 2021.

This may well be the only case of such short-lived support of an international declaration by a sovereign state (lasting less than one year), where the state withdrawing its support had also been the main drafter of the original text. And it is very likely that, following the political tradition of *pendularity* in abortion-related policy (both domestic and abroad, in the same fashion as the constant re-adoption and re-repeal of the Global Gag Rule), a US Republican government would rejoin it when elected in the near future – especially after the 2022 repeal of *Roe vs. Wade*.

Table 6.1 summarizes this overview.

Table 6.1 International Legal Documents and the Matter of Abortion

International text	*Comments/ reservations possible*	*Specific mentions of abortion*	*Specific mentions on life/personhood as beginning at. . .*	*Specific protections of life/ personhood before birth*	*Binding document?*
ICPD Cairo 1994	Yes	Yes – towards legalizing	Unclear	No	No
ICPD Cairo Post-2014	No	Yes – towards legalizing	Unclear	No	No
Universal Declaration on Human Rights (UDHR)	No	No	(Unclear) *"Born free and equal in dignity and rights"*	No	No
Convention on the Rights of the Child	No	No	Unclear	Yes – but specific moment not mentioned	No
UN Covenant on Civil and Political Rights (ICCPR)	Yes	No	(Unclear) *"Every human being has the inherent right to life".*	No	Yes
UN Covenant on Economic and Social Rights (ICESCR)	Yes	No	Not mentioned	(Unclear): *"Special protection should be accorded to mothers (. . .) before and after childbirth".*	Yes
ICCPR General Comment No. 36 on the Right to Life	No (but many comments were presented at the time of drafting)	Yes – towards legalizing	Unclear	No	No
CEDAW	Yes	No	Not mentioned	No	No
Beijing Declaration	Yes	Yes – towards legalizing	Unclear	No	No
Pact of San José	Yes	No	Conception	Yes	Yes
Montevideo Consensus on Population and Development	Yes	Yes – towards legalizing	Unclear	No	No
Geneva Consensus (at the margins of the World Health Assembly 2020)	No	Yes – towards banning	Unclear	Quotes Convention on the Rights of the Child: *"protections before as well as after birth"*	No

Source: Table by author, based on international documents.

A note is pertinent on the point of whether an international document is 'binding': it can depend on how one defines such a concept. For some strict theorists, an international document is 'binding' if a country not only signs it but also follows a ratification procedure which often includes legislative approval at the domestic level.[55] The 'binding-ness' is taken also to mean a constitution of clear commitments of accountability, beyond a mere 'declaration of good intentions'. Some international covenants or instruments also have much clearer and stronger mechanisms of accountability, such as Optional Protocols for Communications Procedures at the OHCHR (where citizens of a signatory state can directly present complains to a Treaty Body).

International law is complex; we can speak of a certain spectrum ranging from 'soft law', which is taken to be non-binding but nonetheless has legal significance, setting legal precedents and stating intentions, and into 'hard law', taken more traditionally to be 'a strict rule to be followed' under defined accountability mechanisms. Another traditional view is that a document is 'binding' if it can be invoked in a court of law, or alternatively if the non-compliance with it can generate sanctions.[56] But this traditional view is more and more coming across as outdated,[57] as governments recognize that even if international documents do not override national law and national sovereignty, 'soft law' is powerful – precisely because advocates on many topics and issue areas can invoke it to pressure their governments into compliance with higher standards of policymaking and policy implementation.

Some advocates seem to take varying positions with regard to a document's 'bindingness', dependent on whether it supports their position or not. It was often seen during fieldwork in Mexico that, whenever a specific document (even if non-binding) helped to favour one position within the debate, advocates would be more open to its great benefits as a piece of 'soft law', whereas if a document is contrary to their position, they're more likely to retort with ideas such as *'Mexico is a sovereign country, though'*, or *'well, it is non-binding for our country'* (or alternatively, *'it's binding but Mexico presented a reservation . . .'*). Advocates on opposed groups do this equally. Perhaps it is somewhat obvious that activists will tend to favour, quote, and 'prop up' those documents that help their cause and disdain those that don't – but it can sometimes indicate a fickle position towards the influence, usefulness, or applicability of international documents in local advocacy, in what we could caricaturize as: *'it's binding law if I like it; and just an empty/illegitimate recommendation if I don't'*.

Despite occasional alarmist views by some 'pro-life' groups, that the United Nations pushes "an abortionist agenda",[58] in reality the closest thing to a current consensus in the UN legal system falls short of recommending a universal legalization of abortion. Access to abortion only comes close to being labelled 'a right' in a few specific documents, and even then it is only mentioned as 'a right' in rather dire contexts such as sexual assault, or dangers to the woman's life if the pregnancy is continued.

The UN human rights and health systems – and its specialized agency, the United Nations Population Fund (UNFPA) – do not advocate for abortion to be legal everywhere, and especially not for it to be used as a common contraceptive. It urges countries to consider the relationship between illegal abortion and maternal mortality, especially in contexts where abortions are in high demand and unsafely performed. A common policy is that abortions should be as 'legal, safe, and rare' as countries can possibly make them and prevented as much as possible through education and contraceptives.[59] The Cairo-2014 "Framework of Actions" presents several cases that stress this view, presenting country experiences where a comprehensive approach to family planning greatly reduced the demand for abortions. In the absence of precise legal boundaries to the 'right to life' but also of an established 'right to abortion', advocates on opposing sides of the "legitimacy gap" find only partial, subject-to-interpretation support in international legal texts. Human rights-related principles and documents have equally served opposing sides of the abortion debate, as advocates interpret principles in the way best supporting their arguments.

The Fragile Compromise: Public Health and the Right to Health

Situating the issue of abortion within the realm of public health often calls for explanations, as mentioned, about *why* abortion is an issue that bears relation to women's health. Various international agencies show data pointing to how maternal mortality in general (or at least, maternal death *caused by abortion*) tends to be higher in states and regions where abortion is illegal. This kind of data however, by its very nature (dealing with an illegal activity), is hard to obtain and often inconclusive. For this reason, it is often questioned by 'pro-life' advocacy movements in many places, who point at the fuzziness and inconclusiveness of the data and ponder not only on whether legalizing abortion necessarily reduces maternal mortality (even the mortality directly caused by abortion) but also on whether abortion 'deserves' to be 'really' considered as a matter of public health.

Indeed it can be hard to obtain accurate data; the correlations are imperfect and often occur along with many confounding factors. Exceptions abound in either direction: many 'pro-life' activists are keen to point out cases of countries (such as Ireland and Chile)[60] where abortion remained illegal until very recently in the late 2010s, yet the efforts to improve several measures of life quality had long before translated into a plummeting of maternal deaths by any cause. Or we can find cases to the contrary, where legalizing abortion has not necessarily led to better numbers in maternal deaths. Various sources report this very situation happening in Mexico City, where despite legalizing abortion in 2007, the Mexican capital still has worse maternal mortality numbers than some of the other Mexican states where it remains illegal.[61] This is explained by the many factors influencing maternal mortality, from co-morbidities in individuals (some risk stemming from the mother's age being too far on either extreme), to the general status of a country's healthcare infrastructure, as well as the availability of well-trained personnel for assisting women during pregnancy and childbirth (or during abortion, for that matter).

However imperfectly, global data points in the direction of legalizing abortion as a step to diminish maternal mortality in most places, if at least the mortality directly caused by unsafe abortions. With this in mind, in various advocacy movements and scenarios, this 'framework of public health' has been the one leading to a compromise for non-punitive abortion policies or for legalization. Such was the case in Mexico City in 2007, when abortion was decriminalized and legalized, only in the jurisdiction of the Mexican capital.[62] This was achieved by framing the issue of abortion as one of public health rather than morality or even human rights in a broader sense. The 'framework shift' in advocacy and public policy was able to achieve a compromise . . . for a time. It has not been the only case where a framework of public health (competing with other possible frameworks such as the 'right to choose', 'privacy', or 'gender equality') has successfully been put forward to attain workable, middle-ground policies where abortion is accepted as legal in at least *some* cases.

In what could be considered 'successful' cases of legalization such as Mexico City in 2007, Chile in 2017 when abortion was legalized only in the three *'causales'*, or Argentina in late 2020, advocates relied on a framework of public health in order to advance their cause and find workable agreements. Thus, one potential stepping stone towards an organizing principle may be the agreement to see abortion *as a public health issue*, rather than an issue of morality or human rights. In some scenarios, this has been the second-best agreement, where advocates and policy makers were able to advance a balanced agenda to liberalize abortion laws, with some boundaries and constraints in place. The public health framework has, in some contexts, proven to be an added value towards repealing full bans and instances of criminalization of abortion. In contrast, when the United States first passed *Roe vs. Wade* to legalize abortion, the framework was more based on 'the right to individual privacy', which was a better cultural fit in the North American environment of legal and political thought.

This compromise, as any other related to abortion, has been the subject of contestation and questioning, as some advocates argue that legalizing abortion does *not* attain the objective of reducing the number of abortions,[63] or that it does not reduce the mortality and complications from abortions, even contesting that abortion is a public health issue at all.[64] Whatever laws on abortion are in place, they are constantly being contested by factions who want to see either stricter or less strict norms. There is a latent risk that such compromises may once again be called into question and rolled back: the public health framework is still a fragile framework, which requires constant discursive justification to be kept in place – as happened in Mexico City during 2016 and 2017, in the context of drafting the new local Constitution, where once again there was public debate and proposals to repeal legal abortion. The discussion on health and the right to health was, only at certain times, common ground for the different actor groups stuck in incompatible worldviews.

Because of the 'fragility' of the current compromises, it has been my aim to explore other possible compromises, with their potential for opening dialogue, where perhaps other frameworks and other common organizing principles may be found. Arguing against the supposedly simple 'binarity' of the debate, this deep exploration of the full 'multilogue' of so many stakeholders, so many clashing principles, and various potential frameworks may bring newer ideas for future iterations of this same controversy.

Abortion in a Global Legitimacy Gap: Current Discourses, Elusive Consensus

In Mexico, the United States, and the Americas at large, some advocates on the issue of abortion attempt to depict a supposed international consensus at the United Nations arena, on a supposed 'obligation' to legalize abortion, or on abortion being 'a human right of women'. Such voices, remarkably, come from opposed 'sides' of the debate, with some of the most extreme 'pro-life' voices attempting to paint the United Nations legal system in quite negative lights, as defenders of things like '*the legalized murder of children*'[65] or as '*the big international pro-abortion lobby*'[66] or '*Big Abortion business*',[67] to which they stand in opposition, framing their contestation of such alleged international norms generally in terms of morality or religion.

Other advocates from 'pro-choice' groups also believe that there is a consensus on abortion, which has allegedly declared that nation-states have some obligation to fully liberalize access to abortion – or also, that this supposed consensus is the default 'feminist position', implying that all/only feminist groups support legal abortion.[68] And while it is true that most feminist movements and associations tend to identify with positions in favour of legalizing abortion, one can find intersectionalities such as 'pro-life' groups that self-identify as feminist[69] – claiming to be 'the true feminists' because they 'also protect unborn girls'.

As shown, no consensus on abortion exists even within the various United Nations Organizations, documents and mechanisms, let alone if other rights systems are taken into consideration such as the Inter-American, European or African regional systems. No international document refers to abortion as 'a human right'; yet the 'right to life' is also not boundless and allows for exceptions such as, many countries' insistence on maintaining the legality of the death penalty, or the principle that in some cases the police is legally allowed to use lethal force. Furthermore, the wording of documents such as, the Universal Declaration of Human Rights or the two Human Rights Covenants, is sufficiently vague as to allow for local and national interpretation.

On various issue areas at the international stage, powerful actors often can (and have) cut the dialogue short and attempted to 'rush' or 'push' their preferred global solutions to local problems (often criticized later for short-sightedness, or for attempting to be 'one-size-fits-all'). This can come at the cost of legitimacy.[70] On the issue here concerned, advocates on the ground – more often those identifying as 'pro-life' – often have an easy time framing international agencies as the *big* (i.e. 'globalist'), *pushy* (i.e. 'powerful' and imposing their power on member states), *profit-oriented* (with supposed financial interests at the core), and especially, *foreign* 'lobby of death',[71] against which they stand in a brave, almost revolutionary manner. With such a narrative, it is easy for them to engage many people from their local communities in a common rejection of those perceived 'foreign interests' and thus fairly easy to contest the legitimacy of any abortion-related recommendation, now perceived as 'imposed from abroad'. In such a polarized sociopolitical climate as we live now, sweeping rejection of global institutions and international expertise becomes a worrisome development.

Notes

1 See Keck and Sikkink, 1998.
2 More acutely so for economic, social, and cultural rights, see Tobin, 2010.
3 See Wiener, 2017.
4 Blake, 2008.
5 Cook, 2014.
6 Johnsen, 1985.
7 Gallagher, 1987.
8 Wiener, 2014, p. 41.
9 Clapham, 2007, p. 14.
10 See Keck and Sikkink, 1999.
11 Kickbusch and Ivanova, 2013, p. 17.
12 Some of the very first multilateral conferences that the world ever saw were on topics related to public sanitation, epidemic control, and "international global health" in a truly modern sense.
13 World Health Organization, 2012.
14 Blofield, 2006, p. 4.
15 For more on the right to health concretely, and human rights interpretations, see Hunt, 2016.
16 World Health Organization, 2003.
17 United Nations Office of the High Commissioner for Human Rights, 2020.
18 Guttmacher Institute and World Health Organization, 2012.
19 Guttmacher Institute and World Health Organization, 2012.
20 Johnson et al. and World Health Organization, 2017.
21 United Nations Economic Commission for Latin America and the Caribbean (CEPAL), 2010, p. 9.
22 United Nations Population Fund, Report to the Secretary General 2014, p. 101.
23 Wiener, 2014, p. 34.
24 United Nations Population Fund, ICPD Cairo Declaration, 1994a.
25 United Nations Population Fund, Programme of Action Adopted at the ICPD Cairo, 1994b.
26 Shah, Ahman and Ortayli. *ICPD Beyond 2014 Expert Meeting*, 2014.
27 United Nations Office of the High Commissioner for Human Rights, 2020.
28 United Nations General Assembly, Universal Declaration of Human Rights, 1948.
29 United Nations General Assembly. "Convention on the Rights of the Child", 1989.
30 United Nations General Assembly, International Covenant on Civil and Political Rights, 1966a.
31 United Nations General Assembly, International Covenant on Economic, Social and Cultural Rights, 1966b.
32 United Nations Office of the High Commissioner for Human Rights, Human Rights Committee, General Comment no. 36, Article 6 (Right to Life), 2018.
33 United Nations Office of the High Commissioner for Human Rights, Human Rights Council. Universal Periodic Review of Mexico, 2013.
34 United Nations Office of the High Commissioner for Human Rights, Human Rights Council. Universal Periodic Review of Mexico, 2018a.
35 United Nations Office of the High Commissioner for Human Rights, Committee on the Rights of Persons with Disabilities. Cycle of Examinations of Austria, 2013.

36 This view was held by several of the interviewed 'pro-life' advocates.
37 UN WOMEN. Declarations, Reservations and Objections to CEDAW, 1979.
38 UN WOMEN, Fourth World Conference on Women. "Adoption of the Beijing Declaration and Platform of Action", 1995.
39 UN WOMEN, Fourth World Conference on Women. "Adoption of the Beijing Declaration and Platform of Action", 1995.
40 Organization of American States. American Convention on Human Rights; Pact of San José, Costa Rica, 1969.
41 See León, 1991.
42 Corral Talciani, 2005.
43 Inter-American Court of Human Rights. American Convention on Human Rights. Pact of San Jose, Costa Rica. Informative Document. 1969.
44 Organization of American States. Inter-American Commission on Human Rights, Informe No. 21–07, 2007.
45 Lamas, 2009.
46 Inter-American Court of Human Rights, Case: Artavia Murillo and others vs. Costa Rica, 2012.
47 Lemaitre and Sieder, 2017.
48 Inter-American Court of Human Rights, Case: Artavia Murillo and others vs. Costa Rica, 2012.
49 Mizrahi Nedvedovich and Zúñiga Tapia, 2017, p. 63.
50 De Londras and Dzehtsiarou, 2013 (on Ireland ruling and abortion in the European Union).
51 Clapham, 2007, p. 47.
52 African Union. Protocol to the African Charter on Human and Peoples' Rights on the Rights of Women in Africa, 2005.
53 United Nations Economic Commission for Latin America and the Caribbean. Montevideo Consensus on Population and Development, 2013.
54 Permanent Representative of the United States of America to the United Nations, 2020.
55 See Boyle, 1999.
56 Boyle, 2014.
57 Lichtenstein, 2001.
58 Noticias ACIPRENSA, 2014.
59 UNFPA Frequently Asked Questions. Does UNFPA Promote Abortion?, retrieved 2017.
60 Fieldwork data: interviewee No. 10.
61 Alarcón Loayza *et al.*, 2017.
62 Lamas, 2009.
63 Balbontín, 2015.
64 Balbontín, 2016.
65 Noticias ACIPRENSA, 2012.
66 Noticias ACIPRENSA, 2014.
67 Weigel, 2019.
68 El País, Editorial, 2021.
69 Domínguez, 2021.
70 Wiener, 2014.
71 Noticias ACIPRENSA, 2011.

References

African Union, Assembly of the Union. (2005). "Protocol to the African Charter on Human and People's Rights on the Rights of Women in Africa." https://au.int/sites/default/files/treaties/37077-treaty-charter_on_rights_of_women_in_africa.pdf

Alarcón Loayza, N., Bartolini Esparza, M., Contreras Díaz, A.J., Mizrahi Nedvedovich, C., Ortiz Trujillo, D., Pérez Hernández, C., and Zúñiga Tapia, F.R. (2017). *Aborto: La Política de un Estado Claudicante*. Mexico City: Consejo Editorial de la Cámara de Diputados, LXIII Legislatura.

Balbontín, A. (2015). *The Government Does Not Solve Any Social Problem by Decriminalizing Abortion*. Chile: El Demócrata. https://www.eldemocrata.cl/opinion/el-gobierno-no-resuelve-un-problema-social-al-despenalizar-el-aborto/

Balbontín, A. (2016). *Minister of Health Provides Key: Abortion is Not a Public Health Issue*. Chile: El Demócrata. https://www.eldemocrata.cl/opinion/minsal-da-la-clave-aborto-no-es-tema-de-salud-publica/

Blake, C. (2008). *Normative Instruments in International Human Rights Law: Locating the General Comment*. NYU School of Law.

Blofield, M. (2006). *The Politics of Moral Sin: Abortion and Divorce in Spain, Chile and Argentina*. Routledge.

Boyle, A.E. (1999). "Some Reflections on the Relationship of Treaties and Soft Law." *International & Comparative Law Quarterly*, 48(4), 901–913.

Boyle, A.E. (2014). "Soft Law in International Law-Making." *International Law*, 5, 119–137.

Clapham, A. (2007). *Human Rights: A Very Short Introduction*. Oxford University Press.

Cook, R.J., Erdmann, J.N., and Dickens, B.M. (2014). *Abortion Law in Transnational Perspective: Cases and Controversies*. University of Pennsylvania Press.

Corral Talciani, H. (2005). "El concepto jurídico de persona y su relevancia para la protección del derecho a la vida." *Ius et praxis*, 11(1), 37–53.

De Londras, F., and Dzehtsiarou, K. (2013). II. "Grand Chamber of the European Court of Human Rights, A, B & C V Ireland, Decision of 17 December 2010." *International and Comparative Law Quarterly*, 62(1), 250–262. https://doi.org/10.1017/S0020589312000620

Domínguez, N. (2021). "Feminismo provida: ¿Qué es y cuál es su lucha?" *Diario de Yucatán*, February 3. https://www.yucatan.com.mx/imagen/2021/2/3/feminismo-provida-que-es-cual-es-su-lucha-236129.html

El País Newspaper, Editorial. (2021). "El derecho al aborto en México: una victoria progresista." https://elpais.com/mexico/opinion/2021-09-08/el-derecho-al-aborto-en-mexico-una-victoria-progresista.html

Gallagher, J. (1987). "Prenatal Invasions & Interventions: What's Wrong with Fetal Rights." *Harvard Women's Law Journal*, 10, 9.

Guttmacher Institute and World Health Organization. (2012). "Abortion in Brief." Joint Publication by Guttmacher Institute and the World Health Organization. www.who.int/reproductivehealth/publications/unsafe_abortion/induced_abortion_2012.pdf?ua=1.

Hunt, P. (2016). "Interpreting the International Right to Health in a Human Rights-Based Approach to Health." *Health and Human Rights*, 18(2), 109.

Inter-American Court of Human Rights. (1969). "American Convention on Human Rights. Pact of San Jose, Costa Rica. Informative Document." http://www.cidh.org/Basicos/English/Basic4.Amer.Conv.Ratif.htm

Inter-American Court of Human Rights. (2012). "Case: Artavia Murillo and Others vs. Costa Rica." Technical Review. https://www.corteidh.or.cr/tablas/fichas/artaviamurillo.pdf. Accessed July 2017.

Johnsen, D.E. (1985). "Creation of Fetal Rights: Conflicts with Women's Constitutional Rights to Liberty, Privacy, and Equal Protection." *The Yale Law Journal*, 95, 599.

Johnson, B.R., *et al*., and World Health Organization. (2017). "A Global Database of Abortion Laws, Policies, Health Standards and Guidelines." *Perspectives, Bulletin of the World Health Organization*. http://www.who.int/bulletin/volumes/95/7/17-197442/en/

Keck, M.E., and Sikkink, K. (1998). *Activists Beyond Borders*. Cornell University Press.

Keck, M.E., and Sikkink, K. (1999). "Transnational Advocacy Networks in International and Regional Politics." *International Social Science Journal*, 51(159), 89–101.
Kickbusch, I., and Ivanova, M. (2013). "The History and Evolution of Global Health Diplomacy." In *Global Health Diplomacy: Concepts, Issues, Actors, Instruments, Fora and Cases*, 11–26. New York: Springer Science + Business Media.
Lamas, M. (2009). "La Despenalización del Aborto en México." *Nueva Sociedad*, (220), 154–172.
Lemaitre, J., and Sieder, R. (2017). "The Moderating Influence of International Courts on Social Movements: Evidence from the IVF Case Against Costa Rica." *Health and Human Rights*, 19(1), 149–160.
León, R.M. (1991). "Aborto: de lo prohibido y lo sugerido." *Derecho & Sociedad*, 4, 44–46.
Lichtenstein, C.C. (2001). "Hard Law v. Soft Law: Unneccesary Dichotomy." *International Law*, 35.
Mizrahi Nedvedovich, C., and Zúñiga Tapia, F.R. (2017). "Las recomendaciones de los organismos internacionales como mecanismos de presión política." In *Aborto: La Política de un Estado Claudicante*. Todas y Todos Valemos en México, 53–67. Mexico City: Consejo Editorial de la Cámara de Diputados, LXIII Legislatura.
Noticias ACIPRENSA. (2011). "Terminología de la cultura de la Muerte." https://www.aciprensa.com/recursos/terminologia-de-la-cultura-de-la-muerte-205
Noticias ACIPRENSA. (2012). "Aborto es el homicidio más cruel, recuerda sacerdote." https://www.aciprensa.com/noticias/aborto-es-el-homicidio-mas-cruel-recuerda-sacerdote. Accessed July 2017.
Noticias ACIPRENSA. (2014). "ONU y OEA son títeres de la agenda pro gay y pro aborto, denuncia experta." https://www.aciprensa.com/noticias/onu-y-oea-son-titeres-de-la-agenda-pro-gay-y-pro-aborto-denuncia-experta-62211
Organization of American States. (1969). "American Convention on Human Rights; Pact of San Jose, Costa Rica." *Multilateral Treaties*, November 22. http://www.oas.org/dil/treaties_B-32_American_Convention_on_Human_Rights.htm
Organization of American States. Inter-American Commission on Human Rights. (2007). "Informe No. 21–07" (Caso Paulina, México). https://www.cidh.oas.org/annualrep/2007sp/mexico161.02sp.htm.
Permanent Representative of the United States of America to the United Nations. (2020). "Letter Addressed to the United Nations Secretary General: '*Geneva Consensus Declaration on Promoting Women's Health and Strengthening the Family*'." https://undocs.org/en/A/75/626
Shah, I.H., Ahman, E., and Ortayli, N. (2014). "Access to Safe Abortion: Progress and Challenges Since the 1994 International Conference on Population and Development (ICPD)." Background Paper #3, ICPD Beyond 2014 Expert Meeting on Women's Health. http://www.unfpa.org/sites/default/files/resource-pdf/Safe_Abortion.pdf
Tobin, J. (2010). "Seeking to Persuade: A Constructive Approach to Human Rights Treaty Interpretation." *Harvard Human Rights Journal*, 23, 1.
United Nations Economic Commission for Latin America and the Caribbean, CEPAL. (2010). "Examination and Evaluation of the Beijing Declaration and Platform of Action, and the Final Document of the Twenty-Third Extraordinary Period of Sessions of the UN General Assembly (2000) in countries of Latin America and the Caribbean." http://www.cepal.org/mujer/noticias/paginas/8/36338/CEPALBeijing15.pdf
United Nations Entity for Gender Equality and the Empowerment of Women (UN WOMEN). (1995). "Adoption of the Beijing Declaration and Platform of Action." Informative Document. Fourth World Conference on Women. http://www.un.org/documents/ga/conf177/plateng/aconf177-20-part6en.htm
United Nations Entity for Gender Equality and the Empowerment of Women (UN WOMEN). (1979). "Declarations, Reservations and Objections to CEDAW." http://www.un.org/womenwatch/daw/cedaw/reservations-country.htm#N21

United Nations General Assembly. (1948). "Universal Declaration of Human Rights." https://www.un.org/sites/un2.un.org/files/udhr.pdf. Accessed July 2017.

United Nations General Assembly. (1966a). "International Covenant on Civil and Political Rights." https://www.ohchr.org/en/professionalinterest/pages/ccpr.aspx. Accessed July 2017.

United Nations General Assembly. (1966b). "International Covenant on Economic, Social and Cultural Rights." https://www.ohchr.org/en/professionalinterest/pages/cescr.aspx

United Nations General Assembly. (1989). "Convention on the Rights of the Child." https://www.ohchr.org/en/professionalinterest/pages/crc.aspx. Accessed July 2017.

United Nations Office of the High Commissioner for Human Rights, Committee on the Rights of Persons with Disabilities. Cycle of Examinations of Austria. (2013). "Concluding Observations on the Initial Report of Austria, Adopted by the Committee at Its Tenth Session (2–13 September 2013)." https://digitallibrary.un.org/record/767045/files/CRPD_C_AUT_CO_1-EN.pdf. Accessed July 2017.

United Nations Office of the High Commissioner for Human Rights, Human Rights Committee. (2018). "General Comment no. 36, Article 6 (Right to Life)." CCPR/C/GC/35, September 3, 2019. https://www.refworld.org/docid/5e5e75e04.html. Accessed September 3, 2021.

United Nations Office of the High Commissioner for Human Rights, Human Rights Council. (2013). "Universal Periodic Review – Mexico, Second Cycle of Examination." www.ohchr.org/en/hr-bodies/upr/mx-index. Accessed July 2021.

United Nations Office of the High Commissioner for Human Rights, Human Rights Council. (2018a). "Universal Periodic Review – Mexico, Third Cycle of Examination." www.ohchr.org/en/hr-bodies/upr/mx-index. Accessed July 2021.

United Nations Office of the High Commissioner for Human Rights. (2020). "Abortion. Information Series on Sexual and Reproductive Health and Rights." https://www.ohchr.org/Documents/Issues/Women/WRGS/SexualHealth/INFO_Abortion_WEB.pdf

United Nations Population Fund. (1994a). "Cairo Declaration on Population & Development." https://www.unfpa.org/sites/default/files/resource-pdf/94-09-04_Cairo_Declaration_on_Population_Development_ICPPD.pdf

United Nations Population Fund. (1994b). "Programme of Action, Adopted at the International Conference on Population and Development, Cairo 1994." https://www.unfpa.org/sites/default/files/event-pdf/PoA_en.pdf

United Nations Population Fund. (2014). "Framework of Actions for the Follow-Up to the Programme of Action of the International Conference on Population and Development Beyond 2014." http://www.unfpa.org/sites/default/files/event-pdf/93632_unfpa_eng_web.pdf

Weigel, G. (2019). *The Catholic Difference: Truth Telling and Big Abortion.* Catholic Diocese of Spokane. https://dioceseofspokane.org/news/truth-telling-and-big-abortion. Accessed April 2020.

Wiener, A. (2014). *A Theory of Contestation.* Springer.

Wiener, A. (2017). "Agency of the Governed in Global International Relations: Access to Norm Validation." *Third World Thematics: A TWQ Journal*, 2(5), 709–725.

World Health Organization. (2012). *Abortion Without Risks: Technical and Policy Guideline for Health Systems* (*Aborto sin Riesgos: Guía Técnica y de Políticas para Sistemas de Salud*), 2nd ed. https://www.paho.org/clap/dmdocuments/AbortoGuia2.pdf. Accessed May 2021.

World Health Organization, World Health Organisation Staff, and UNAIDS. (2003). *Safe Abortion: Technical and Policy Guidance for Health Systems*. World Health Organization.

7 Concluding Considerations

What Possible Pathways to Dialogue?

The polarized and confronted ideas on legal abortion, throughout Mexico as in Latin America at large often include entire worldviews where the advocates (especially those opposing legal abortion) detect the influence of efforts by international organizations and transnational NGOs. They see these efforts as an overarching global 'imposition of a liberal agenda' on all states, mixed along with issues of LGBTQ+ rights and a supposed 'destruction of the family'. For those advocating the liberalization of abortion laws, their narratives are less focused on such an 'imposition', interpreting sometimes the opposite: the prevalence of an oppressive patriarchy that denies women basic reproductive rights and that is only beginning to change, too slowly for their liking, through global and international advocacy.

The irreconcilable discourses are likely to stay irreconcilable; however, the crucial matters for the future will be in matters of normativity: *'Who decides?'*, and in that sense, *'Whose advocacy practices are going to "count" for the creation of law and policy?'*. Any concluding considerations aim not to provide my 'take' on how to 'solve' the debate, nor to reduce the dogmatic discussion to mere 'policy recommendations', but to set some ideas of what may become a pathway to dialogue.

We can draw on a multitude of observations – no less because of the multi-faceted nature of the issue, touching upon many others if at least tangentially (sexual violence, disability rights, conscientious objection . . .). Though it is impossible to predict what may happen in future decades without getting into merely speculative claims, it is likely that future scientific and technological advancements will continue to change the landscape of this debate. Scientific and medical discoveries have the potential to add new insights into a debate that ponders about human development pre-birth, in similar ways as to how other debates pertaining to the realm of global health can change after the development of new medical treatments or technologies.

Many pro-choice advocates, for instance, use foetal viability outside the womb as the threshold to indicate when an abortion should no longer be lawful, and modern developments in medical technology have been able to lower the viability threshold significantly. Pairing this observation with the earlier assessment that human rights have had a history of progressive inclusion of diverse groups once considered not to have such rights, it is not a foregone conclusion that the

DOI:10.4324/9781032642338-7

'progressive' path will always invariably be towards liberalized (or more unrestrained) access to abortion.

Despite numerous advancements in that direction so far, the liberalization path should not be assumed as the immutable, teleological path of human rights laws and principles having to do with abortion. Progressiveness in laws and in local politics is associated to the liberalization of abortion rights, but it is unclear whether medical or technological advancements might change the debate in the future, or whether 'unborn rights' might one day gain strength as an established legal concept and a category of internationally protected human rights. It is an unsafe bet to speculate that state-nations will all eventually follow a path leaning towards legalization. A woman's right to make decisions over her own body, however, will most likely continue to be a pressing demand of various feminist movements and human rights movements.

Time will tell if setbacks such as those seen in the USA 'post-*Roe vs. Wade*' have more to do with contemporary conservative currents throughout the Western and Northern 'worlds', or whether in the future the inclusion of 'unborn rights' could be witnessed as part of the ever-widening definition of internationally recognized rights. Ever-enlarging definitions of human rights, aiming to include 'everything and everyone', could however water down any judicial potential of the concept. These reflections should serve as a reminder that contestation is a process which precisely allows for the shaping and re-shaping of legitimate governing norms, allowing for the inclusion of new developments.

The main issue discussed by the 'fundamentally irreconcilable' sides of this debate ought not to be *'Where does life begin?'*, but rather, *'Where should its legal protection begin?'*. . . In reality, it is hard to find people standing on either extreme: either stating that life should be absolutely protected since the very moment of fertilization (*actually, enforceably* protected), or stating that life should only be protected beginning at birth. Even though the self-proclaimed 'pro-life' advocates insist on protections beginning 'from the moment of conception', most of them admit at least some exceptions to the prohibition of abortion, indeed progressing into 'more protection' as a pregnancy advances.

Though activists initially tend to present their claims in a black-and-white, seemingly binarized manner, when further pressed, most think of somewhere in-between. They then propose diverse criteria as a potential benchmark of *'criminalizability'*: the existence of a recognizable human heart or heartbeat, the existence of foetal pain and potential suffering, viability outside the woman's body, or a numerical benchmark (X number of days/weeks/months of pregnancy). But also, most importantly in the contestation framework, most people agree to *some* second-best solutions, exceptions, and varying-case criteria (abortion being allowed in cases of risk to the mother's life, rape or incest, fatal malformations, etc.). Medical technology might, in the near future, introduce significant paradigm shifts in this debate. We can ponder on how, thanks to modern medical technology, the threshold of viability has been moving downwards and could one day 'meet' many of the widely accepted gestational limits for abortion.

What I have witnessed in Mexico, as have others elsewhere throughout the past two decades, is that *activism matters for policymaking:* it impacts the perception of messages, regulation, practice, and the culture at large. This Mexican tale of polarization and *'pendularity'* in the abortion debate can find strong parallelisms in other countries, as well as clear echoes in other issue areas of the international and global multilogue. Advocates find links to the global level as a part of their policymaking and policy proposal. In this manner, while looking at a deep understanding of the uniqueness of the Mexican case, applicability of these ideas at the global context and for advocates working on other areas can be considered as well.

Other observations certainly become more country-specific. However, they still deliver interesting points of reflection to be kept in mind when analyzing other cases, be it at a global scale or concerning other national or regional contexts. In the Mexican case, *federalism* brought an extra layer of complexity into the whole normative scenario about the legality of abortion. As a federation, each subnational state has much autonomy over its local laws (having its own local Constitution and local Criminal Code). This should be kept in mind for other nation-states of a federal nature.

Activists often target laws at different levels, be it the federal or the local scope, to achieve what they perceive as more attainable reform goals. The potential clashes of different laws, or their potential overlap in scope and applicability (not just a strictly geographical scope, but also the differing applicability for different individuals, institutions, or professional disciplines) makes for a hugely complex and fascinating case. A case where, at times, seemingly clear-cut binaries are used for the sake of analytical simplification, but where it is most useful to remember that both the solutions and the intricacies of real-life practice tend to happen along a spectrum of diversity and complexity.

Assessing Potential Organizing Principles: Back to the Origins with *'Despenalización'*?

The search for organizing principles that allow for a sort of 'weighing' of the rights of the woman and those of the unborn has not yet yielded a principle that 'solves' the debate in a way that is satisfactory to most people. Organizing principles should function as a link, filling the gap between the moral claims of fundamental norms and the practical enactment of procedures – as, recalling the famous phrase, *'politics is the art of the possible'*. In this case, *'the possible'* tends to fall through a 'legitimacy gap' where, at any given time and with any given solution, a great part of the advocates remains dissatisfied.

The attempt at reaching an agreement that access to abortion is 'an issue of public health' rather than one of morality – or even just 'human rights' – tends to become a more successful framework in advocates' attempts to liberalize access to abortion, but one that was only been accepted at times, in some places. It is thus one possible organizing principle but one that still leaves many unconvinced (and with some 'pro-life' advocates challenging the notion itself that abortion is part of legitimate healthcare), and one which does not really address the question of *where* exactly the legally protected right to life should begin.

The prioritization of public health has been, for now, a 'fragile compromise' – one that has only been successfully applied in *some* contexts. The results achieved by such 'fragile framework' can be subject to change, reform and 'roll-back', as access to legal abortion remains a contentious issue by excellence. Policy on the ground often seems to be more responsive to the political and partisan sways of the moment than to actual expertise by lawyers, doctors and specialists. As of now, no framework shift is definitive in terms of getting to a consensus, and no 'winning discourse' is sure to stay 'winning' for very long. The irreconcilable normative viewpoints (even leaving aside religious norms or traditional gender codes on behaviour) are likely to stay irreconcilable. Abortion's legitimacy is in constant and ongoing contestation, trapped in a never filled *legitimacy gap* between opposed worldviews.

It is the only case where the rights of two differently recognized individuals clash in such a unique way, as the body of one of those individuals is entirely within and dependent on the other individual's body. *Some* specific framings in the advocacy about abortion manage to temporarily work out policies, yet the contestation continues, and political changes almost invariably bring again a questioning of the norms and an attempt to change them: thus the proposed solutions and policies seem to be an eternal 'work in progress'. In light of the current social, political and ideological turmoil throughout many regions of the world, any explanation of a current abortion policy should probably be appended with the words *"...for now"*.

Based on the current medical knowledge of aspects such as foetal viability, foetal sentience or the lack thereof, the non-existence of pain before a certain gestational age, etc., some experts attempt to shed clarity on the debate by proposing parameters of a certain 'prioritization of rights', where the woman is considered to have full rights whereas as a foetus has 'suspensive', 'future' or 'potential' rights. Another potential organizing principle could be the consideration that the unborn person has only 'suspensive rights' or 'potential rights', so long as it is still inviable outside the woman's body as well as incapable of feeling pain. 'Potential rights', however, remains an unconvincing notion to 'pro-life' advocates. 'Future rights' could become a dangerously discriminatory notion if it were applied in any other context or to any other individual than an unborn person.

'Suspensive rights' is a concept that still has potential for further development and analysis. The notion of 'suspensive rights' might be another organizing principle in this contested topic, such 'temporal' notion of human rights might act as a principle of precedence, whereby the woman's rights (to health, to privacy, or life choices) take precedence over the unborn's rights. However, current literature mentions 'suspensive rights' only scarcely and in the context of contractual law, asylum application, civil disobedience, and other areas far removed from issues of public health or gender equality. The right to life itself being 'suspensive' is not a common notion anywhere in the current rights literature, and by its very nature it could not be considered suspensive in any other case.

These notions could also backfire dangerously – if some groups proposed the idea that, for example, it should rather be the woman who has 'suspensive rights' while she is pregnant, in favour of granting the unborn with legally protected personhood from conception until they are born. Though most people and most legal theorists would soundly reject that notion, it is not entirely difficult to imagine that it could gain acceptance among some 'hard-line' conservative groups or gender-role traditionalists, or within legal systems based on religion and theology.

Decriminalization, or *'despenalización'*, may be for now a potential solution, the closest thing to a Type 2 workable compromise: one that sits in the grey area between not criminalizing women (and potentially also doctors) for a specific act, but while also keeping enough restrictions in place that the practice is generally discouraged. This can be a realistic 'point of dialogue', given that that most of the 'pro-life' groups at least agree with the *'pro-choicers'* in saying that the idea should *not* be to penalize women in a punishment-focused framework. This solution, however, tends to be far removed from what could be called 'real access'. It always depends on what exactly it means to implement a *'de-criminalization'*, and most importantly it fails to address the argument given by many pro-legalization advocates who claim that low-income women will still be suffering from unsafe abortions, mostly due to lacking access to abortion in a discrete, private clinic.

And still, many 'pro-life' advocates agree with not imprisoning women for abortion, but they still believe that it should be punished in some way: they advocate instead for 'lighter punishments' consisting of monetary fines or serving time in community works. So in a way, many agree with 'not imprisoning', but not necessarily with 'decriminalization' as such. One problematic aspect of this is that such a 'cosmetic' type of decriminalization (meaning simply 'not jailing'), would fail to address the problem of a stigmatization towards women who abort: 'light criminalization' or considering abortion as 'a misdemeanour' of sorts, is not quite exactly 'decriminalization'.

Illustrative also of these ambiguities is the fact that, as of September 2021 and September 2023, the Mexican Supreme Court has ruled that criminalizing abortion is unconstitutional, which likely *does* pave the way for decriminalization across the country rather soon. But the 2021 ruling for instance, although it sets a major binding precedent, does not clarify if it should be done by merely eliminating the penalties in the Criminal Codes – and with Mexican Criminal Law being based on the principle that punishment cannot be given by inference or extrapolation, but only through precisely described sanctions for precisely described crimes, this would effectively make abortion 'not punished', but also 'not legal'. Or instead, the Court rulings might be translated into different reforms within the Criminal Codes, where the lower number of gestational weeks (below 12, for example) will be considered a cause for 'exclusion of responsibility'.

Although the two types of changes might appear similar from the outside, the exact 'legal message' is quite different. In this sense, 'decriminalization' can be framed as an organizing principle, but this is not without conceptual difficulties: at least the way in which it is understood in the Mexican legal system, 'decriminalization" is not in itself a legal principle codified in law, it is rather *'an effect'* – of a reform enacted on a piece of written law. It is not in itself a legal concept but rather an effect that is manifested after changes, such as elimination of references to penalties, or otherwise making such penalties inoperable in a specific context or in the presence of a specific condition (the number of gestational weeks, occurrence of a sexual assault, etc.).

For the time being, the legitimacy gap sitting not only at the level of Type 2 norms, but also between both colliding worldviews, finds only rather insufficient solutions.

At a more 'meta' level of the debate, one cannot ignore important power components at the state-wide scale and the international scale, concerning *who* is really 'an agent' that has the capacity to define, contest, decide, have options and raise a voice that will be heard. *Contestation itself is a matter of access*. It cannot be assumed that the affected entities always have access to it (as vulnerable groups are often '*invisibilized*'). The two affected entities (the unborn as well as the woman who needs or desires access to abortion) face great barriers to self-representation and agency: it is of course impossible in the case of the unborn and highly difficult and discouraged for the affected woman due to abortion being a 'taboo' topic, to social stigma and pressure, to socioeconomic disadvantage, and to concerns about privacy. As I found during interviews and protest attendance, even if women are very present in advocacy both for and against legal abortion, the 'taboo' nature of the issue means that even women on pro-legalization groups are most often speaking *'for other women'*, as it remains a strong taboo to say that one had an abortion herself, or ever desired one.

Contestation is a norm-generative practice, it creates legitimacy as well. Yet in this idea, the assumption is implicit that *interested stakeholders always have active access to contestation processes and practices*. On the abortion issue, however, 'access to contestation' remains complex. Who has access to it, and who doesn't?. . . Many still assume that gender as a factor in itself plays a decisive role. It is often assumed that the activists pressing for abortion legalization are mostly female/feminist activists, and that the people against it are almost entirely conservative men. I found this not to be accurate, at least in the case of Mexico. The interviewed stakeholders are split more or less evenly between genders, with both 'pro' and 'anti' legalization groups each containing more or less equal amounts of men and women.

The 'pro-life' protest that I attended in Mexico City in 2018, with thousands of attendees, had a roughly equal distribution of participants of both sexes, as well as a strong presence of young people. Throughout my fieldwork, I had direct contact with many women who are highly vocal and highly visible pro-life advocates, among them politicians, public servants, congresswomen, civil society leaders, conference speakers and law reform drafters (either partisan or independent), many of whom I had personal conversations with. Although women do comprise most of the ranks of pro-legalization and feminist advocacy, as one would more or less expect (even if here, too, we find a diversity of sexes and age groups), female presences and voices (of many age groups) are strong in pro-life advocacy in Mexico.

Despite this strength and presence, it is still the case that with abortion being a 'private' or 'personal' topic, the women who advocate in favour of its liberalization are often 'not speaking for themselves': even providing 'explanations' that they perceive are needed, such as *"I am a mother myself, but I believe that abortion should be legal"*[1]. . . This makes for a case where talking about 'access' and 'self-representation' comes with caveats.

The Devil Is in the Details . . . Is the Dialogue in the Middle Ground?

I previously analyzed how pro-legalization advocates in Mexico have often achieved their goals by working at the level of the 'technicalities', using norms or reforms that may be considered rather obscure, such as the creation of a NOM0046 that became important in expanding access to abortion, or through the legal change of rewriting the 'causes for the extinction of penalties' into 'causes for the exclusion of responsibility' in the Criminal Codes.

The saying that *'the devil is in the details'* is common in Mexico (*'el diablo está en los detalles'*). And while it is true that working with these 'devilish details' of legal technicality has often advanced the desired cause of pro-legalization advocates, it also tends to lead their ideological opponents into certain feelings of alienation, non-representation, even a tinge of 'treason' when they perceive that a change was made through procedures or technical laws that they hardly even know exist. It may be true that *'the devil is in the detail'*, but perhaps by metaphorical inference we could say that *'the angels are in the middle ground'*: these technical changes will not convince most 'pro-life' advocates about the necessity of legalized abortion. Borrowing the language of norm contestation theories: true, lasting agreements will not happen at the level of Type 3 technical norms, but by finding Type 2 organizing principles that can truly function as an axis of justice.

If more permanent, less 'pendular' solutions are to be found, dialogue needs to happen at the level of the middle ground and not that of the obscure legal technicality. It may remain true that both views are fundamentally irreconcilable – yet workable policy may be achieved by a mapping of commonalities and middle grounds: the alleged desire to *not* punish women, to uphold motherhood, to protect life in a meaningful way that truly rings with justice and with common good.

Note

1 Interviewed Expert No. 5.

Epilogue: A Research Journey and the Way Full Circle

Why abortion in Mexico?... When studying to become academics, young researchers and scholars-in-training often confront the dreaded (if well intentioned) question about the scholarly purposes of their research, focusing on the knowledge gap that they're supposed to be filling. *"You analyze this particular issue or case, and you use this or that concept and x y z methods . . . and so what?"*. We often learn to give a sanitized, embellished and, most especially, *simplified* response to such questionings – designed rather to project an illusion of *'cleanliness'* in our research journey, than to provide accurate insights into the process.

Such response often goes along the lines of *"I was interested in this case, then I read a lot and found my knowledge gap, then I went to the field in search of answers to this question, then I came back and wrote a thesis about it"*. Such a linear path in research is almost impossible to find – if not outright undesirable. If the researcher's questions didn't change in fundamental ways while on the field, bringing her "back to the drawing board" in ways which often feel like existential crisis, perhaps she wasn't asking important enough questions to begin with.

Towards the end of writing my doctoral dissertation, I myself wanted to understand and recount the very process of creating such a project: how this particular 'puzzle' of abortion laws in Mexico came to be, how the research questions were developed, how the research itself changed throughout time and through the findings themselves, and how a certain 'back to the beginnings' brought the research endeavour full circle . . . but now seen through a new lens of normativity, dialogue, and suggestions of *'organizing principles'* as middle-ground solutions. This exercise also serves to dismiss the illusion of the 'clean', straightforward, and unchanging path when doing research for a PhD, where the researcher starts with literature and a question, and then neatly proceeds from 'point A' into 'point B', then into 'C' until a dissertation is born. Some academics now dare to open the 'black box', the 'messy' process of how their research came to be what it is, how the questions birthed answers, only to then have the answers influence back the questions and shape newer questions. The academic herself should recognize where she stands, how she came to stand there, and how the process itself of researching influences not only the results but also the *types* of questions that one can fathom in the first place. Telling a certain 'story' about the process of research itself – leading 'there' into the empirics, and then 'back again' to the initial questions – makes for a much more interesting vision of a research piece than would merely a retelling of data sources, methods used, and a purely academic, 'sanitized' justification for using those methods.

A recount of this 'research story' brought about the reflection that had some elements of my fieldwork been any different – for example, different experts pointing at slightly different ideas and 'seeding' different questions, or if they had withheld what later became key pieces of information – then it is not only the case that empirical results might have been different, but perhaps so would be the questions that I thought of asking. This might stand in contrast to the vision of academics who argued that qualitative and quantitative studies could follow fundamentally similar logics of research (in works that have sometimes been called "neopositivist research"), sparking great academic debate and often intense critique.

My interest in the abortion debate in Mexico, from a standpoint more personal than academic, dates back to the early 2000s when it was effectively still illegal in all of Mexico, but indeed the *"Caso Paulina"* had caught strong media attention, to which followed a social, legal and academic debate. It eventually culminated in the legalization of abortion until the 12th gestational week in Mexico City, in the year 2007, followed by a backlash of opposed laws in almost every other subnational state. Respected journals such as *La Jornada* published a series of articles presenting both viewpoints, printed literally side by side – consulting experts from medical, legal, and religious backgrounds, as well as some simpler but well elaborated citizen opinions and 'takes' on the issue. Some aspects of the topic were still taboo, yet already in those times, and notably also among very young people such as high school or university students, personal or family stories of clandestine abortions done in secrecy (or discrete trips abroad for the same purpose) invariably leaked from the abstract public discourse into what we all knew were the personal stories of at least one person we may know. Voices from the Catholic Church in opposition to abortion were strong and loud, finding echo among many Mexicans of all ages, but at the same time, the Catholic Church – and especially the personal figure of Archbishop Norberto Rivera – had started to face a strong crisis of credibility: corruption scandals, as well as the cover-up of cases of sexual abuse, had started to fissure the Church's reputation.

Of course, some circles within the country have had a secular tradition for centuries – the abortion debate did *not* introduce secularity to Mexico, nor was it the first issue to push many people into challenging the Catholic Church, and it would be profoundly disingenuous to pretend so (already in the 1850s, the civil Reformation War had had an undercurrent of clash between secularism and religious tradition, and so did the *Guerra Cristera* strongly in the 1920s). But the corruption scandals of Rivera's, and the protection of sexual criminals within the Catholic Church, had brought the dominant religious institution into a fuller crisis of credibility where, if many Mexicans did not stop identifying as Catholic, at the very least they felt more comfortable in ignoring Church mandates whenever convenient. The Church had long ago lost the battle against the use of modern contraceptives (with a majority of Mexicans using them whenever available, despite what their Church may declare), and some dared to think – perhaps some, for the first time – that if the Church could safely be ignored about contraceptives, and if their sexual abuse scandals showed some hypocrisy in their discourses about protecting the innocent, then perhaps the Church had lost credibility as well on the abortion debate. This has happened only to a certain extent, of course. Many Catholics may ignore Church mandates on contraceptive use or on sexual relations before marriage, but they strongly agree with its opposition to abortion. During fieldwork, it seemed clear that one of the reasons why the Catholic Church (and other Christian churches) advocates so strongly against abortion is because they are aware that this is one of their last ideological strongholds: an issue on which they retain credibility, one on which thousands of people will still listen and mobilize.

In the early 2000s, human rights as a concept were of course widely known (and children's rights, as recognized in the corresponding UN Convention, were a topic of study for primary school children); however, they were not as prevalent in the legal thinking as they are today, now set as a fundamental pillar of Mexico's legal system. In our copies of the Mexican Constitution, at the time – available as small pocketbooks, to be used as part of the basic schooling curricula – one article still mentioned the death penalty (if only for very serious crimes, most of them crimes by military personnel), and the entire first section of the Constitution was called *"Garantías Individuales"* (Individual Guarantees), where the paradigm was that the individual had not 'human rights' but 'individual guarantees', granted *by* the Mexican state *to* the person. The Constitution was 'supreme law of the land', and the legal paradigm of the time made it unthinkable that a 'foreign' or 'global' treaty might stand by its side in authority. The Constitutional Reform of 2011 brought a radical, historical paradigm shift: the "*Garantías Individuales*" chapter was renamed "Of Human Rights and their Guarantees" (*"De los Derechos Humanos y sus Garantías"*), where the Mexican state now recognizes that human rights are inalienable and the state does not 'grant' them, but rather respects, protects, and fulfils them.

And very important for the topic analyzed here: international treaties signed by Mexico were now to be considered supreme law along with the Constitution, the goal being to always grant every person the broadest extent of human rights protection (the *pro persona* principle). Today, expert advocates on both sides of the abortion debate, and especially those with legal expertise mention this reform as fundamental, as it gives them stronger grounds to use international documents in their advocacy. This stands true for 'both sides' of the debate. The death penalty had been abolished in 2005 – which, according to some 'pro-life' advocates, could and should be interpreted *in contrario sensu* to mean that all human life is, by inference, to be protected from the moment of conception, because the Mexican Constitution now forbids even the passing of any future laws sanctioning the death penalty. If this alleged link between the death penalty and abortion seems strained (and to most legal experts, it is, given that they are vastly different topics dealing mostly with contexts, circumstances and scenarios that have next to nothing in common), in the view of some 'pro-life' advocates it is a rational connection to make in the legal realm.

In those articles at *La Jornada* and other media that cared to present 'both sides' of the debate (and subsequently, more complex and nuanced opinions, and any 'takes' on the debate aiming to show the issue as much more than 'black and white' or 'good versus evil'), it was clear that most of the opposed opinions had some grains of good reason to them. After all, they often described an undesirable situation that most women do not wish to find themselves in, and one that often brings great personal difficulty regardless of the individual decision made. 'Pro-legalization' advocates seemed to make reasonable demands that would improve women's lives; meanwhile, not every 'pro-life' opinion came from religious dogma: some of them were well constructed on entirely secular terms, standing in their turn on international documents. Another alternative, personal interest of mine happens to be the medical field, concretely on issues related to pregnancy, embryological development and early childhood development, and there was an undeniable disjoint between the agreement towards women's right to personal autonomy, and a parallel agreement with some of the 'pro-life' views about the common interest of protecting pre-born life. Protecting life before birth did not seem like a nonsensical proposition based on mystical faith, but an idea containing a degree of public good. One which, however, clashed with other fundamental rights of women, especially considering what many Mexican experts and reporters brought attention to: the harsh realities for many women in disadvantaged sectors of society, or who had suffered abuses, women who had real plights that were just as pressing (if not much more) than a concept of 'life' in the abstract.

It was the acutely controversial nature of this case – one where the opposed advocates all seemed to possess a measure of truth – that sparked what later became the academic interest of looking at abortion as the one issue to which I could assign the label: *'the most controversial that I can think of'*.

When beginning the doctoral path towards building a research design and eventually a dissertation, one initial proposal was to make a comparison between Mexico and Chile. More concretely, between Mexico *City* and Chile, because at the time of beginning this project (late 2016), Chile was still one of a handful of countries on the planet where abortion was banned with no exceptions. Mexico City, on the other hand, was the most familiar example of a place that had successfully liberalized abortion, in 2007 – the closest such place in my particular surroundings, where I had somewhat followed the debate highlights for years. The initial research proposal already looked at the concept of "transnational advocacy", as previous academic research had been influenced by Keck and Sikkink's works about it. An initial hint was, therefore, that such advocacy had had something to do with the success of legalization in Mexico and that perhaps *something* was preventing the same from happening in Chile: maybe opposing transnational strategies by 'pro-life' groups, or perhaps the advocacy for legalization simply wasn't 'working' in Chile. Another notion that was woven into this initial research plan was an early concept that I had deemed *'the politics of personalities'*: the idea (also influenced by Keck and Sikkink) that advocates use different types of 'characters' in their construction of a narrative for advocacy – for example, 'the victim', the 'duty bearer', the 'aggrieved activist' (a 'martyr' of sorts), etc. It seemed like a solid idea to analyze the advocacy movements in both countries, taking into consideration these depictions of 'characters' in their respective narratives, and if and how it had influenced the results: liberalization in Mexico City, continued full ban in Chile.

Any comparison will of course bear its many disclaimers and beg the question: '*why compare?*'. . . From the outside, what seemed logical about the comparison was to look at one seemingly 'successful' case of abortion legalization, Mexico City, and an 'unsuccessful' one, Chile, where abortion had remained completely banned despite years of efforts by advocates, similar to the efforts carried out in Mexico. To talk about 'successful' versus 'unsuccessful' advocacy seemed to lead in the direction of creating a hypothesis. One such hypothesis was that perhaps advocates in Mexico had succeeded because of the use of 'public health' as a framework for advocacy. And while there is *some* truth to that idea, trying to aim for a simplistic hypothesis that could be verified or falsified seemed to be precisely that: too simplistic (even when trying to weave in the 'politics of characters'), ignoring the enormous complexity of the topic. It would especially risk ignoring the politics of both countries, with Mexico City having always been a bastion of progressive policy within Mexico, while Chile was a deeply conservative country that, for example, only legalized divorce in 2004. Another huge difference that risked being ignored was that Mexico is a federation, and Chile is not. Any such 'hypothesis' would then seem to provide only shaky and self-confirming explanations of *one* specific framework being 'successful' in one place, while ignoring that other countries (in Europe, for example) had legalized or at least decriminalized abortion through very different paths. Another possibility explored was then a concept of "norm robustness", where the legalization of abortion would have been analyzed as a case of 'the agreement on public health' being a "robust norm". But still, the construction of a framework of public health as 'successful' or as 'a robust norm' not only rang as self-confirming but also risked becoming a simplistic explanation deeply lacking the depth that the issue intuitively seemed to have.

Another issue was that any comparison in academia, by nature, must be especially well constructed in order to make sense. Comparisons done for the sake of comparison instinctively push others to ask equally, 'if the two cases are so similar, *then why compare*?' and 'if the two cases are so different, *then why compare*?'. . . Two cases that happen to be 'similar enough, yet different enough' had to be found, and also, the comparison itself must be constructed in a way that it effectively yields results that are not just relational for the sake of it but also meaningful in other ways: perhaps transferable to other areas; or speaking to larger, more abstract norms; or providing roadmaps for other advocates in other places. The final 'nail in the coffin' for this comparative framework came in 2017, when Chile legalized abortion in the cases of the 'three exceptions' and simply ceased to be one of the few countries in the world with a total abortion ban. While this changed things for Chileans in Chile, it didn't necessarily change many of the basic ideas on advocacy, robustness, or other applicable concepts. A comparison between the advocacy in Mexico City and the advocacy in Chile *up until that point* could still have been done (and might even have confirmed the supposed 'hypothesis' of the 'successful framework of public health'), but admittedly, the change solidified the notion that a different framework than just 'comparing countries' in order to extract 'similarities and differences' might just provide much richer insights.

Chile was finally left out of the research project entirely, to focus only on Mexico. The next important questions then seemed to be, firstly, 'What are my research cases? This is a case of *what?*'. . . One possibility was to select a few of the subnational states in Mexico and analyze them as cases, comparing the advocacy in Mexico City to the advocacy (or lack thereof) in other states, perhaps Guanajuato as an example of 'a very conservative one', or Yucatán as one that was 'not so conservative but still has not legalized abortion'. Such a perspective, however, carried similar risks to those of the comparison with Chile, even with the Mexican subnational states being 'more comparable' as part of the same federation, the risk of following a simplistic hypothesis of "why this happened *here* and didn't happen *over there*". Also, searching for such an explanation might involve, yet again, a rather simple causal theory having to do with the influences of different political parties, something that many Mexicans would deem rather obvious. Such an angle did not seem to bring anything new to the 'academic table', let alone explore the dimension of *the international* that was clearly there as well. It would thus be missing two things: the much larger narratives that I was interested in exploring, having to do with depictions of characters and with different advocacy groups interpreting the same concepts in completely different ways, and the global dimension of international norms. Because now that the comparison across two countries had been left behind, another important question was: 'How can this topic stay connected with the global perspective?'. . .'How can I still link the issue to International Relations while focusing more deeply on Mexico, and when I risk posing the type of question that will be given a simplistic answer having to do with domestic partisan politics?'

Through exploring the literature and starting to follow the current abortion debates, it became clear that there was a complex story here, one which not only had solid connections to the international, but a hugely complex map of conflicting discourses and narratives, where advocates constructed interpretations of various concepts in opposed ways – very much framed by themselves as indeed two opposed, competing discourses. Through more analysis of the literature, as well as exchanges with other academics in Hamburg and other locations, what emerged as a more adequate idea was to use the two competing discourses (pro- and anti-abortion legalization) as the cases for analysis: both discourses had clearly been 'successful' in some places and not in others, both had managed some clear legislative victories in Mexico in recent decades. It no longer seemed adequate to call them 'successful' or 'unsuccessful' but rather to realize the hugely complex ontology on each side, having to do with rights, norms, concepts, characters, international texts, and an ongoing "*lawfare*" (as proposed conceptually by Rachel Sieder and others). It also didn't seem adequate to propose a hypothesis but rather to look at the research question as a complex *'how'* rather than simplistic attempts at a *'why'* – especially because of the *'pendular-ness'* of the case, where any victory in either direction may be only temporary, subject to change when opposed political winds start to blow in a certain region. In such a complex issue, the *'whys'* can change according to persons, regions, times, and contexts, but understanding the *'hows'* of this particular matter might then provide insights that are useful for advocates in other times, places and issue areas.

In such a complex network of *'hows'* and the two competing ontologies, the conceptual framework of norm contestation seemed adequate. If the cases were to be the opposed discourses (instead of subnational states or something else), it made sense to look at them 'in parallel', to study and compare the ways in which advocates had, indeed, for several decades *contested* concepts, laws, norms, ideas, and meanings. The previously proposed aspect about 'the politics of personalities' can easily be woven in, as one of the many facets and dimensions of the entire ontology of what activists are contesting: the concept of who is, for example, a *transgressor*, a *victim*, or an aggrieved activist is assigned different (and often opposed) meanings.

Previous research experiences in international Geneva, and especially inside international institutions like the UN Office of the High Commissioner for Human Rights (OHCHR), had already earlier provided me with a solid understanding of the international human rights system, and of how the modern-day global institutions are constantly in exchanges with civil society actors in domestic settings. It was through exchanges with OHCHR officials, with global advocates, and attending sessions of the Universal Periodic Review (UPR), that I gained insights into, for example, how the Committee on the Rights of Persons with Disabilities sometimes challenged countries' policies (as well as the rulings of other OHCHR divisions), on whether abortion for reasons of severe disability is a legitimate norm. Other voices brought awareness about the practice of sex-selective abortions (overwhelmingly against female foetuses) that happen in some regions of the world and the many layers of incredible complexity that one can face when trying to balance women's choices (*whose choice actually?,* in the face of family pressures to produce male children within strongly patriarchal societies?), against what can easily be recognized as a form of sex discrimination with huge demographic consequences. Discussions and debates like those, at the global level, gave me insight into the great diversity of positions, discourses, and dimensions to be analyzed within any human rights topic, and especially within the abortion debate. Most positions within the possible range thereof in the abortion debate can find resonance in one or another international NGO, or UN-related institution, and therefore have a voice which is amplified into the modern-day global *multilogue* of stakeholders.

The first period of fieldwork was carried out in the second half of 2018, from August to November. I first selected some prominent advocates and salient voices on the abortion debate in Mexico, holding opposed positions on the legality of abortion. Advocates with higher degrees of expertise on one aspect or another were preferred. As such, some of them are legal experts; others are medical experts, parliamentarians who have furthered legal reforms, directors or managers of NGOs, or experts on the advocacy itself, who have had years (sometimes decades) of experience with activism on the issue, long-time witnesses of the historical development of the topic. A research stay at *El Colegio de México*, a prestigious research institution in Mexico City, also provided connections to and through academics and experts involved in the issue; it became possible to contact some of the experts through other experts, and some of the advocates with the help of other advocates, in what is sometimes deemed 'snowball sampling'. It also goes without saying that the ability to interview them in the Spanish language (of which all experts are native speakers) also enabled rich and flowing conversations where they could naturally talk about their experiences and expertise. By approaching advocates who were 'experts' of one sort or another, two things became clear: on the one hand, the earlier 'hunch' that there is much connection to international forums, debates, and documents was confirmed, and on the other, it became apparent that there was a disconnect between opinions from expert advocates (which can indeed be more nuanced and less 'black and white') and the opinions of non-experts on social media or public protests, where the issue is much more easily simplified into 'a matter of opposed *teams*'.

For instance, it was only through these initial interviews that I first heard about NOM0046 and how important it was for the legal landscape of abortion in Mexico. As is explained throughout the book, NOMs are technical norms in Mexico (the acronym stands for *Norma Oficial Mexicana*) that relatively few people know the first thing about. They regulate and set standards for industries, environmental protection, administrative procedure, or other areas where technological and procedural regulation is required. And some of the NOMs regulate medical practice, as well as legal proceedings concerning victims of crimes, thus the connections to abortion: after it was reformed in 2016, NOM0046 procedurally legalized abortion in cases of sexual assault and did it in such a way that many other regulations and 'procedural padlocks' outlined in 'higher-level' laws (such as the Criminal Codes) could seemingly be skipped, in favour of providing quick attention towards victims of assault. That such a significant change could come through a 'technical', *third-tier* kind of law took many advocates by surprise – especially those identifying as 'pro-life', who interpreted the change as a 'sneak attack' of sorts: an infiltration of massive legal change 'through the back door'. This speaks to the fact that NOMs are very much *not* an issue that attracts media attention for the public at large. They don't make for eye-catching slogans on posters for public protest, or for popular *'Twitter hashtags'*. But experts in medical, legal, or scientific fields are very aware of them, because it is NOMs rather than the Constitution or even the Criminal Codes that directly regulate and constrain their practices. If not for extended interviews during fieldwork (where experts and advocates freely told their stories and expressed their views on the debate), details such as NOM0046 and the role it has played in the current abortion landscape would likely not have been found. And NOM0046 is only one example among several of details that might have been missed because they may come across as 'technicalities' but that play an important role in what experts see and aim to change – *the devil is in the details*.

Media articles often simplify an issue, for example declaring: '*Senate approves law on conscientious objection to abortion*', without detailing what that means in legal terms: Which law is new or changed? Is it a 'Federal' or a 'General' law? (This is relevant in Mexico, where those are two different legal ordinances.) To whom exactly is the law binding: authorities, experts, or all people in a certain place? Is this reform still pending approval from the Lower Chamber or from other authorities?. . . otherwise, a law being approved 'at some legislative level' doesn't mean that its provisions have come into effect. This is especially true when, in such a complex issue, the news piece will use limited space to declare that a certain authority has 'legalized' or 'banned' abortion in a certain place, but does it mean that penalties were removed from the Criminal Code; that the Constitution was amended; or that a NOM was published regulating how and when a doctor can proceed to interrupt a pregnancy?. . .'Technical' details such as these often don't interest the general public but can greatly change the goals, tactics, and discourses for expert advocates.

Also during fieldwork in 2018, the global debate happening at the OHCHR on what was then the *"Draft Comment No. 36 to the International Covenant on Civil and Political Rights (ICCPR), on the Right to Life"* officially ended with the publication of the finalized "General Comment No. 36, on the Right to Life". I had the opportunity to interview advocates in Mexico who had been directly and indirectly involved with sending comments and communications to this global forum, as well as others who had been part of Mexican delegations sent abroad to participate in the negotiations for the Cairo 1994 International Conference on Population and Development (ICPD Cairo '94), or to other international events and conferences at the Organization of American States. In October of that year, I also could attend a very large 'pro-life' protest in Mexico City, taking place in the framework of (and in opposition to) the "*Day of Global Action for Safe Legal Abortion*", declared by a coalition of NGOs from Latin America and the Caribbean in 1990. Crucial contacts for expert interviews came from the attendance to this protest.

This first 'round' of fieldwork brought some changes to the research framework itself, mainly through the insights that would have been impossible to gather otherwise – such as all of the discussions relative to NOM0046. The international and transnational dimensions of the debate in Mexico had been made clear: besides the previously mentioned exchanges with global forums and events, both 'pro-life' and 'pro-legalization' advocates were in contact with advocates in Argentina, because that country was also the scenario of controversy and advocacy for and against abortion in 2018. Some Mexican advocates keenly showed proof of personal communications with Argentinian advocates; others were inviting Argentinian experts to talk at public events or conferences. Throughout this first 'round' also came the conceptual proposition of aiming to find 'organizing principles' as potential 'solutions' to the debate and to the 'deadlocks' that both sides seemed to find themselves in, at times.

The second 'round' of fieldwork, in 2019, gave access to more experts for interviews, as well as attendance to two other relevant events: a smaller protest event in the state of Coahuila, where some people from feminist groups organized a pro-legalization protest (also in late September, in the framework of the *"Day of Global Action for Safe Legal Abortion"*), thus complementing my attendance to the 'pro-life' protest from the year prior, and a public conference at a catholic university in the state of San Luis Potosí by Jorge Serrano Limón, one of the most prominent 'pro-life' advocates in Mexico who has been active since the late eighties. This second round of fieldwork in 2019 served to solidify and expand many of the notions already gathered in 2018; by this point, the research framework, concepts, and methods had also been strengthened and solidified. It was also by this point that the earlier idea of focusing on trying to find organizing principles as 'a solution' to the debate was modified into having them be part of 'a pathway to dialogue'. Through all the analytical effort already underway, it seemed that instead of a rather arrogant attempt at 'solving' the debate (which may not have any easy foreseeable solutions in the near future), the endeavour of the thesis would concentrate, firstly, on trying to *understand* rather than *explain* the topic and, secondly, on attempting to find said pathways to dialogue where some measure of middle ground can be found.

A curious thing happened throughout the long process of transcribing, coding, and carefully analyzing all of the information gathered. It became noticeable that, decades ago at the very beginning of my following the abortion debate in Mexico (and of course since long before that), the concept of abortion *decriminalization* ('despenalización') rather than *legalization,* was one of the proposed principles that many advocates suggested as the much-needed policy change for Mexican women. Certainly 'decriminalization' was one of the first concepts that I had been hearing for decades when it came to this issue. To 'decriminalize' an action is not the same thing as to 'legalize' it, as experts know – despite a popular simplistic vision about law in Mexico, where many believe the idea that '*anything not forbidden is permitted*'. This binary vision, of course, does not correspond with a complex reality where a merely 'forbidding' norm is not the same as a 'constituting' or 'regulating' norm: it is one thing to *not* outline punishments for a certain act or practice and a very different thing to actually regulate, outline, and provide access through public funds. These realizations had emerged since early in the doctoral research: the fact that, for example, one could study the case of Germany's abortion laws and find that it is not 'criminalized' but it is also not quite 'legalized' in the sense that some actions related to it are still forbidden, such as creating publicity about it. Abortion in Germany (and in many other nations) seems to exist in somewhat of a legal grey area, purposefully kept so because that "works" in practice . . . for better and for worse.

For many of today's Mexican pro-legalization advocates, 'decriminalization' is a deeply insufficient solution, one that does very little for true access to justice or equality, especially for the most vulnerable women. Many of them now advocate much more boldly than their 'pro-decriminalization' predecessors did, demanding that abortion be considered 'a right' and also that the state should provide free access to it. In some feminist pro-legalization circles, 'decriminalization' seems to be an outdated, much too insufficient solution that *'only the first-generation feminists would have been contented with'*. But at the same time, 'not punishing women' is also an idea that many 'pro-life' advocates can agree to, even if they would never agree to 'legalization'. Only after much analysis and thought, emerged the idea that *decriminalization itself* could be, if not *'one'* or *'the only'* organizing principle (and there are still certain difficulties in trying to implement that idea 'on the ground', or even in written legal normativity), at the very least the start of a dialogue where opposed groups agree on one core concept. In a curious way, the research seemed to have come full circle, but now with a newer vision provided by the framework of norm contestation, and the potential to view 'decriminalization' as a Type 2 organizing principle that may help advocates to bridge the initial and fundamental legitimacy gaps. A curious story of "back to the beginnings" seemed to then be realized, looking again with new eyes at that which had been the point of departure.

Annex 1: List of Experts Interviewed

From September to December 2018, and from August to October 2019, I carried out in-depth, personal interviews with the following advocates to gather primary data for this research. For privacy purposes, the interviewees are identified only by a number and a description of their abortion-related work, along with the institutions that they belong to or that they closely work with:

1. AM, legal expert at the GIRE organization (*Grupo de Información en Reproducción Elegida*), the most important pro-legalization advocacy organization in Mexico. Pro-legalization advocate.
2. AR, medical doctor, Violence Prevention and Gender Equality department at the Mexican Secretariat of Health (*Secretaría de Salud*). Was also part of the Mexican delegation at the Regional Conference on Population and Development in Latin America and the Caribbean in 2013, when the Montevideo Consensus was created. Also part of a Mexican delegation to CEDAW. Pro-legalization advocate.
3. BS, officer at the Legislative Unit on Gender Equality, at the Lower Chamber (*Cámara de Diputados*) of Federal Congress. Previously a politician at the Unit for Equality Policy, at the government of Mexico City. Pro-legalization advocate.
4. CE, academic and expert on demographic studies at *El Colegio de México*. Previously worked at the Secretariat of Health, on family planning issues. Was also a part of the Mexican delegation at the Regional Conference on Population and Development in Latin America and the Caribbean in 2013, when the Montevideo Consensus was created. Pro-legalization advocate.
5. EO, representative of the NGO "*Constituyentes Feministas*", who were active on gender-related topics during the public debates of the Asamblea Constituyente, for constitutional reform in Mexico City in 2016. They were authors of law initiatives to keep abortion legal in the new Constitution of the capital. Pro-legalization advocate.
6. IP, legal expert involved with the NGO coalition *"Red Familia"*, a network of various NGOs who advocate against abortion and in favour of various family-supportive policies: work-family balance, adoption, etc. Involved also

with several of the state-level constitutional reforms, amended to protect "life from the moment of conception". 'Pro-life' advocate.

7. JM, sub-director and expert from the *"Frente Nacional por la Familia"*, a major coalition of conservative NGOs advocating generally against abortion, against homosexual marriage, and in other family-related and social issues. 'Pro-life' advocate.
8. LR, former independently elected representative at the Lower Chamber of Congress (Cámara de Diputados), advanced generally progressive reforms concerning gender equality and LGBTQ rights. Pro-legalization advocate.
9. LA, member of ANCIFEM, a civil association advocating for women's political participation, it frames its conservative message as 'against feminism'. Was involved in the International Conference on Women at Beijing + 15. 'Pro-life' advocate.
10. MB, academic and representative of the *Early Institute*, a Mexican think tank that creates policy-oriented research on many issues related to childhood, family, maternity leave policies, preventing of sexual abuse of children, among many others. Where it concerns abortion, they are very invested in building an anti-abortion message on a basis of bioethics. 'Pro-life' advocate.
11. MR, retired academic and lawyer, author of an independent law reform initiative to 'roll back' legal abortion in the new Constitution of Mexico City, at the time of the public debates of the *Asamblea Constituyente*, for Mexico City's constitutional reform of 2016. 'Pro-life' advocate.
12. MCM, director of Mexican NGO Catholics for the Right to Decide (*Católicas por el Derecho a Decidir*). Was part of the Mexican delegation present at the International Conference on Population and Development in Cairo, 1994. Pro-legalization advocate.
13. MER, director of the NGO "Equality, Citizenship, Work and Family" (*Equidad, Ciudadanía, Trabajo y Familia*). Pro-legalization advocate.
14. MC, former representative at the Lower Chamber (*Cámara de Diputados*) of National Congress, by the PRD party. Proposed a legislative reform at the national level, to decriminalize abortion (the proposal did not pass). Former representative also at the local Congress in Mexico City, at the time of abortion decriminalization in 2007, was one of the proponents of the main decriminalization reform. Pro-legalization advocate.
15. MM, former representative at the Senate (*Senado de la República*), in National Congress, by the PAN party. Proposed a legislative reform to facilitate adoption, among other 'family-supportive' reforms. 'Pro-life' advocate.
16. MT, former representative at the Lower Chamber (*Cámara de Diputados*) in National Congress, by the Morena party. Pro-legalization advocate.
17. PN, officer at the federal Secretariat for Women (INMUJERES). Was part of the Mexican delegation during the presentation of Mexico's report on Civil and Political Rights to the United Nations in 2011; also part of the Mexican delegation at the time of the Universal Periodic Review of 2018. Pro-legalization advocate.

18. PM, former representative at the Senate (*Senado de la República*) in National Congress, by the Morena party, member of various feminist organizations. Pro-legalization advocate.
19. RS, lawyer and former technical secretary at the legislative Human Rights Commission, at the Lower Chamber (*Cámara de Diputados*) in National Congress. Not really an advocate on a particular position regarding abortion but rather provided extensive knowledge on laws, regulations, and legislative reform procedures in Mexico.
20. WB, former representative at the Lower Chamber of Congress (*Cámara de Diputados*), by the Morena party. Interviewed twice: once in 2018 and again in 2019 for follow-up, as in September of 2019, they had just presented a proposal for legislative reform to decriminalize abortion nation-wide, although the reform ultimately did not pass. Pro-legalization advocate.
21. BB, local parliamentarian at the Congress of San Luis Potosí, by the PRI party. Presented an "Action of Unconstitutionality" (*Acción de Inconstitucionalidad*) to the Mexican Supreme Court, when the local Constitution of San Luis Potosí was amended to "protect life from the moment of conception". Pro-legalization advocate.
22. CR, local parliamentarian at the Congress of Coahuila, by the PRD party. Pro-legalization advocate.
23. GD, a 'pro-life' citizen advocate who is a point of contact for many local 'pro-life' NGOs in the state of San Luis Potosí, also co-organized the public conference with Jorge Serrano Limón, attended during fieldwork. 'Pro-life' advocate.
24. JT, coordinator of the local chapter of the NGO *"Frente Nacional por la Familia"* in San Luis Potosí. 'Pro-life' advocate.
25. LM, officer at the local Secretariat of Social Development (*Secretaría de Desarrollo Social*) in the state of Coahuila. Pro-legalization advocate.
26. MMB, director of the San Luis Potosí chapter of the NGO "Centres of Support for Women" (*Centros de Ayuda a la Mujer* or CAMs), an organization founded by prominent 'pro-life' activist Jorge Serrano Limón. The Centres (of which now there are 167 across Latin America) dissuade women from having abortions and provide them with some measures of support, such as free ultrasounds and some donations of money or children's clothes. Some of the Centres can also temporarily house women and their children, if they have a vulnerable family situation. 'Pro-life' advocate.

Interviews ranged in time from about 20 minutes to some of them extending to nearly three hours. All were recorded, with the participants' consent, with only three exceptions. The interviews with experts No. 4 "CE" and No. 19 "RS" could not be recorded for technical reasons, as they were telephone interviews while the rest happened in personal, face-to-face encounters. Only in the case of expert No. 26 "MMB", they requested not to be recorded, thus in this case, only written notes were taken.

It can be seen that, in general, a higher number of pro-legalization advocates (16) were interviewed than the amount of advocates identifying as 'pro-life' (9). Only one of the experts did not identify as an 'advocate' for any particular position within the debate (No. 19 "RS"), instead providing expertise on law, especially Criminal Law, and on how legal reforms are proposed and advanced in National Congress. This imbalance in the number of advocates identifying as belonging to one 'side' of the debate or another can be explained by how the selection of available experts could be carried out on the ground. Contacts gained through the research stay of 2018 at *El Colegio de México* (COLMEX) opened the doors to many advocates who had contacts with academia; this in itself carries an implicit tendency towards people who identify as 'pro-legalization'.

In 2018, the new left-wing-leaning government of Andrés Manuel López Obrador had been recently sworn in for a six-year presidential and administrative term (also winning majorities in both legislative Chambers), which also implied a stronger likelihood of finding persons with a pro-legalization stance (and implementing the respective agenda) among the advocates who were government officials, or legislative representatives, or who held positions in government.

Messages were sent through e-mail, Twitter, Facebook, and other platforms to various advocates with public profiles, holding different positions within the debate – in equal attempts of 'cold contacting' prominent figures on 'both sides'. Fewer people tend to respond to 'cold contacting' in general (about 15% of all attempts made) regardless of ideology or position within the debate. However, I found that those with a 'pro-legalization' stance tended to respond more readily. Some advocates identifying as 'pro-life' seemed to hold a certain distrust of academia or researchers, which sometimes made it difficult to get an interview.

One crucial 'door' towards accessing more advocates identifying as 'pro-life' was my personal attendance to the large 'pro-life' protest in late September 2018 in Mexico City. It was then possible to approach leaders of NGOs such as the *Frente Nacional por la Familia,* while they were present at the march. Only then could I gain access to talking with expert No. 7 "JM", who in turn provided the contact with expert No. 6 "IP" from the state of Aguascalientes. Traveling in person to Aguascalientes, to interview expert No. 6 "IP", also facilitated them providing contacts for interviews with experts No. 10 "MB" and No. 15 "MM".

This 'snowball sampling' was of course influenced by these advocates' willingness and readiness to provide more contacts, once the crucial in-person connection had been established. One balancing advantage, however, was that whenever advocates identifying as 'pro-life' did finally agree to personal interviews, those exchanges are among the longest and most detailed: for example, the interview with advocate No. 6 "IP" lasted 2 hours and 40 minutes; interview with No. 7 "JM" lasted 1 hour and 20 minutes, and with No. 10 "MB", it lasted 2 hours and 10 minutes. The three also provided written material, documentation of their advocacy, and further contacts.

I personally attended, as well, a public conference by prominent 'pro-life' activist Jorge Serrano Limón in San Luis Potosí in 2019 and recorded it in its entirety: it provided an additional hour and 20 minutes of material. Also through having attended this conference in person, it became possible to meet several more 'pro-life' advocates and have interviews with them: in this case, experts No. 24 "JT" and No. 26 "MMB". Once met in person, most of the 'pro-life' advocates overall were eager to provide abundant written material, such as books, reports, written communications with other advocates, or copies of proposed law reforms.

The 'pro-life' protest of 2018 was also attended by thousands of people, as it happened in the megalopolis of Mexico City, it was a much larger protest than the 2019 pro-legalization protest attended in Coahuila. This yielded the opportunity to gather much more photographic evidence (of messages, slogans and phrases used by attendants). In the same vein, it could be observed that attendants at the 'pro-life' protest of 2018 gave away substantially more printed publicity and other freely distributed paraphernalia, than those at the 2019 'pro-legalization' protest.

All of this helps to 'balance out' the information and evidence gathered for the opposed sides of the debate, helping to overcome the undeniable hurdle that 'pro-life' advocates tended to be more distrustful of a researcher with whom no previous contact existed (or without someone they knew acting as a 'link'). They seemed warier of academics in general and more difficult to reach overall for interviews.

The data was then comprehensively analyzed: extended interviews (as well as the public conference by Jorge Serrano Limón) were transcribed in their entirety and coded afterwards *in vivo* through a multilayered system of codes. This manner of coding was aimed at detecting the most important concepts as portrayed by the advocates, and the connections between them, as well as being aware of those ideas most used and repeated throughout the various messages and documents. Secondary sources were analyzed in detail for various signifiers, sets of ideas, concepts, as well as the discursive frameworks used for their respective messages. The interpretive comparative analysis is enriched by notions of semiotics (meaning-related aspects), especially semiotics in politics. Thus, the methodology used was based, for the most part, on interpretive and comparative discourse analysis, in order to analyze the discourses put forth by advocates on both sides of the debate.

Annex 2: Printed Materials and Other Items Shared by Advocates in Mexico

1. "Aborto: La Política de un Estado Claudicante". Detailed in Chapter 2.
2. The interviewee from GIRE (*Grupo de Información en Reproducción Elegida*, an important pro-legalization NGO) provided a copy of GIRE's 2018 Annual Report: "*La Pieza Faltante: Justicia Reproductiva*". Used extensively for this research, it provides detailed factual information about legal and judicial cases concerning abortion in Mexico, women who have been victimized or jailed for crimes of abortion, and personal testimonies from women throughout Mexico, as well as much detail about GIRE's activities through the country.
3. Annual report booklet *Católicas por el Derecho a Decidir, 20 años* (*20 Years of 'Catholics for the Right to Decide')*, USB stick with audiovisual material from their advocacy campaign, and 20 publicity postcards with advocacy messages. Detailed in Chapter 2.
4. Initiative of a Decree on "the Right to Abortion", by the NGO *"Constituyentes Feministas"*, submitted to the Constitutional Assembly of Mexico City in 2016, proposing various articles to be included in the new Constitution. The document contains a brief legal justification of why abortion should allegedly be 'a right'.
5. Citizen (independent) law Initiative to abolish access to abortion in Mexico City, documenting why it is allegedly 'a legal fallacy', submitted to the Constitutional Assembly of Mexico City in 2016. It is of interest to see how these two last documents, No. 4 and No. 5, are presented side-by-side as opposed Initiatives to the Constitutional Assembly: one calling abortion 'a right', while for an opposed advocate, it is 'a legal fallacy', in a clear display of irreconcilable viewpoints and colliding principles of justice.
6. Law reform initiative by a 'pro-life' advocate at the Senate, in National Congress: the initiative to create a new "General Law for the Protection of Pregnant Women". The initiative does not mention abortion, but focuses on other tangential measures in order to (according to the proponent), 'discourage abortion and encourage motherhood': such as public financial support for childbirth and childcare, ensuring fathers' compliance with legal responsibilities towards their children, facilitating adoption procedures, more access to publicly funded daycare centres, more support for working mothers and improvements in work/life balance policies to care for their young children,

etc. The initiative was ultimately not voted in Congress, so it has not been turned into law. It can be mentioned that, in a commendable display of coherence between message and practice; this advocate gave the interview at their office in the Senate, while holding their very young infant (their fourth child).

7. A copy of the "Action of Unconstitutionality, No. 62/2009" (*"Acción de Inconstitucionalidad 62/2009"*), presented by parliamentarians of San Luis Potosí to the Supreme Court, denouncing the alleged unconstitutionality of the reform that had amended the local Constitution to *"protect life from the moment of conception"*. The Action was ultimately rejected by the Supreme Court (on the grounds of subnational state autonomy to decide their laws).
8. Two law reform initiatives by a pro-legalization advocate in the Lower Chamber (*Cámara de Diputados*) of the National Congress, one proposing to reform the Federal Criminal Code and the other to reform the General Law on Health, both intending to decriminalize abortion until the 12th week of pregnancy nation-wide (copying the same redefinition procedure done in Mexico City). Presented in 2019, but ultimately rejected by Congress.
9. One pro-legalization advocate shared a copy of a law reform proposal, to be presented at the Lower Chamber (Cámara de Diputados) at National Congress, proposing to reform the General Law on Health (*Ley General de Salud*), to have an article added where access to Legal Interruption of Pregnancy would be declared to be 'part of Sexual and Reproductive Health and Rights'. (The reform proposal was ultimately rejected.)
10. One pro-legalization advocate shared a copy of another law reform proposal, to be presented at the Lower Chamber (Cámara de Diputados) at National Congress, proposing to reform the Federal Criminal Code (*Código Penal Federal*), to redefine abortion as the interruption of pregnancy that happens after the 12th week of gestation, so that any penalty mentioned would immediately only be applicable after that period. (Reform proposal was ultimately rejected.)
11. One pro-legalization advocate provided a copy of the law reform initiative that was presented (and eventually approved) in 2019 at the local Congress of the State of Oaxaca, which decriminalized abortion by reforming articles to the local Criminal Code and the local Health Law, through a redefinition of abortion as the interruption of pregnancy that happens after the 12th week (the same procedure done in 2007 to legalize abortion in Mexico City).
12. One 'pro-life' advocate shared the full text of a "Constitutional Controversy, No. 53/2016 and 45/2016" (*Controversia Constitucional No. 53/2016* y *No. 45/2016* – as a single unified document) presented to the Supreme Court, by the local Executive Power and local Legislative Power of the state of Baja California, against the Federal Executive Power, denouncing the alleged unconstitutionality of NOM0046. The Controversy challenges the alleged 'legal overreach' of NOM0046, as it imposes on subnational health institutions across the country the obligation to provide abortions requested by victims of sexual assault. The Constitutional Controversy also strongly challenges the point about underage persons being able to access abortion without

parental consent, considering it a *'state override over parental authority'*. The document includes the full transcript of the debate in Court, the votes, and the result, where the Controversy was ultimately dismissed by the Supreme Court and NOM0046 was upheld as constitutionally valid.

13. "*Nuestros Irrenunciables*" (*Our Inalienable* [Rights]), a written statement by the NGO "Constituyentes Feministas", submitted to the Constitutional Assembly of Mexico City in 2016, at the time of drafting the new Constitution. The text states their support towards the legality of abortion.
14. One 'pro-life' advocate provided a copy of a written complaint, made by another 'pro-life' independent advocate, and submitted to the Constitutional Assembly of Mexico City in 2016, at the time of drafting of the new Constitution. The complaint denounces legal abortion and *"other attempted and illegitimate constitutional reforms about gender ideology"* as *"destructive to the family and to the future of the country"*.
15. One 'pro-life' advocate from San Luis Potosí shared a communications piece by Catholic Church officials, titled: "In Favor of Girls and Women who are Victims of Rape and In Favor of the Conceived Unborn (Child)" (*"A Favor de las Niñas y Mujeres Víctimas de Violación y del Concebido No Nacido")*. The authors are: one archbishop from the state of Chihuahua and two from Monterrey, who together conform the "Episcopal Dimension for Life" (*Dimensión Episcopal Para la Vida*), part of the Mexican Episcopal Conference (CEM, *Conferencia Episcopal Mexicana*). The document denounces the 'culture of death', specifically the creation of NOM0046, as a norm that allegedly *"will not provide women with real solutions to sexual violence"*, that legal abortion *"will only serve to re-victimize the victims of sexual assault"*, and that abortion is unacceptable even in cases of rape (the official stance of the Catholic Church).
16. One 'pro-life' advocate shared a video message from a representative at the local Congress of the state of Oaxaca, filmed at the time when the Oaxacan Congress was debating (and eventually approved) the decriminalization of abortion, in September 2019. In the footage, the representative declares that *"pro-life women are the real feminists"* and denounces the alleged *"interference of foreign advocates and foreign agendas in matters that are national, and local to the people of Oaxaca"*. The representative featured in the video states that Argentinian advocates were allegedly present at that moment in the Oaxacan Congress, implying that they were there to influence the procedure of voting for the decriminalization.
17. Screenshot proving personal communications between advocates from *"Católicas por el Derecho a Decidir"*, Mexico, and advocates from the sister institution in Argentina, communicating the OHCHR's publication in 2018 of the finalized *"General Comment No. 36 to the ICCPR on the Right to Life"*.
18. Screenshot of personal communications between prominent pro-life advocate Jorge Serrano Limón and an interviewed 'pro-life' advocate in San Luis Potosí, praising the activities of the NGO "Centres of Support for Women" (which provide some support to pregnant women in the form of money,

children's clothes, or temporary shelter, to discourage them from abortion), while denouncing that abortion *"pits a mother against her own child"*.

19. A printed flyer, created by the "Centres of Support for Women" (*Centros de Apoyo a la Mujer*, or CAMs), promoting their activities in a deceitful manner. Detailed in Chapter 2.
20. Invitation to the public conference by Jorge Serrano Limón. Detailed in Chapter 2.
21. The medical expert from the Secretariat of Health (*Secretaría de Salud*) provided a CD with a presentation called: "Programme for Legal Interruption of Pregnancies in Mexico City: An Island of Freedoms" (*Programa de Interrupción Legal del Embarazo en la Ciudad de México: Una Isla de Libertades*), containing information on how the programme for legal abortion in Mexico City has worked since its implementation. The data is mostly quantitative, but framed in a way to show that the programme has been successful and that women have largely benefited from it.
22. Response given by the Mexican government (by INAI, the government agency specializing on transparency and the provision of official information to citizens) to an official request for information, showing that it's a relatively low number of women, allegedly, who are ever imprisoned in Mexico for crimes of abortion. Detailed in Chapter 2.
23. Another 'pro-life' advocate shared the same type of information as above, but specifically for the state of San Luis Potosí, as of March 1, 2019: the official government response to an information request, showing that only two men (and no women) are in prison in San Luis Potosi for the crime of abortion. This advocate's argument is in the same vein as above: to make an argument *for* the criminalization of abortion in written law, hinging on a principle of impunity – that this punishment will not be carried out in reality.
24. In the same vein as the last two, a 'pro-life' advocate from San Luis Potosí shared a news article where they themselves are mentioned (as a local representative of a pro-life organization), as denouncing the 'fake news' about the number of women who are allegedly in prison in San Luis Potosí for the crime of abortion, stating that the local authorities have clarified that "only two men, and no women, were in prison as of 1 March 2019, for abortion-related crimes".
25. Screenshot of a "tweet" where a person shares an invitation to a women-only talk in the city of Mazatlán, Sinaloa, on the topic of "Myths about Abortion" and "how to safely abort at home". Detailed in Chapter 2.
26. Invitation to a lecture by Argentinian 'pro-life' advocate and medical doctor Chinda Brandolino, titled "Globalization of Abortion: the Culture of Death" (*La Globalización del Aborto: la Cultura de la Muerte*).

Other materials, publicly available or gathered during protests or conferences:

1. Full recording of the public conference by Jorge Serrano Limón, founder of "Pro-Vida Mexico" and a long-time 'pro-life' activist, at the Universidad de San

Pablo (a private catholic university) in San Luis Potosí. Notes and photos were also taken during the conference.

2. Publicity materials gathered at the in-person attendance of the 'pro-life' protest called "Blue Wave" (*Ola Celeste*) that took place on October 20, 2018, organized by a coalition of civil society organizations, chiefly among them the *Frente Nacional por la Familia.*

   a. Seventy-one photographs taken during the protest, mostly capturing the messages written on signs and carried by the attendees. More detail in Chapter 2.
   b. Handkerchiefs in a light blue colour, with the printed message "Salvemos las Dos Vidas" (*Let Us Save Both Lives*).
   c. A compact disc containing the USA-produced, 'pro-life' short documentary film: *"A Silent Scream"*.
   d. Chalkstone-made models of an embryo, allegedly 'real size' at about 10 weeks gestation.
   e. A pamphlet called *"Ama la Vida por Mí"* (Love Life for Me). Described in Chapter 2.

3. Materials gathered during the pro-legalization protest event called *"Tendedero Feminista"* ("Feminist Clothesline") attended in September 2019 in Saltillo, Coahuila.

   a. Twenty photographs taken during the event, capturing the messages written on signs and carried by attendees.
   b. Green handkerchiefs with 'pro-choice' messages.
   c. Fifteen images found online, most of them photos taken by other people during other public protests for and against legal abortion, in Mexico and other countries (Argentina, Spain).
   d. Seven other law reform initiatives (some approved and some not), both for and against legal abortion, found publicly online: some presented at the Senate or the Lower Chamber at National Congress, others submitted to the Constitutional Assembly of Mexico City, at the time of Constitutional reform in 2016. (*References in Bibliography*).

Index

Note: Numbers in **bold** indicate a table. Numbers in *italics* indicate a figure on the corresponding page.